Speaking of Race

Speaking of Race

Language, Identity, and Schooling Among African American Children

Jennifer B. Delfino

LEXINGTON BOOKS
Lanham • Boulder • New York • London

Published by Lexington Books
An imprint of The Rowman & Littlefield Publishing Group, Inc.
4501 Forbes Boulevard, Suite 200, Lanham, Maryland 20706
www.rowman.com

6 Tinworth Street, London SE11 5AL, United Kingdom

British Library Cataloguing in Publication Information Available

Library of Congress Control Number: 2020944861
ISBN 9781793606488 (cloth) | ISBN 9781793606501 (pbk)

For Southeast

Contents

List of Figures, Table, and Text Boxes   ix

Preface and Acknowledgments   xi

A Note on Transcription and Transcription Conventions   xv

Introduction: Theorizing Raciolinguistic Transformation   xvii

1   "I Have a(n American) Dream": Race, Schooling, and Achievement in The Nation's Capital   1

2   Talking "Like a Race": Language and Identity in Southeast   23

3   "He-Said-She-Said (Do This)": Directives, Marking, and the Resemiotization of Authoritative Discourse   47

4   "You about to Get Cooked!": Joning and Raciolinguistic Chronotopes of Policing and Survival   73

5   "You Don't Know How to Read!": Racializing Discourses about Literacy   95

6   Race, Literacy, and Power: Learning from Children about Educational Justice   117

Conclusion   139

References   143

Index   155

About the Author   163

List of Figures, Table, and Text Boxes

FIGURES

Figure 1.1	The Four Quadrants of Washington, D.C.	4
Figure 1.2	The Eight District Wards of Washington, D.C.	5
Figure 2.1	Street Tough Scientist	33
Figure 2.2	The Dual Component Model	34
Figure 2.3	Paul Posing for Camera	39
Figure 4.1	"Absolutely NO JONING!"	78
Figure 6.1	Learning Logs for French and Spanish	123
Figure 6.2	Learning Logs for French and Spanish	124
Figure 6.3	Tsunami	126
Figure 6.4	The Mayor Election	129
Figure 6.5	If I Were President of the United States	131
Figure 6.6	If I Were President of the United States	132
Figure 6.7	If I Were President of the United States	133

TABLE

Table 2.1	Street-Tough and School-Ready Identity Models	30

TEXT BOXES

Text Box 6.1   Tsunami (Author Reproduction)   127
Text Box 6.2   The Mayor Election (Author Reproduction)   130

Preface and Acknowledgments

In February 2012, not long after I finished my ethnographic research, seventeen-year-old Trayvon Martin was shot to death by George Zimmerman. Zimmerman had seen Martin as a threat. But the boy's gray hoodie and the fact that he was carrying a bag of Skittles, which Zimmerman claimed he thought was a concealed weapon, evidently construed Martin as suspicious. Rachel Jeantel, Martin's best friend and key witness, had testified that shortly before his death, Martin had in fact been running away from his killer. But Zimmerman was acquitted, quite possibly and partially due to the fact that Jeantel's use of African American Language (AAL) had negatively impacted her witness credibility (Rickford & King 2016). Trayvon Martin's murder and trial, plus the following deaths of people such as Michael Brown, Eric Garner, Tamir Rice, and Sandra Bland, registered as deeply tragic events that forced me to consider the place of my research in a U.S. society that claims to be postracial, but which disregards or reframes Black lives as not mattering.

In 2020, the year I completed the final manuscript for this book, a new wave of anti-Black incidents, including the murders of Ahmaud Aubrey, George Floyd, and Breonna Taylor, precipitated nationwide protests on behalf of the Black Lives Matter movement. In the midst of deep sadness and anger about the unapologetic anti-Blackness that is displayed by so many in the United States, I thought again about the kinds of socializing myself and other adults transmitted to the African American children who had been my after school students and research subjects from 2008 to 2011. The after school program and the students' schools were located in a low-income neighborhood of Washington, D.C., with mostly African American residents, precisely the kind of place that is either disparagingly or proudly typed as "ghetto," depending on who you talk to. Many of the students were already at an age where they could be targeted either by local teens and youth, many of whom participated in gangs, or by local police, who were known to stop even children for the same reasons cited by Zimmerman and other murderers, "Barbecue Becky," or any other white person who feels uncomfortable with cultural or linguistic signifiers of Blackness, such as hoodies or baggy pants. As adults, after school staff and parents had to navigate the impossible and for me, heartbreaking, project of helping the students value their Blackness while also teaching them that the wider society would see them as a threat if they walked, talked, or dressed in a certain way. On top of socializing the students out of styles of talk and behavior that register as criminalized Blackness, adults controlled even the most normal actions taken by many children when they get upset, such as yelling, stomping around, lashing out with arms and fists, and fighting their peers. We all carefully controlled these behaviors, as we knew they would be read as indicators of Black violence and criminality by anyone taking up the white gaze. I often discussed my ambivalence about restricting the children's behavior in this way with fellow staff who were African Americans, many of whom were also parents and who felt as I did: no one wanted to teach the students what it really means to be a racialized minority, but we had to for their safety and well-being. In learning the facts and limits of race, the students experienced age differently than many other children because they were socialized to be aware of their stigmatized identity as possible social threats to society early and often. This burden meant that they often could not talk, play, or express emotions as freely as children who are not viewed thus, and it was compounded by the extreme poverty they lived in.

Ultimately, this book is about lived experiences of childhood from the perspective of thirty-one African American preadolescents and teens. For the after school students, childhood was shaped and in many ways incredibly limited by the inescapable social fact of race compounded with the experience of living in deep poverty. With this book, I hope to disrupt the folk logic of postracialism and its ideological anchor, colorblindness, by trying to shed light on how race was felt, seen, and heard in the daily lives of the students I worked with. In the following pages, I argue that childhood is not simply a chronologically or biologically determined phase of life, but instead shaped in and through language and the experiences of race and class.

In this book, I also aim to disrupt culture of poverty and deficit theorizing, which has seen a resurgence in education policy and discourse and which continues to shape the academic canon even when theorists seek to self-consciously eradicate such perspectives from their work. As I show in the book, such pathologizing perspectives were held by well-intentioned, liberal and progressive educators and by many of the students and after school staff from the local neighborhood. This monograph is a self-consciously ethnographic project in that it tries to interpret how these individuals intersubjectively made sense of race from an analytical standpoint while accounting for their positionalities and perspectives on their terms.

Finally, as the book's ethnographic and theoretical engagement suggests, trying to educate people out of racist beliefs, especially in an era when most people believe themselves to be not racist or anti-racist, is largely ineffective. Not only is race ideologically and structurally embedded at all levels of lived experience; its discursive expression has changed, to indicate forms of difference that many do not consider or believe to be about race. Language is one of those things. Thus, in this book, I hope to critically expose the ideological underpinnings of the "new [linguistic] racism" (Alim & Smitherman 2012) in a way that compels people to rethink and change the system that produces race rather than focus on helping the marginalized and oppressed to adapt to it. Rosa and Flores (2015) have called this theoretical position a *raciolinguistic perspective*, and I hope that my work adds to this way of thinking. By looking at how racism and anti-Blackness articulate in our social and political institutions via the interests and views of privileged whites, I believe radical transformation is possible.

Writing this book would not have been possible without funding and the commentary, help, and encouragement of various individuals. I would like to thank The PSC-CUNY Faculty Research Award and CUNY Book Completion Award programs for funding the work of this monograph. Thank you to Journal of Sociolinguistics and International Journal of the Sociology of Language for granting permission to reproduce parts of my previously published works for this monograph. A special thank you to my editor, Kasey Beduhn, for approaching me about my research and encouraging me to take on this project. Thank you to Dave Luljak for his wonderful work indexing this book.

In terms of commentary and support, I would like to first thank the anonymous reviewer who read my first manuscript for their extremely positive yet critical feedback. Your comments helped me much improve this book and refine my thinking on its themes and content. I want to thank Kevin Nadal and Angie Reyes for mentoring me through the process of writing a monograph and for taking me under their respective wings, and I want to thank Natalie Schilling for being a steadfast mentor and supporter in this regard as well. I would not have had the courage to write a book otherwise. I owe my gratitude to Jessi Grieser, who was always available to read a chapter or talk through my ideas. Sincere thanks to Sabiyha Prince, Chuck Brown, Stanley Thangaraj, Arthur Spears, and H. Samy Alim for their feedback on chapters of this book or related publications.

I owe a huge debt of gratitude to my colleague and linguistics "big sister" at BMCC, Maureen Matarese, who has unfailingly encouraged and supported me through my writing and teaching. I also owe my thanks to my close teaching colleagues, Leigh Somerville, Patrick Flink, Tim Leonard, and Bill Koch, for their love and encouragement. Colleagues who have unfailingly supported me through graduate school and beyond are Nell Haynes, Matt Thomann, Julie Maldonado, Maureen Kosse, Greg Niedt, Corinne Seals, and Amelia Tseng. Thank you so much.

Many friends and family have supported me through this book project. Brendan Dolan, Christian Espinoza, Chris Collinsworth, Steffan del Prado, Katie Bliss, Ted Skaarup, Henrike Neumann, Kelley Foreman, and Fabián Guerra come to mind, though there are many others. I owe a special thank you to my parents, Anne Weston Henningsen and Robert Delfino, for the many ways in which they helped me make this book possible. I am so grateful to Pancho Savery, the first professor and friend who really taught me how to write for an academic audience and who also encouraged me to break the mold and find my own voice. I would not have started on the path to academia without your steadfast support. My most heartfelt thank you to Vivian

Vasquez, without whose love and support I would not have continued in academia. I owe you special thanks for teaching me what it means to teach for social justice.

Finally, I owe my thanks to all the people who allowed me into their lives to do the research for and write this book: Victor, the founder and executive director of Urban Pathways, and the after school staff with whom I worked closely for so many years (pseudonyms are retained for anonymity): Matt, Minnie, Mr. Morris, and especially Raymond. I am most grateful to the families of the after school program, especially the "big kids," for opening up to me and sharing their lives. I learned so much from you and I was lucky to be your teacher. This book is for you all.

A Note on Transcription and Transcription Conventions

NOTE ON TRANSCRIPTION

I have chosen to transcribe speech according to English spelling conventions that approximate how particular sounds are pronounced for the lay reader. In cases where research participants produced a hyper-stigmatized form, such as *aks* for *ask*, I transcribe according to the "standard" form, *ask*, and then provide an endnote that explains the linguistic variation; in this example, it is called *metathesis*. In doing so, and in providing the following table of commonly used AAL features, I wish to reduce any prescriptive or racialized language bias that may result from readers' perception of stigmatized languages.

TRANSCRIPTION CONVENTIONS

" "	constructed dialogue
CAPS	amplified volume or stress
Bold	falsetto
.	end of intonation unit
,	end of intonation unit; fall-rise indicates possibility for turn continuation
-	self-interruption/repair; break in the word, sound abruptly cut off
:	lengthening
h	laughter; each token marks one pulse
(( ))	transcriber comment
[ ]	overlap
/	rising final intonation
\	falling final intonation
__	level final intonation
=	continuing turn
(<.5)	pause less than .5 seconds

Introduction

Theorizing Raciolinguistic Transformation

By mid-March of 2011, toward the end of my fieldwork researching language and identity among the nine- to thirteen-year-old students in Urban Pathways'[1] two after school programs in Southeast Washington, D.C., seven-year-old Keri and I were assembling a puzzle in the small recreational space that housed the family literacy program. Keri's mother, Ms. Betty, and her nine-year-old sister, Alisha, began to argue at a table nearby. Ms. Betty had been helping a five-year-old practice his writing, ignoring Alisha's persistent demands that Ms. Betty help her peel an orange. "Hey Ma, I said help me peel this!" shouted Alisha, thrusting the orange in line of her mother's view. Ms. Betty swatted her hand away. "You better get out of my face," she threatened. As they continued to argue, I chimed in, appalled by how Alisha was addressing her mother.

"Alisha. Don't talk to your mother like that," I chided. Alisha appeared not to hear me as she and Ms. Betty hashed it out. Keri, however, shot me a wayward glance from across the table and appeared to grow uncomfortable, or perhaps hesitant. "Ms. Jennifer, they wasn't arguing," she vouched gently several seconds later, underneath the din of the dispute. I had to strain to hear her. "That's just how Black people talk to each other sometimes."

Keri explaining to me how Black people talk to each other would have not likely happened prior to me introducing and explaining my study to the after school students. Keri knew that I was interested in the language and identity practices of the nine- to thirteen-year olds; in fact, she had been disappointed that I could not include her in my study since she was only seven years old. With the exception of a few thirteen-year-olds, the preadolescents would soon be teenagers and as such, racialized institutionally as potential criminals and threats to society (cf. Garot 2010; Rosa 2019). I wanted to know what it meant for them to "talk" and "act Black" during a transitional moment of their lives where adults would attempt to socialize them out of the street-based identity practices they adopted, especially when and why acting and talking Black were meaningful to them as "communicative displays of agency" (Tetreault 2010) in school-based settings. While there are an abundance of studies on language and racial identity among teens and youth, there is no comprehensive account of how children use language to make sense of race.

To explain the introductory story, I see my misperception of Alisha's language as emblematic of the ways in which racialized minority students are institutionally misheard as somehow aggressive, threatening, or generally unprepared for learning and scholastic success. In this particular story, I was the institutionalized listening subject who heard Alisha as aggressive and loud. As I argue in this book, my perception was not the view of an individual who was simply unfamiliar with African American Language (AAL). Rather, my perceptions of language and race are grounded in a longer history and sociopolitical context of policing the linguistic practices of racialized minorities (Alim & Smitherman 2012; Flores 2020). African American and Latinx students, as the majority-minority students in most U.S. school districts, experience particularly severe racial and linguistic policing in schools. Much of this policing is due to the implementation of neoliberal schooling reforms that have aimed in the past two decades to "turn around" academic performance in underfunded majority-minority urban schools (Lipman 2011; Paris & Alim 2017; Rosa 2019). In this era of school reform, the linguistic practices of racially minoritized students are treated as a barrier to their academic success.

Thanks to the work of sociolinguists over several generations, AAL is now seen by many progressive educators as its own dialect with distinct features. Yet in the context of many language education programs, AAL is nevertheless seen as "inappropriate" at best for the purpose of academic communication and learning (Flores & Rosa 2015; Delfino 2016). And while AAL is widely appropriated in popular culture for advertisement and humor (Lippi-Green 2012; Roth-Gordon et al. 2020), it is still viewed as socially deviant or grammatically deficient language when spoken by African Americans in public and institutional spaces. Such a contradiction belies common-sense thinking of race as "no longer mattering" and points to a social process through which ideas about race are articulated in relation to ideas about language (Alim & Smitherman 2012; Alim 2016a).

Children like Keri are perceptive regarding the ways in which they are heard and perceived in schools as racialized speaking subjects, and they often find ways to challenge or transform received racial logics (Schaffer & Skinner 2009; Kromidas 2016; Chaparro 2019). Having taught, researched, and babysat American children for over two decades, I contend that children's ways of making sense of race and language in relation to wider ideas about personhood, identity, and success merit a closer look. Looking at how children see, hear, and try to transform race is especially important when considering the schooling experiences of African American students who live in impoverished neighborhoods. As I seek to demonstrate in this book, current policies and pedagogies, even when crafted with good intentions, often work against their needs and interests because an assimilatory racial logic governs attempts to understand how they ought to be educated, even within a liberal/progressive context of multiculturalism.

This book explores how the nine- to thirteen-year-old African American students of Urban Pathways used language to negotiate identities in relation to dominant discourses about race and academic success. The thirty-one children in this book, whom I taught in two after school programs from 2008 to 2010 and who participated in my ethnographic study from 2010 to 2011, lived and attended school in a deeply impoverished area of Southeast Washington, D.C. During these years, the "achievement gaps" represented by African American and Latinx students were spotlighted as a national education crisis in policy discourses focused on neoliberal strategies of school reform—among them, holding school districts accountable for improving achievement statistics by closing low-performing schools and introducing competitive funding as a reward for meeting the criteria (Lipman 2011). Along with other urban majority-minority school districts, District of Columbia Public Schools (DCPS) participated in neoliberal education reform from 2007 to 2011 and continued to do so after my fieldwork ended by implementing these accountability-based models. According to neoliberal rationale and the framing of school reform, minority underachievement was more widely symbolic of the failure of racialized minorities to achieve success according to national education standards.

At times, the African American adults involved in Urban Pathways' after school programs, such as parents and staff members, appeared to sponsor an achievement ideology that blamed impoverished African Americans for not achieving academically and socioeconomically. At others, these individuals spoke or acted against the educational and economic oppression that undergirded much of their lived experiences. As chapters 3–5 show, the nine- to thirteen-year-old students ambivalently sponsored but also resisted oppressive discourses that represented them as always-already failures in their approaches to learning and socializing in the after school program. However, they also attempted to display, through language and identity practices they culled from their communities, schools, and popular media culture, alternative models of Black personhood and academic achievement. Yet because their practices often involved invoking pathologized stereotypes of Black "street culture" (Anderson 1990; Hannerz 2003[1966]), their efforts were often misread as unpreparedness for or unwillingness to participate in learning.

Though the topic of language and identity among African American children is not new, especially with respect to their schooling experiences, there is not yet a full ethnographic study that treats language and race as dynamically co-constructed in children's practices. Problematically, much of the social science research on children has focused on how they come to learn either race or language through the socializing of caregivers and in school, but not both together. Outside of critical scholarship on childhood, children are still typically perceived as passively soaking up social meanings and practices from adults rather than as producers in their own right. From such a perspective, children are not seen as agents of social reproduction and transformation and their cultural practices are trivialized as developmental relative to adults. But as I argue in this book, such a perspective severely undercuts a valuable opportunity to see children as capable of transforming the unjust realities that not only affect them in school and in their everyday lives, but acting out of concern for the people they learned about in school and in after school. I explore this topic in more depth in chapter 6.

Grounding my analysis in research on how linguistic and racial injustice affects African American children, I position my students/research participants as young people who crafted identities for the purpose of social and educational transformation. In this regard, my work builds on anthropology, sociolinguistics, critical pedagogy, and critical race theory by taking up the theories and methods of raciolinguistics to challenge several presuppositions about how to study language in relation to race (Alim 2016a). In addition to analyzing how the students used language to modify or manipulate dominant, adult-centered discourses about race and academic success, I explore, conversely, how ideas about race shaped their linguistic practices and language ideologies. In this way, I attend closely to how the students' language and identity practices challenge typical understandings of race and language as self-evident objects of analysis by showing the ways in which both are coproduced via students' interactions, and in ways that transgress how one is normatively mapped onto the other. Ultimately, this book is premised on the idea that if dominant stakeholders attend to how children, especially racially minoritized children, "'race' language and 'language' race" (Alim 2016a), they would develop better solutions for educational equality.

AAL: A RACIOLINGUISTIC PERSPECTIVE

A major goal of this book is to foreground a *raciolinguistic perspective* that interrogates how racialized minorities are seen and heard by listening subjects. Following Flores and Rosa (2015), I define listening subjects as people whose perceptions of language and race normalize the structures and practices of white supremacy. It is in this sense that teachers, in their institutional role as facilitators of learning and academic success, sponsor raciolinguistic ideologies that see and hear the linguistic practices of racialized minorities as deviant, deficient, or disorderly no matter how they actually speak or how their language is structured (Rosa 2017; Flores et al. 2018). Despite decades of research on language variation and change, the fact of the matter remains that even well-intended liberal and progressive educators and parents see and hear racialized minorities as needing remediation and as "problem students" who are unwilling to assimilate.

A raciolinguistic perspective reframes much of the prior work on AAL by challenging the idea that there exists a standard English, against which one can compare the distinctive features of other dialects or varieties. For a long time, sociolinguists have compared the distinctive features of AAL to the features of English-in-general (Heath 1983; Baugh 1983; Wolfram 2002; Alim 2004). Such a descriptive approach yields wonderfully detailed information on how multilingual speakers code-switch or styleshift in stark contrast to prescriptive or "deficit" approaches that see such linguistic practices as evidence of imperfect or disorderly speech. However, descriptive sociolinguistics does not interrogate the political and ideological foundations of concepts such as "difference," "diversity," and "pluralism." As raciolinguistics scholars note, bringing these foundations into the scope of analysis is important because language education programs that have been designed to help students learn "standard" or "academic" English while using the "home language" as a bridge still see racialized students through the lens of deficit. That is to say, the linguistic practices of racialized minorities are measured against an imagined norm of white middle-class speech; "standard" English, in other words, does not actually exist (Lippi-Green 2012; Flores & Rosa 2015; Flores et al. 2018).

A raciolinguistic perspective thus interrogates the foundations upon which racial and linguistic differences are predicated. For one, race as a social construct operates differently than ethnicity in this regard, with ethnicized groups being offered the potential for inclusion and class mobility. Racialized groups, on the other hand, are those that are defined as irreconcilably Other and unassimilable, often through essentializing determinations about their cultural and linguistic practices (Urciuoli 1996; Rosa 2019). In the United States, African Americans have always been racialized as unassimilably Other within an opportunity structure that does not simply privilege whiteness, but which relies upon anti-Blackness to function politically, economically, and socially (Fordham 1996; Marable 2000; Alexander 2012). As I argue in this book, African American students' contemporary academic failures are understood against this institutional and ideological normalization of anti-Blackness.

Just like racial ideologies, which posit particular notions of difference in relation to wider political, economic, and social structures as well as relations of power, language ideologies also merit critical investigation and reframing. This is particularly important since it is through language that people make sense of race and racial difference (Bucholtz 2011; Alim 2016a). In traditional fields of linguistics, for example, languages are studied as self-evident constructs with objectively identifiable features or properties. The everyday person also assumes languages such as "English" and "Spanish" to exist as objectively different with reference to particular sounds, words, phrases, and grammatical structures. Languages, in this sense, do exist. But as relatively recent work in linguistic anthropology, raciolinguistics, and translinguistics has shown, monoglossic and purist language ideologies, in which languages are seen as distinct, separate, and bounded entities, often unwittingly reproduce hegemonic norms or assimilatory aims even as scholars and educators advocate for linguistic pluralism in language education. For example, this is evident in the idea of "standard" English or "academic language" (Silverstein 1996; Flores & Rosa 2015; Flores 2020), the idea that minoritized students' authentic selves are tied to the language spoken at home, and that these home languages should be used as a bridge to access to mainstream or academic forms of English (Guerra 2016; Chaparro 2019; Flores 2020). In reality, code-mixing, crossing, sharing, and other translingual practices are inherent to language and put to use as purposeful statements of identity, especially by young people who are grappling with the meaning of race and class positionality and attempting to transform their lived experiences (Rampton 1995; Paris 2011;

Tetreault 2016; Morales 2020). As I discuss in the following chapters, the after school students did not see themselves through the lens of Blackness-as-unassimilable-difference that was offered to them by schools and the wider society, and they used language to try and transform this racial ideology.

In sum, a raciolinguistic perspective helps bring into relief how linguistic and racial differences are socioculturally constructed in relation to wider issues of power, identity, and belonging. In reality, there is no such clear division between what linguistic practices may be objectively considered standard and which might be considered nonstandard, especially considering that people, especially young people, often blur these distinctions. Applying a raciolinguistic perspective to language planning and policy refocuses what is perceived as the "problem" of minority achievement to critique the institutions and criteria set for academic success.

FROM LEARNERS TO DOERS: LANGUAGE, RACE, AND SOCIAL IDENTITY AMONG CHILDREN

This book aligns current research on language, race, and identity with the critical study of childhood. In the past decade, there has been a generous amount of research on how teens and youth engage in the reproduction and transformation of race and other social categories of identity (Mendoza-Denton 2008; Reyes 2009; Bucholtz 2011; Paris 2011; Tetreault 2016; Rosa 2019). Drawing from earlier British work on youth and style or semiotic approaches to studying language and identity,[2] this work has done much to foreground the agency of teens and youth who are, in popular thinking, typically viewed as passively internalizing received social models of personhood, including the making of racial identities and racial differences. It shows instead that youth are actively engaged in the making of their own social identities, and in ways that challenged adult-centric understandings of difference and belonging. This body of work also foregrounds youths' particular concerns with language, race, and identity via scholarly interpretations of young people's sociocultural logic.

Bucholtz (2011) notes, for example, that while teen style is typically understood by adults as youth rebellion against authority and institutions, young people are actually more concerned with style for the purpose of creating social distinctions among peers. Using a concept she calls *hemispheric localism*, Mendoza-Denton (2008) notes that Latina high school students draw on, and often end up reproducing, racial stereotypes about Mexicans to create distinctions among each other, even as they attempt to resist school-based discourses, which employ those self-same categories of identification. And drawing from her work thus, Rosa (2019) finds that as Puerto Rican and Mexican youth in Chicago complete high school, ethnic distinctions between the groups become more rigid in response to institutional efforts to identify these students under the panethnic category of *Latino*.

In contrast to this youth-based literature, children younger than high school age are the focus of language acquisition and socialization studies. In this line of work, they are generally not viewed as fully fledged, competent makers of language and social identity in and of themselves (see Goodwin 1990 and Thorne 1997 for similar critique). Rather, children are usually positioned as learners rather than as producers of sociocultural reproduction and transformation. Yet instead of simply drawing parallels between preadolescent children's practices with the teen and youth literature to highlight their agency, I seek instead to describe how the nine- to thirteen-year-old after school students socially constructed their age in response to adults' expectations and anxieties regarding their behavior, and in connection with wider racial and linguistic ideologies about their development and future successes. As I discuss in chapter 2, the preadolescent and thirteen-year-olds experienced pressure from adults to disalign with the street-based cultural practices and values of older teens and youth in the neighborhood in favor of academic success, to take on adult-like family and school responsibilities, and yet to recognize their place as children in relation to adults.

Moreover, pressures to successfully navigate the dominant society's expectations for African Americans' talk and behavior[3] shaped their language and identity choices, but not in the same way as described in the research on teens (e.g., Fordham 1999; Alim 2004; Paris 2011). Thus, in addition to race, gender, class, and location-based ways of identifying the students as possible future criminals created what I see as a particularly overwhelming set of expectations for the preadolescent and thirteen-year-old students, one which younger children and older teens did not necessarily share. In the view of both adults and the students themselves, this placed them at a different life stage than the teens and youth in the neighborhood, and their cultural practices were specific to those shaping forces. Thus, to simply fold preadolescents' language and identity practices into existing theories about teen and youth would therefore create an inaccurate and unfair picture of how they negotiated their social identities and how they understood themselves in relation to other culturally defined age categories, including adults, teens, and younger children. Thus, I seek to draw on the relevant insights from the teen and youth literature without collapsing preadolescent children into that analytical fold.

Like the child language acquisition and socialization literature, studies that examine how children negotiate identity in schools similarly position them as passive recipients of adult-centered or institutional models of race and other social categories (see Kromidas 2016 as exception). Moreover, these studies do not analyze language or linguistic practice in any depth. For the after school students, language was an important means of negotiating racial identification and for displaying age-specific identity models. But even more importantly, language figured centrally in the construction of race in at least three ways: (1) as an object of ideological struggle in terms of how students' behavior was racialized as appropriate or not for particular types of classroom or learning-specific activities, (2) in terms of how students resisted the idea that acting or talking Black was somehow inappropriate for schooling, and (3) in terms of what "acting Black" and "talking Black" even meant in the first place (i.e., what linguistic practices constituted talking Black). That is to say, along with other racialized minorities, African American children learn that the way they speak is a reflection of who they are racially according to a white gaze, and they will be taught and use language with that knowledge in mind (Morgan 2002). As I show in chapters 4–6, the students socialized each other into their own age-appropriate models of acting and talking Black in distinction from adults and older teens. Failing to analyze language with robust attention to use, form, and ideology is therefore a missed opportunity to understand how children engage in the reproduction and transformation of race.

RACIALIZING PROCESSES AND RACIOLINGUISTIC TRANSFORMATION

This book examines how contemporary meanings of race were negotiated and transformed in the language and identity practices of the nine- to thirteen-year-old students. Following anthropology and critical race theory, I define race as a sociopolitical construct that (re)produces essentialist understandings of biology and culture (Omi & Winant 1994; Hill 2008; Bonilla-Silva 2018). When racialization sorts people into hierarchical socioeconomic structures and facilitates in the service of white supremacy, you have what is commonly referred to as *systemic* or *structural racism* (Brodkin 1999; Marable 2000; Alexander 2012). As I discuss in chapter 1, schools are key institutions for the production of structural racism in the United States, as they figure centrally in what Omi and Winant call *racial projects*.

Omi and Winant define racial projects as "interpretation[s], representation[s], or explanation[s] of racial dynamics and an effort to reorganize and redistribute resources along particular racial lines" (1994, p. 56). In today's world, such racial projects include the neoliberal gentrification of urban cities, a process that has undercut social services in favor of commercial profit (Goldberg 2008; Lipman 2011).[4] As cities such as Washington, D.C., are developed for this purpose, schools in impoverished neighborhoods are taken over, closed, and often reopened as private charters to service increasingly white and wealthy populations.

As D.C. Public Schools (DCPS) proceeded to implement school reform in step with neoliberal "urban renewal" efforts in Washington, D.C., I took notice of how students made sense of and responded to their racialized characterization as "problem students" when it came to school and policy-based discourses about their achievement. As I discovered through informal chats and interviews, they were frequently talked to about the so-called Black-white achievement gap by teachers and school officials, and they took note of the fact that their intellect and moral preparedness for school was always compared as lacking to that of white students. While the students openly resisted such racialized comparisons in explicit talk about academic achievement, their everyday language and identity practices evidenced much more complex and nuanced negotiations of race and what it means to be a Black speaking subject in a society that considers itself to have moved past race and racism. And as it did for many African Americans, the 2008 election of Barack Obama marked this symbolic but imagined postracial transition to an equal society for many of the students and their families, but often contradicted the lived experience of race and class oppression (cf. Alim & Smitherman 2012).

Drawing from Omi and Winant's (1994) conceptualization of the racial project, this book describes how the after school students were engaged in their own *transracial project* insofar as they aimed, through language, to transform the raciolinguistic ideologies that are taken up by listening subjects who hear and see African Americans as problem students. Unfortunately, the students' raciolinguistic transformations, while perhaps locally or symbolically empowering, did little to change how they were seen, heard, or policed by the gatekeepers of academic success and future social mobility. These gatekeepers were not intentionally racist individuals, but rather, educators, parents, and other "institutionalized listening subjects" (Flores et al. 2018) who wanted to help the students best navigate being Black in a society that continues to see them as social threats and criminals in the making. Thus, while the after school students showed remarkable dexterity in how they used language to challenge and transform received ideas about race and academic success, including code-mixing, constructing hybrid discourses, and creating a Black linguistic space for academic learning, their efforts were often policed or stemmed by adults in favor of helping them adjust to the assimilatory demands of schooling.

Both the students and adults actually expressed the same language ideologies when it came to schooling and academic success. As I discuss in chapter 2, AAL was seen as integral to how students navigated their home, peer, and neighborhood relationships. Students also saw themselves as needing to speak "proper" for inclusion in the mainstream. But how students and adults determined the appropriateness of language and behavior clearly differed and resulted in adults' policing of their linguistic practices. Students were constantly perceived to be off-task, "having an attitude," and otherwise not on board with the goals and tasks of academic learning. Over the long term, this led to students' disengagement and teachers writing off students as unteachable.

While decades of research on schooling tells us that racialized minority students almost never win the fight from the perspective of structural change, the frictional dynamic I have just described complicates theoretical efforts to understand the school-based production of race and racism as shaped by discrete acts of either domination or resistance (Willis 1977; Ogbu 1978; MacLeod 1995; Fordham 1996). This dynamic is implied in Omi and Winant's (1994) conceptualization of the racial project, which sees any one set of racial discourses and representations as dominant and others subordinate within a given sociohistorical period. According to them, within any given racial formation, liberal or conservative racial projects may predominate; this would explain, for example, why the gains of the Civil Rights Movements from the 1960s–1970s were followed by the neoconservative[5] backlash to this period of liberal multiculturalism from the 1980s forward. It also helps explain how racial representations and ideologies change over time. Thus, today, the idea of race as a "social construct" has gained traction as a rebuttal to biological determinism (and perhaps unwittingly helps to fuel colorblind and postracial thinking).[6]

The concept of the racial project helps explain how a particular racial representation can become dominant, or "hegemonic," but it misses an important perspective: racial projects can overlap or share ideological foundations. This explains the fact that most whites today do not consider themselves to be racist, and that they share similar racial and linguistic ideologies across party lines (Hill 2008; Bonilla-Silva 2018). Colorblindness and postracialism are shared racial ideologies across the political spectrum, and not just among whites (Alim & Smitherman 2012; Alim 2016a). In terms of schooling, deficit perspectives are evident in liberal and progressive language education programs, which often end up centering whiteness and white power even if the educators are not white (Flores & Rosa 2015; Chaparro 2019).

The racial project model also misses the fact that people can articulate multiple or contradicting racial and linguistic ideologies. Many adults in the after school program were committed to helping students maintain their sense of cultural Blackness, but only in ways that would not threaten their present and future academic accomplishments. By contrast, students often expressed an assimilatory logic with respect to race, language, and academic achievement, but often challenged or attempted to transform this logic in their actual language and identity practices. A new way of thinking about racialization, then, is needed, for which I propose the concept of the transracial project. It draws from several other areas to help theorize what it meant for the students to transform race in relation to the wider structures and institutionalized practices that more often constrained their efforts than enabled them.

First, my concept of the transracial project draws from recent work on *raciolinguistic chronotopes*, defined as cultural narratives that produce raciolinguistic models of personhood in relation to ideas about time and space (Flores et al. 2018; Rosa 2019). As I explain in chapter 4, raciolinguistic chronotopes help explain how students and adults were socially positioned as institutionalized subjects who often found themselves having to act within broader histories and structures they did not necessarily choose. On the one hand, this includes the imagined history, present, and future of criminalizing Black bodies and language as socially threatening, a chronotope I refer to as *policing*, and on the other, ensuring the linguistic and cultural survival of an "imagined" Black community (Anderson 1990; Fordham 1996), which I refer to as the chronotope of *survival*. Positioning students' raciolinguistic transformations within these wider chronotopes helps nuance how they navigated the meaning of race in relation to broader structures and practices. It also helps explain why students' efforts often went unseen and unheard by well-intentioned educators and parents who sponsored deficit-based raciolinguistic ideologies because they were worried about how they would be perceived outside of the space of the after school program and neighborhood.

Second, I draw from work on language crossing (Rampton 1995; Paris 2011) and translanguaging (García & Wei 2009; Seltzer 2017) to analyze how students attempted to transform race using linguistic practices. Together, these bodies of work call into question monoglossic and bilingual language ideologies as ones that unwittingly reproduce deficit ideologies. As I discuss in chapter 6, it is commonly assumed that racially minoritized students need to linguistically retain an authentic core self by maintaining their "home language" while using it as a bridge to acquire an imagined Standard English. Such an assumption undercuts educators' opportunities to see and hear the "translingual sensibilities" (Seltzer 2017) that such students often bring to their academic learning and to navigate schooling. Similar to Alim's (2016b) work on transracialization and Tetreault's concept of *transculturality*, the after school students often sought, in code-mixing and discourse blending, to challenge naturalized assumptions about the link between racial identity and language.

Using these conceptual tools, I seek generally to highlight the complexity and sophistication of children's language and identity practices against the tendency to see them through the harmful lenses of deficit or unassimilable difference. More specifically, I want to show how the after school students were fundamentally engaged in a political project of racial transformation in relation to their lived experiences. The concept of the transracial project frames my analysis of how the students transformed race by selectively blurring or erasing perceived differences in Black and white styles of speaking in some contexts—for example, in how they framed linguistic practices such as "slang" as something that everyone speaks (chapter 2)—while highlighting racial differences in others—for example, in voicing the verbal disciplinary styles of African American and white instructors (chapter 3). That is to say, sometimes racial differences mattered to students and sometimes it did not. Describing how they "did" race in their after school interactions reveals the limits and possibilities of structural transformation and, I hope, provides opportunities to interrupt the kinds of race-thinking that stand in the way of lasting change.

TEACHING AND RESEARCHING IN THE AFTER SCHOOL PROGRAM

I first learned of Urban Pathways and its community programs through a School of Education/Anthropology graduate summer intensive course for practicing and future teachers in August 2008. In this course, "Understanding Non-Standard English," I served as a graduate teaching assistant. One of the professors, who was also my graduate mentor, served on Urban Pathways' board of directors and had asked the executive director of this nonprofit organization if the class could observe and teach at one of their summer program sites as part of the course practicum. For a week, I carpooled with teachers in the class to Urban Pathways' summer program location on 25th Street in the Southeast quadrant, located south of the Anacostia River and freeway. This part of Southeast bordered Prince George's County, Maryland to the north and east; one could easily cross over into Maryland on foot. Though gentrification was already underway north of the freeway by the waterfront (Prince 2014; Grieser forthcoming), this lower part of Southeast across the Anacostia and several miles south of the waterfront was, in the popular local imagination, a dangerous hinterland of "Black on Black crime" and poverty. In reality, 94 percent of residents in Wards 7 and 8 were African American, with a majority living at or below the poverty line (U.S. Census 2010), and with many suffering chronic health issues (Williams 2009). Related to issues with health and wellness, nearly all of Southeast was a food desert, and many neighborhoods suffered from nearby river and trash pollution (Williams 2001). According to local news and stories I heard from residents, gang violence among youth was a common occurrence, especially once it turned dark. As a result of Southeast's emblematic reputation as a minority "ghetto," a few of the teachers expressed concerns or frustration with being asked to travel "down there" for the fieldwork component of the course. Complicating the racializing discourse about Southeast as a dangerous ghetto, at least for me, was the fact that all but two of the teachers in this class were African American and all women, with several years' experience teaching in DCPS schools.[7] As reported by teachers, and as I observed through pilot research projects, any of these schools mirrored the conditions of impoverished schools even if they were not in neighborhoods with the racial and socioeconomic demographics of Southeast. As I was to learn in the course of my teaching and ethnographic fieldwork, many of the verbal and disciplinary conflicts the Urban Pathways' students experienced in school were with African American teachers, and that the achievement ideologies their teachers sponsored tended to be oppressive from the students' perspectives. I explore this particular topic in more depth in chapter 1.

Nevertheless, along with the professors who co-taught the course and the teachers enrolled in the course, I went to Urban Pathways' summer program for the week's practicum, where we would observe the students and try out the critical literacy activities the teachers developed in the coursework component. All of the students were African American, between the ages of five and thirteen, and divided into two age groups: the "little kids" (ages five and eight) and the "older students" (ages nine to thirteen). Despite some of the teachers' feelings of reservation to have to travel to Southeast, we all quickly fell in love with the students, who were quirky and excited in the presence of unfamiliar visitors. Many of the "little kids," as we called them, expressed their quickly formed attachments in the way of bear hugs and asking to sit on laps. We all tried to master the given names of the children, used for record-keeping and attendance, plus the two or three nicknames they had, typically assigned by family members or friends. Since there were around fifty children in the summer program, this was no small task.

Because I liked the progressive educational goals of Urban Pathways and the personalities of the children so much, I asked if I could return as a volunteer literacy instructor in the winter of 2008. Once again making a connection through my faculty mentor, this time with the site coordinator, I came on board one day a week through the end of the 2009 school year to work with the nine- to thirteen-year-old children in the 25th Street after school programs, called "family literacy" and "academic enrichment." The programs were located within two blocks of each other near the same low-level, "garden"-style residential housing units. In the summer of 2009, after meeting Victor, the founder and executive director of Urban Pathways, I was hired to be a lead teacher and program coordinator at multiple sites throughout Southeast. I found myself driving "Big Blue," the organization's blue van, from one site to another (three total), teaching at one, supervising at another, or gathering verbal and written reports at another depending on my particular role. I also used Big Blue to drive groups of fourth and fifth grade children to and from the local community pool one afternoon a week during the summer programs. Along with what I heard and observed during lesson time, this gave me an unofficial opportunity to listen in on, participate in, and ask questions about the conversations of the preadolescent age groups I worked with. In addition to learning slang, I learned how central joning was to peer rapport (chapter 4), as well as what kinds of topics and concerns occupied them on a regular basis.

Since Urban Pathways housed their programs and unofficially partnered with DCPS schools and their teachers and staff for several of their academically focused programs, I also came to know matters of school procedure, policy, and practice from the perspectives of teachers and sometimes parents. This included advice on how to manage behavior problems, learning how students were tracked and measured academically in school and why and how teachers and administrators tried to manage accountability standards and free breakfast and lunch programming in the service of the children, a process that often conflicted with official procedures and rules. Even though the organizational mission of Urban Pathways was to challenge and provide alternatives to accountability models of schooling, a topic that I explore in depth in the next chapter, as an organization, we were nevertheless bound by grant and school-institutional requirements to help students succeed academically according to institutional and policy standards.

As I continued working with Urban Pathways in multiple roles through 2010, I eventually landed back in the 25th Street programs, which had always had high need among its 100 or so students, related to high turnover among staff. Because I was one of the few teachers to have stayed as long as I did, I came eventually to meet, chat with, and gain the respect and trust of parents and caregivers, who had already heard of me, as many said upon first meeting me, through their children. By summer 2010, my plan to do my dissertation research on language and identity among teenagers in a DCPS high school was falling through the cracks. I had two options for doing high school research: work with a ninth-grade English teacher who wanted to casually ignore all of the central office red tape needed for me to come into her classroom, or work with a twelfth-grade English teacher at a different school who, along with the school principal, wanted me to follow procedure and policy for doing research in a DCPS school to the letter, and who still expressed reservations about my research questions and methods. Though the twelfth-grade teacher trusted me (we are still friends to this day), she was anxious that I would find or document fodder for the school administration or central office to further scrutinize as evidence of her school's and students' failures. I was not comfortable with either research scenario and decided to explore the possibility of doing my research with the children at Urban Pathways instead of teenagers and youth in a high school.

When I approached Victor and the Urban Pathways staff about the possibility of doing my research in the 25th Street after school programs, everyone agreed readily to let me do my research, though some said they were nervous about how I might perceive and evaluate them. I believe a few staff members with classroom experience were under the impression that I would be there to assess their competence in teaching from an administrative perspective. A few teachers asked if they should act normally, and I explained that I would try to observe as much as possible how everyone would act in the absence of knowing that they would be audio-recorded. Similarly, my tenure in the community and established reputation as a good teacher whom the students liked lent support and validity to my research topic and goals. Only one parent expressed concern when I asked for her child's assent and her consent, but then agreed to sign her consent form and let her child sign his assent form after I verbally explained my research and answered her questions. Like this parent, I met with others in person at one of the after school sites or, accompanied by one of the students, went to their homes to explain my research and obtain consent and assent. One student, ten-year-old Alisha of the orange vignette at the beginning of this chapter, took a hesitant stance when taking me to visit the home of a neighbor, whose child was also in the program, out of concern for what I might see or hear in her apartment complex—for one, the "crackheads" who hung out in the hallways. Generally speaking, parents and children appeared more concerned with what I might think or feel about what I would see or hear rather than with me doing anything potentially suspicious. Thirteen-year-old CeCe's mother, for example, responded to my research with the following: "Oh, I hope she doesn't say anything that embarrasses me!" and laughed nervously.

Thus, from October 2010 to June 2011, while working without pay as the lead teacher at Urban Pathways' two Southeast after school programs, I collected data by observing and audio-recording interactions three to five days a week between the hours of 3:30 p.m. and 6:00 p.m. I ended up with 432 hours of audio-recorded data, 171 of which I transcribed roughly and took notes on. I also collected data by observing and taking field notes on my computer whenever possible while also running the digital voice recorder, conducting informal interviews with students, staff, and parents, and conducting four ninety-minute-long focus groups with twelve participants.[8]

A smaller component of my ethnographic project involved tracking how students' language and identity practices might change after three months of doing critical literacy in the last phase of the research. However, I did not successfully complete this research component due to other demands. For one, doing critical literacy conflicted with the program rule and parents' desire that the students return home with most or all of their homework completed. Homework typically consisted of endless rows of math problems and reading comprehension passages, all of which aimed to "teach to the test"—a term that refers to the pedagogical strategy of drilling students for high performance on high-stakes standardized tests. In 2010, this test was the DC CAS. DC CAS was part of the national education policy mandate for schools to report students' performance on math and reading, which factored into district-wide decisions to close or radically "turn around" (usually close and repopulate with different students) schools that did not meet the determined proficiency level.[9] When after school staff actually worked through all of the sheets that students brought in, it typically took all of the program time to complete the assignments. At one point, I became so exasperated with nine-year-old Joseph's math teacher that I wrote her a letter assuring her that he and I worked up to two hours at a time and still could not complete all of his homework.

Over the course of three years, I went from being a teacher to becoming a teacher-researcher. At times, I was frustrated because I felt this dual positionality limited my ability to adopt the interpretive and analytic stance of a pure ethnographer. However, as I discuss in the next section, being a teacher-researcher in the after school program uniquely positioned me to reflect and analyze my data in ways that challenge ethnographic analyses of classrooms from the standpoint of ordinary participant observation. Moreover, how I identified ethnoracially in the course of my teaching and research also challenged me, but ultimately helped me reflect on and analyze my limits and potential as a scholar-practitioner of educational justice.

Listening Subjectivities: Becoming a Teacher-Researcher

Like other anthropological researchers who conduct research in schools or after school programs, I was not simply an observer in the after school program, nor even simply a participant-observer as defined in the traditional ethnographic sense, I also had a teaching role, and a more involved one than described by other school ethnographers (Mendoza-Denton 2008; Bucholtz 2011; Rosa 2019). As much as I tried, I could not, shake the formal identity and classroom role indexed by my teacher title of the previous two years, "Ms. Jennifer," when shifting to conducting fieldwork as a teacher-researcher. While it felt limiting to be a teacher doing research rather than a researcher doing (some) teaching, in retrospect, I believe this vantage point offers important insights for the analysis of my listening subjectivities in my dual role as a teacher-researcher.

Initially, I wanted to adopt the stance of an outsider for at least an hour each day to get a better total picture of academic learning, other task activities, and classroom interactions. But this quickly turned out to be impossible: students would approach me to ask for help as they normally would, even when I outsourced my teaching role to someone else to try and quietly observe and take notes in the back of the room. Moreover, the after school programs were constantly short-staffed. More often than not, I had to abandon my plan of alternating between programs each day to go tutor students in one program or another. My data collection plan felt unbalanced, and I became frustrated that I was not doing fieldwork at all in the classroom. To try and reintroduce some aspect of observation, I would immediately start listening to my audio-recordings on the train and continue taking field notes while recalling key details of interaction as well as I could. Each day upon arrival, I would quickly sketch a map of the after school space and note where the students sat or played at different times, which helped me put together the pieces in retrospect. To preserve what I could remember, I also used my field notes to selectively and roughly transcribe and code my linguistic data when I got home.

In retrospect, taking on a teacher-fronted role while doing research offered me the opportunity to explore the workings of listening subjecthood and ideology from a reflexive standpoint that anthropologists in more of a researcher-fronted role typically do not experience. For one, as a teacher in the after school program, I inevitably felt complicit with some of the schooling processes that anthropologists have the luxury of describing when they are simply observers, overhearers, or occasional tutors. Especially when disciplining the students or keeping them on task, I felt myself to be the animator of social and linguistic ideologies I did not personally share—for example, in telling students to settle down, be quiet, or stop joning during homework, reading circles, and other learning activities. This was especially the case in the first month or so of my audio-recording the students: they believed that I was doing it to report them to their parents or other listening authorities, despite my efforts to explain to the contrary. For the first several weeks, I heard students on my recordings remind each other not to cuss or say anything bad because they were near the digital voice recorder. I believe that once they realized, no one was going to confront them about any talk or behavior picked up by the audio recorder (and once I began to interview them, which they enjoyed), the students began to relax.

After that first month or so, students began to greet the audio recorder knowing I would listen back to it (e.g., "Hi, Ms. Jennifer! Your hair look nice today."). They would also playfully "snitch" on each other, collapsing into giggles over real or invented transgressions they accused each other of performing. For the most part, after the first month, they paid little attention to it except for those moments. Students' reactions to the voice recorder, then, reveals the extent to which they are hyperaware that their talk and behavior will always-already be policed by listening subjects ready to discipline them into appropriate models of talk and behavior.

Though offering somewhat of a flexible classroom, the structure of learning and style of most after school teachers and tutors mimicked what the students received at school. Especially toward the end of my fieldwork, which coincided with the end of the school year, students' weary, sullen, or defiant faces bore all the evidence of the constant battle they faced in constantly having to correct their talk and behavior to be school appropriate. I felt incredibly guilty, and continue to feel incredibly guilty, for silencing students for the purpose of classroom control and implementing achievement standards, which demand assimilation to white, middle-class norms. Thus, while classroom researchers typically watch this process, I directly participated in it and reproduced the processes I wanted to interrupt.

In most ethnographies of schooling, anthropologists tend to explore the workings of ideology and complicity on students, but not on teachers, and sometimes write off educators who they determine to be complicit with the racial project of schooling while analytically rewarding practitioners of critical pedagogy. Having felt the pressure myself to balance students' needs with meeting after school grant requirements for proof of academic growth to ensure funding for the next year, I made teaching choices that I did not agree with at the time and still grapple with. In this book, then, I explore the implicit and often false linking of critical consciousness with socially just action: as I do with the after school students in this book, I examine how my critical stance was limited not by "false consciousness," but by position as an insti-tutionalized listening subject who needed to ensure that the program could function within the prescribed limits of teaching, learning, and assessment. I describe these structural limits in more detail in chapter 1.

Another aspect of my listening subjecthood was shaped by my perceived eth-noracial identity among the students as white—or, at least, as not Black. In terms of parentage, I am Filipino and European American, and I self-identify as a Filipina American woman of color who, given my phenotypical appearance to others, typi-cally passes for white. My one effort to reposition myself as not white (and to get information about how students linked race and language) during a conversation with four girls about talking "like white girls,"[10] which occurred toward the end of my fieldwork, appears to have had little impact on how most students, aside from Janice (line 10), identified me as racially white (lines 7 and 8):

1	Jen	How many white girls do you know?
2	Alisha	Uh, ((name of student))-
3	Jen	Do they go to your school?
4	Alisha	No.
5	Keri	I know how many white girls!
6		Ms. Rachelle ((an after school tutor)),
7	Keri	Uh, [name of student], you-[YOU]
8	Alisha	
9	Jen	Who says I'm white?
10	Janice	(.>5s) She light-skinned, y'all.
11	Alisha	No she not.
12	Alisha	She – ((inaudible)), mix.
13		I'm, I'm chocolate.
14	Jen	I'm Asian. And white.
15	Alisha	So you white?
16	Jen	Half white.

Having already worked with the students for nearly three years, I found it useless to try and change their perceptions of me as a person of color, and I could not have related to them as such: it was not a racial category of distinction for them as it is for academics, many of whom theorize racial identity in alignment with liberal mul-ticulturalism, and which often uncritically leaves whiteness unmarked ("not a race") in stark contrast to the broad category of "people of color." I was more interested in having my self-identity socially acknowledged if possible. Though an increasingly multi-ethnic Washington, D.C., is often conceptualized as a Black and white city (Modan 2007), the students spoke about "Chinese" (Korean) and "Spanish (Latinx) people" whom they encountered in their daily lives, and used ethnoracial/ethnolin-guistic labels in terms consistent with their own assumptions about phenotype and language. I assumed the students would not be familiar with Filipinos as an ethnic group, so I chose "Asian" as a safely accurate representation that I thought they would understand (I am not, after all, Chinese). But after some discussion about my ethnoracial background that day with the two girls, the topic quickly faded and was never raised again.

Thus, I could not change my local racialization as white except perhaps through insistent correction, which would be irrelevant and awkward to what I was doing: teaching and researching in the after school program. Since education was one area in which the families I worked with desired for race to not matter (chapter 1), I remained silent on the topic of my ethnoracial identity. I did, however, decide to approach my analysis of language and identity as someone who is not Black and also not white, as I experienced or witnessed linguistic policing and mocking among Filipino family members who had non-native phonology and syntax. For example, I understood how students recruited pathologizing stereotypes of African Americans in the styles of verbal art called joning (chapter 4) and marking (chapter 3) to negotiate their Otherness. Poking fun at "the Filipino accent," and even performing imitations of the first generation adults in my family as a child for collective entertainment, was a big part of my Filipino American upbringing. As an adult and scholar, I came to understand how such linguistic practices evidenced larger issues about ethnoracial identity, belonging, and social mobility. Such personal experiences, then, provided some sort of bridge to me understanding as a reflexive listening subject how and why the students used language to negotiate their linguistic racialization as Other. At the same time, I was aware that there were limits to what I could know about the students as someone who is not African American or Black (cf. Ellsworth 1989).

LINGUISTIC ANTHROPOLOGICAL APPROACHES TO ANALYZING LANGUAGE AND IDENTITY

Following contemporary approaches to the study of language and identity, I use the analytical tools of semiotics as developed in linguistic anthropology. These approaches, which I use for discourse and conversation analysis in this book, investigate how linguistic forms can be used to index, or presume and entail, social group identity. More importantly, a semiotic approach investigates how racial groups and racialized bodies are constituted, affirmed, and transformed in and through socially meaningful uses of language. Semiotic approaches provide a tool for examining how situated cultural practices lead to the (re)circulation and reproduction of broader social meanings and institutions.

Related to this, I approach AAL not as "a language spoken by African Americans," but instead as a set of language and discourse practices that African Americans take up to negotiate Black identities. In this book, I take the position that AAL is not in and of itself comprised of any particular features that are distinct from normative English; it is simply one way of describing what speakers do from the standpoint of linguistics. African Americans who use AAL linguistic and discourse features describe these features differently (or as meaningfully different), and white listening subjects unfamiliar with AAL often perceive it through the lens of raciolinguistic pathology—for example, deficit perspectives (Labov 1972; Paris & Alim 2017). These are a few of the ways in which language, race, and identity are forged through competing, intersecting, or overlapping language ideologies (Morgan 2002). Following approaches developed by Mendoza-Denton (2008), Bucholtz (2011), Paris (2011), and Rosa (2019), I try to account for all of these interpretations of language as well as their frictions and effects by grounding analysis of linguistically defined forms in students' use and their own ideologies about language. Doing so reveals key ways in which they semiotically transform race in connection with other meaningful signs and discourses.

In her ethnography of style and identity among white teens, Bucholtz (2011) divides the analysis of race-in-language, so to speak, into three categories: *ethnoracial labels* (what terms people use to describe themselves and others), *racial discourse* (talk about race), and *racial indexes* (the racialized meanings associated with the use of particular linguistic forms). In this book, the predominant focus is on how students indexed racialized meanings, more so than focusing on race labels or racializing discourses, which tends to be the focus of most studies on talk about race (e.g., Pollock 2004; Kromidas 2016). Most studies, moreover, do not take up an explicit analysis of language (i.e., linguistic forms and practices) proper (cf. Bucholtz 2011; Alim 2016a). Race talk and race labels are relatively more explicit ways of showing the co-constituting relationship between language and race; that is to say, it is easier to "see" race in language. However, they are not as frequent as indirect indexes in everyday speech (Hill 2008), nor are they necessarily reliable for determining, for example, people's beliefs about the relationship between language and race, in other words, their raciolinguistic ideologies. That is to say, explicit forms of talk about race cannot fully explain the often present contradictions between practice and ideology—that is, what people do and what they think about what they do and why. Because I am interested in how students' everyday talk shapes ideas about language and race, I therefore focus on how talk that does not necessarily refer to race but that enacts it in tacit ways.

CHAPTER SUMMARY

Chapter 1 provides the historical and institutional context for my ethnographic exploration of African American children's language and identity practices by discussing schooling in Washington, D.C. Specifically, I theorize schooling in Washington, D.C., in relation to the urban developments that produced "Southeast," the city quadrant where 94 percent of residents are African American, with a majority living at or below the poverty line. Drawing from other studies of schooling and gentrification in D.C. and other urban cities (Lipman 2011; Prince 2014), I analyze how schooling was imbricated in a broader neoliberal racial project to commercially and residentially develop the nation's capital for whites to the exclusion of African

Americans. Then, using data I gathered from informal interviews and conversations, I analyze how these race- and class-based urban disparities shaped the achievement ideologies of the families I worked with in Southeast and the justice-focused goals of Urban Pathways.

Chapter 2 introduces the nine- to thirteen-year-old students and presents the second core focus of this book: how they used language and other identity practices to index and deconstruct pathologizing raciolinguistic discourses about Blackness. Here, I explain their understandings of AAL and examine their raciolinguistic practices and ideologies in relation to age, gender, and class stereotypes of Black children and youth. In particular, it focuses on how the preadolescent students responded to and resisted the racialized policing of their bodies as potential street youth, whereby adults attempted to correct or control their perceived orientations to the street toughness stylistically embodied by local teens and youth as well as popular hip-hop artists the students were perceived to mimic. At times, this involved students minimizing or "indexically bleaching" (Bucholtz 2016) racialized linguistic practices, as in Blake's description of slang; at others, their practices deliberately highlighted and played on raciolinguistic stereotypes of Black youth as "criminal" as a form of resistance. This chapter highlights the sophisticated ways in which the after school students understood and navigated their identities as "Black" and as "kids" in relation to adult-centered anxieties about their academic and socioeconomic futures.

Chapter 2's broad focus on raciolinguistic identity sets the stage for chapters 3–5, which analyze language and discourse to examine how students locally transformed dominant discourses about race and academic success. Together, these three chapters address the different ways in which the nine- to thirteen-year-old students used language and discourse practices to construct their own raciolinguistic identity models in relation to learning and academic achievement.

Chapter 3 examines two types of speech acts, directives and marking, as voicing practices in which students directly or indirectly quoted the words of parents and teachers to perform or comment on the act of verbally disciplining students in the after school program. It shows how directives and marking resemiotized the prestige value of racialized languages in the after school space and, by association, the speakers typically associated with those "imagined" language varieties (Chun 2001). By way of producing contrasts between African American and white adult speakers, students represented African American adults as articulate, capable, and effective in their role as authority figures, and white instructors as quite the opposite: inarticulate, hesitant, and weak. By marking white speakers as out of place, silly, and ineffective while normalizing African American linguistic practices as appropriate for asymmetrical interactions between children and adults, the students disrupted the dominant raciolinguistic ideology of white speech as orderly, proper, and appropriate in the after school space.

Chapter 4 explores a verbal performance style called *joning* by students. In the after school program, joning was policed as aggressive or threatening language that encouraged students to fight and bully one another. However, the preadolescent students nevertheless continued to jone with one another as a way of relating to peers and facilitating academic learning. As a verbal performance style, joning indexed pathologizing speaker types associated with "talking ghetto" or "talking street"; as such, it was a socially risky linguistic practice: students were likely to be seen as having an attitude or starting fights despite the fact that joning functioned as peer talk and as playful banter in which students competed with one another academically. Focusing analysis on such uses, this chapter highlights how joning helped students co-manage age- and location-specific expectations for peer socializing and to create a "Black linguistic space" (Alim 2004) for academic learning in relation to wider raciolinguistic chronotopes of policing and survival.

Chapter 5 examines how the students circulated racializing stereotypes about Black students as "not literate" and as "low achievers" in academic learning activities such as reading groups. Here, I highlight how students used pathologizing discourses about "resistant" African American students to disengage from or deflect away from participation in activities such as reading, tease peers, or to manage anxieties about their own academic performance. Yet rather than approaching the students' practices as reproductions of dominant raciolinguistic ideologies, this chapter highlights instead how students' recursive construction of normative school-based ideologies of intelligence and achievement constituted a form of raciolinguistic transformation. Specifically, it shows how students projected pathologizing identities onto peers in order to avoid stereotype threat, or the fear of confirming negative racial stereotypes such as the belief that African American students are less smart than whites.

Finally, chapter 6 uses critical pedagogical perspectives on literacy and language learning to analyze the students' written discourse and art projects, taken from lessons and activities we did together in the after school program and the potential for transformative teaching. Some of the activities, such as "What does a scientist look like?", came from my efforts to practice critical pedagogy with the students. Others, such as "If I were President of the United States," were not explicitly designed as critical pedagogy, but nevertheless evidence the ways in which students actively create their own models and discourses about social justice in the absence of teacher guidance. This chapter has two main goals. First, it aims to show how children's thinking on race and other social justice issues produce transformative possibilities, which are rarely considered in such a capacity from an adult-centered perspective. Second, this chapter shows that children already engage in critical pedagogy apart from the leadership or guidance of adults. Following Vasquez (2002) and Flores (2020), it argues that instead of seeking to teach children critical pedagogy, educational practitioners might benefit instead from adopting a perspective that views children as always-already engaging in the production of social meaning and social justice. Finally, the conclusion suggests ways in which academic scholars and students of anthropology, linguistics, childhood studies, critical race studies, and education might use this book to inform their own research projects. It suggests ways in which scholars, practitioners, and teachers can reframe their own ideas about language and race to the benefit of the students they teach and towards the goal of educational justice.

NOTES

1. All identifying names and locations are anonymized to protect the confidentiality of the research participants.

2. See, for example, Hebidge (1979) and Rampton (1995) on youth style and Irvine and Gal (2000) and Agha (2004) for semiotic theories of social meaning.

3. See Alim and Smitherman (2012) on normative expectations for Black language use and styleshifting in the contemporary era of "post-racial" thinking.

4. Critical reproduction theorists discuss how schooling functions to socialize and "sort" minoritized groups into social hierarchies related to race and class. For a fuller discussion, see Willis (1977), Ogbu (1978), Bourdieu (1980), Foley (1990), MacLeod (1995), Fordham (1996), and Duncan-Andrade and Morrell (2008).

5. In Omi and Winant's work, neoconservative refers to the social and political ideology adopted by proponents. In current theorizing, neoliberal is the term used to denote the social and political ideologies accompanying economic practices (e.g., Harvey 2004 and other citations).

6. Nevertheless, scholars and non-academics alike unwittingly apply similar notions of essential difference to the linguistic and cultural practices of racialized minorities. See, for example, Harrison (1998) and Urciuoli (2001).

7. As Moore (1999) and Prince (2014) document, after the Civil War, Black institutions such as Howard University made it possible for African Americans to enter professions such as law and education, with the demand for teachers being the highest. This helps explain why many of the educators and administrators in Washington, D.C., have been African American, with a possibly Black majority teaching force. However, with schooling reforms and the introduction of teachers from programs such as Teach for America from the 1990s forward, as well as demographic changes to the city more generally, educator demographics have changed.

8. I obtained consent and assent for 31 nine- to thirteen-year-olds to participate in interviews and focus groups and observed up to 100 total students (the program enrollment cap) at any given time during my ethnographic fieldwork, including the five- to eight-year-olds.

9. Prior to 2010, No Child Left Behind (NCLB) Act mandated that schools demonstrate "Annual Yearly Progress" (AYP) at the Basic level or above. After 2010, President Obama's introduction of Race to the Top was a similar neoliberal policy initiative that replaced NCLB but largely kept the same criteria for "accountability" (see Lipman 2011).

10. Ten-year-old Mary was also present but did not participate in the conversation.

1

"I Have a(n American) Dream"

Race, Schooling, and Achievement in The Nation's Capital

The summer before I started my fieldwork with the nine- to thirteen-year-old students, I met with Victor, the founder and executive director of Urban Pathways. Urban Pathways was a Christian nonprofit organization that provided summer and after school programs for children, adult educational and English language programs, bilingual preschooling, and other social services aimed at mitigating poverty. The office was housed in a church in the upper part of the Northwest quadrant of Washington, D.C., in a relatively wealthy and mostly white neighborhood far away from the predominantly African American neighborhoods where the after school programs were located. Despite its location in an affluent neighborhood, the church itself was a modest space in need of renovation. When I met with Victor, his office space was piled high with books and papers. That day, I was interviewing to take a paid position as a curriculum developer and lead teacher for Urban Pathways' summer program. Right away, I could tell the interview was a formality, and that Victor was mostly concerned about explaining that the position was a lot of work and not a lot of pay.

Victor shared my critical view of the schooling reforms that had started three years earlier in 2007 under Adrian Fenty's mayoral administration. He and his son, a third-grade science teacher at one of the public schools, shared with me the perspective that the high-stakes tests that were used to claim the existence of an "achievement gap" between whites and African Americans radically underestimated our own students' intellect and academic capabilities. Victor and his son also insisted, like me, that the impoverished African American communities of Washington, D.C., were oppressed on the basis of race, not "class" or a "poverty gap," as many with whom I casually discussed my dissertation research dismissively argued. As Victor explained to me, he had founded Urban Pathways with the idea that the organization's staff had as much to learn from the communities we worked with as they did from us. He conceptualized its educational mission as a cultural exchange rather than as a one-way street that aimed to assimilate students into the mainstream. Given the climate of schooling reform, which discursively insisted on highlighting the failures and deficits of African American and Latinx students, the "majority-minority" student populations in most urban school districts, I found Victor's perspective promising.

Yet, as I discovered that summer and the following year when I conducted field-work as a teacher-researcher, it was not always so easy to practice the philosophy of cultural pluralism that Victor and I had discussed. Prior to that summer, I had not been involved enough with the after school program as a tutor to observe the daily grind. Over the course of October 2010–June 2011, when I taught and researched daily in the two programs in Southeast, I found that the after school program's educational structure and practices often mirrored that of the schools the students attended. For parents but also many staff members, the whole point of after school was to help students succeed in school, their entry point into the wider world of the so-called "mainstream" society. Many staff, regardless of ethnoracial identity, shared the belief that we were there not just to educate the students in the sense of facilitating intellectual and academic growth, but that we also needed to socialize them appropriately for inclusion into a dominant society where their ways of talking and "behaving" would not be understood or welcome. While there were many nice moments where cultural exchange happened, by and large the pluralistic educational vision Victor communicated to me was nearly nonexistent in the day-to-day business of after-schooling. Specifically, as a teacher-researcher, I observed and often participated in the reproduction of deficit ideologies. I conducted my ethnographic fieldwork with an ongoing sense of frustration and guilt about being complicit with the very processes I hoped to eventually interrupt.

This brief description of my time with Urban Pathways serves to briefly introduce readers to the after school program, its goals, and my reflections as a teacher-researcher. In this chapter, I explain how my research participants and I made sense of and in some ways reproduced the unjust racial ideologies we hoped to interrupt. More broadly, this chapter provides the ethnographic context for understanding our local negotiations of race, identity, and academic achievement in relation to the project of schooling. Grounding my analysis in a historical approach to racialization, I focus on how the intersecting processes of urban restructuring, schooling, and home rule have produced African American exclusion in the city of Washington, D.C. As Washington, D.C., became a neoliberal city (Lipman 2011) in the late 2000s, school reform became central to the racial project of "revitalizing" the city to attract whites and capital flow. School reform was discursively anchored in racial-izing discourses about the moral and economic failures of African Americans, D.C.'s urban "majority-minority" student population. As I show through historical analy-sis, educational discourses about the unwillingness and unpreparedness of African American students constituted a rebranding of long-standing deficit and underclass perspectives, which have been shared across the political spectrum and which have functioned to justify political economic and social structures of racial exclusion in the post-civil rights period.

Following Flores (2017) and Rosa (2019), I suggest that neoliberal multicul-turalism, which repackages racial difference as cultural and linguistic deficiency, produces false notions of inclusion and belonging that make it impossible for racialized minorities to achieve regardless of how they position themselves in rela-tion to school-normative ideologies of success. Such race- and class-based structural disparities shaped how we negotiated academic achievement, as did a deficit-based approach to understanding students' engagements with schooling. Here, I argue that even progressive framings of racial inequality may work to reproduce the edu-cational injustices they seek to eradicate because they unwittingly rely on deficit and underclass ideologies to conceptualize academic success as students' main pathway out of poverty.

SOUTHEAST WASHINGTON, D.C.: URBAN RESTRUCTURING AS RACIAL EXCLUSION

By the time I started ethnographic fieldwork in October 2010, almost two years after having volunteered and worked for pay with Urban Pathways, I had gotten used to the long commute. I would start my journey from the upper part of DC's Northwest quadrant, where I lived and went to graduate school, and end it in the upper half of the Southeast quadrant, a distance of just over ten miles. An avid runner, I often considered the fact that it would have taken me just as long to run from point A to B as it would when taking the combined subway-bus commute (and it would be much less expensive). Each way, I traveled for an hour and a half, so my total com-mute time of three hours equaled the amount of time I spent with the students in the after school program.

Part of the reason the trip took so long because the buses in Southeast were inconsistent with their arrival times to the subway stations. I would typically budget a minimum of thirty minutes to wait for one at either the Anacostia or Congress Heights subway station. After a twenty-minute ride, the bus would drop me off about two blocks from one of the after school program locations, and I would walk that short distance, sometimes with a few of the students who were coming from school or the corner store. On days that I went to the family literacy program, staffed by Matt, a twenty-five-year-old Jewish American man originally from Los Angeles, Ms. Betty, the cook and homework tutor (and mother to four of the participating students), and myself, I fretted and fussed about getting there on time, as I was the staff member with the key to the space. At least once a week, Ms. Betty and the students would be outside the locked door for ten to fifteen minutes waiting for me to open up. But everyone understood the bus issues, which was part of the normal routine of living in "Southeast," as students most often referred to "where they were from." A more localized designation they used was "25th Street," the (anonymized) name of the street on which they and their families lived.

As shown in figures 1.1 and 1.2, Southeast is not a neighborhood per se, but an administrative quadrant made up of two district wards, 7 and 8.

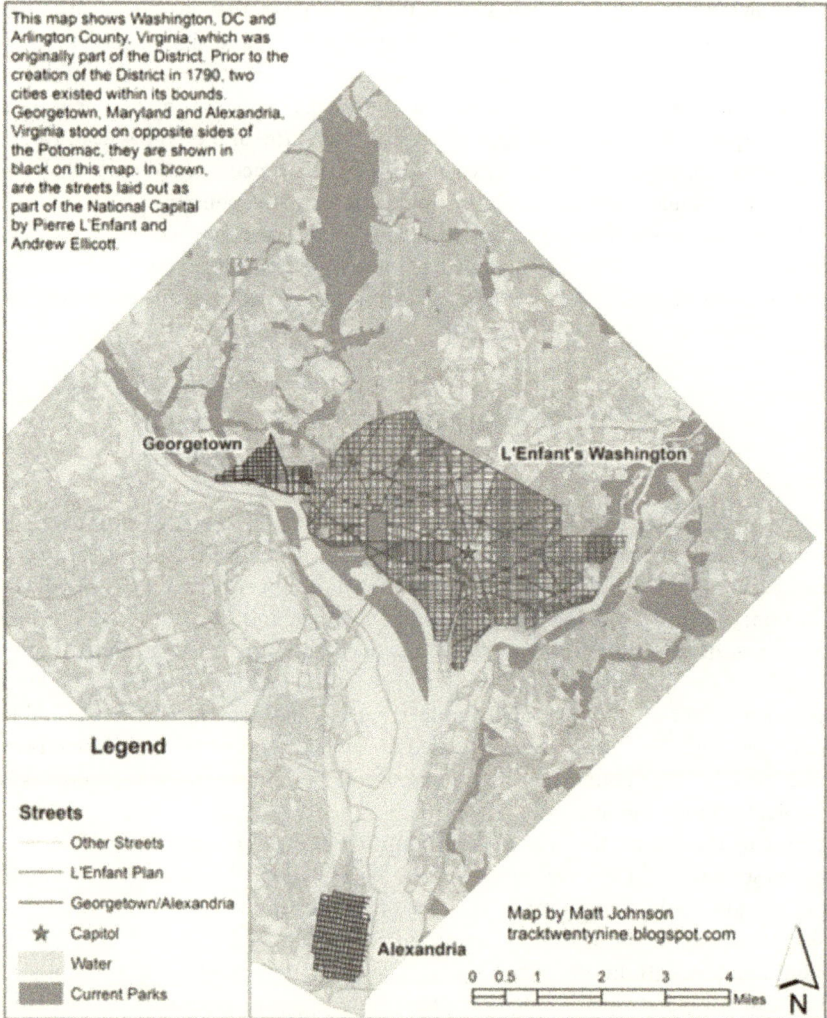

This map shows Washington, DC and Arlington County, Virginia, which was originally part of the District. Prior to the creation of the District in 1790, two cities existed within its bounds. Georgetown, Maryland and Alexandria, Virginia stood on opposite sides of the Potomac; they are shown in black on this map. In brown, are the streets laid out as part of the National Capital by Pierre L'Enfant and Andrew Ellicott.

Georgetown

L'Enfant's Washington

Legend

Streets
Other Streets
L'Enfant Plan
Georgetown/Alexandria
★ Capitol
Water
Current Parks

Map by Matt Johnson
tracktwentynine.blogspot.com

Alexandria

0 0.5 1 2 3 4 Miles

N

Figure 1.1 The Four Quadrants of Washington, D.C.

Demographically, wards 7 and 8 were 94 percent African American (U.S. Census 2010). All of my students and their families were African American, and all of them qualified for local social services such as the Temporary Assistance for Needy Families (TANF) program and the Capital Area Food Bank, a donation-based food pantry located in the Northeast quadrant. This smaller slice of demographics was a microcosm of the general demographics of Southeast: compared to others, wards 7 and 8 have had the highest number of multigenerational African American residents, the lowest average household incomes, and the highest rates of unemployment (Prince 2014). If you compare Census information, these particular figures have remained relatively consistent since the 1980s.

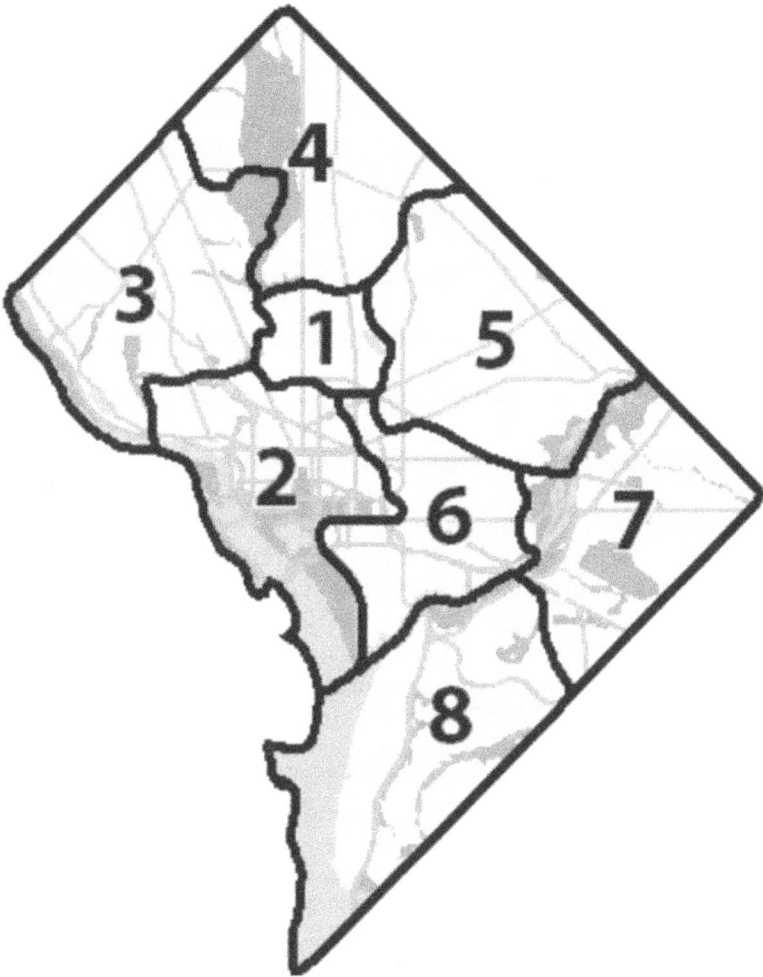

Figure 1.2   The Eight District Wards of Washington, D.C.

Inconsistent local transportation, along with other forms of social and institutional neglect, characterized the daily lives of my students and their families. But instead of being recent developments, these conditions were the result of several decades of African American exclusion from city "revitalization" efforts (Williams 1988, 2001; Prince 2014). Except for the commercial and residential buildings along the Anacostia waterfront that had begun to be erected in the late 2000s, much of Southeast, especially in the surrounding neighborhoods of the after school program, lacked access to any basic services needed for well-being other than local nonprofit organizations housed in the area.[1] Generally, and as is usually the case, these organizations were too small to make any kind of lasting or structurally relevant impact in terms of poverty relief. Given this context, it would be fair to assume that my lateness was among the least of the after school students' or Ms. Betty's worries.

This brief bit of ethnographic description provides a glimpse of where the after school program and my research participants lived and what it was like to live there. It would be impossible to explain who the students and their families are without explaining how they came to be residents of Southeast in the first place. Though many of my students proudly "repped" (represented) Southeast, they, their parents, and their grandparents did not exactly choose to live there. With a few exceptions, most of my students and their parents, the latter of whom were aged anywhere from twenty-five to forty, had been born and raised in Southeast. Arguably, much of the history of African American residency in Southeast below Anacostia begins in the middle decades of the twentieth century, when the government began planning urban redevelopments such as slum removal and redlining through the African American neighborhoods of inner Washington, D.C. The stretch of African American neighborhoods coalesced in the 1940s and 1950s followed two periods of "great migration" from the south, each after the two world wars (Williams 1988, 2001).

In the middle of the twentieth century, segregation, racialized gentrification, and African American outmigration from poor and unlivable areas shaped demographic changes within the city. These shifts were fueled by an increased number of elite and middle-class African American communities who were had access to white-collar professions, including federal employment, law, and teaching (Prince 2014). Shortly following World War II and the second wave of migration, the government planned a series of highways, freeways, and expansion of the streetcar lines to service whites living in the suburbs, running the major thoroughfares through the District's Black neighborhoods and forcibly relocating residents. In the 1960s and 1970s, urban developers collaborated with the District to plan what they termed "revitalization"—that is, develop the city residentially and commercially to attract whites into the city (Williams 2001; Leap 2009; Prince 2014). As a result, the city's working, poor African American communities were relocated to Southeast, across the then new Anacostia Freeway. Many of the African American neighborhoods within the city, particularly in Southwest and the specific neighborhood of Ivy City, have been characterized by health-hazardous living conditions such as proximity to high-sewage areas and substandard housing; near the Anacostia River and further down, these conditions were even worse, since the Anacostia River collected much of the waste and pollution from the freeway commuting. The city developers erected flimsy, temporary housing units under the promise of eventually building more livable residences; much of these were replaced by Section 8 housing, which afforded slightly better living conditions (Williams 2001; Prince 2014).

While whites tend to view gentrification positively and as good for city growth, Prince (2014) provides a rather bleak description of what racialized gentrification is like from African American perspectives. While these perspectives differ by generation and class, she documents the general sentiment that African Americans have been pushed out of the city due to a combination of structural and discursive factors.

This includes unaffordable housing and the erasure of African American culture, history, and presence within historically Black neighborhoods.[2]

Prince notes further that urban restructuring in Washington, D.C., has followed the pattern of "accumulation by dispossession" that is characteristic of neoliberalism, defined as a model of capital accumulation-focused governance that reduces the welfare state and social services in favor of privately owned, profit-generating structures and institutions (Harvey 2005; Lipman 2011; Hackworth 2013). Beginning in the late 1990s, former mayors Anthony Williams and Adrian Fenty initiated citywide reforms that put a heavy focus on commercial and residential development in what were discursively described as "vacant" or "blighted" neighborhoods in Northeast and the Anacostia Waterfront (dmped.dc.gov). As a matter of fact, these areas were well-populated with African American communities, and residents had been living there for several generations (Williams 2001; Prince 2014). Both mayors were widely perceived to be paving the way for gentrification with little concern for the well-being of African American communities (Prince 2014; Hyra 2017; Asch & Musgrove 2019).

After several decades of exclusion from urban development in the form of redlining, housing covenant restrictions, and the institutional neglect of poor conditions in Black neighborhoods, much of Washington, D.C.'s African American working-poor population had been forcibly pushed out to the margins of the city and navigating structural poverty for several generations. But much of this history is invisible to many of the city's residents, who tend to imagine inequality, not to mention the population itself, in terms of a simplistic Black-and-white dichotomy. This not only erases the diversity of African American perspectives grounded in class, generational, and political differences, but the fact that Washington, D.C., has been a multi-ethnic city since the 1990s, with large immigrant populations from El Salvador, Mexico, Vietnam, Ethiopia, Nigeria, and the Caribbean (Manning 1998; Modan 2001, 2007; Prince 2014).[3] Throughout the city's history, with respect to urban restructuring and, as I will show, education policy, African Americans have been discursively rendered invisible as beneficiaries of city improvements and rendered highly visible as a problem population to be removed, ignored, or, in the case of schooling reform, remediated within deficit discourses of "Black lack" (Fordham 1996). Black lack naturalizes practices and structures of racial exclusion as abject, or stigmatized, racial difference such that poverty or academic failure, for example, signal the moral, social, and economic failures of the racialized group in question rather than the conditions to which they have been made subject (Fanon 2003[1967]; Fordham 1996).

African American residents, regardless of class and generational differences, share alike the frustration that Blacks have been pushed out through gentrification and erased in city history and culture and engage in political activism against neoliberal practices of accumulation by dispossession (Prince 2014). Unfortunately to date, there are no comprehensive published ethnographies of African American communities below the Southeast neighborhood of Anacostia, and it is beyond the scope of my own study to offer ethnographic analysis of African American perspectives beyond the particular community I worked and researched with. The perspective that I can offer is that among the participating families, schooling was perceived as the pathway out of poverty and a means of status transformation against racializing discourses of Black lack.

SCHOOLING, RACE, AND ACHIEVEMENT: A HISTORY OF EDUCATION IN THE NATION'S CAPITAL

The families of Southeast not only shared in common the belief that schooling would provide their children with opportunities and status, but the belief that Black success in the political and economic mainstream was evidence of having overcome structural and ideological racism. For many of the staff I worked with, who were residents of the local community, as well as for the students, the 2008 election of Barack Obama to the presidency represented a landmark achievement for what they discursively imagined to be a singular African American community. Despite my own critical view of how Obama sponsored the idea of a Black-white "achievement gap" and African American resistance to learning in education policy and speeches, he was generally revered among the families I worked with as the first Black President of the United States. I shared the sense of symbolic importance with my students, who imagined themselves as one day in the same role in their writing and artwork. But they did not have a postracial perspective, in which his election is viewed as evidence of the United States having moved beyond racism and race (Alim & Smitherman 2012). Rather, Obama was locally lauded as one who had made it against the near-impossible odds of doing so as an African American in a U.S. society that is predicated on anti-Blackness (Marable 2002; Dumas 2016). For many of the adults and students, he had, as Fordham (1996) puts it, "proved the racists wrong."

The families I worked with shared a vision of being able to achieve according to normative standards while also having their perspectives and experiences as African Americans represented politically, socially, and economically. The adults I knew in the community unfailingly voted in local elections and proudly wore their "I Voted" stickers, followed local news and read the Post, involved themselves in their children's schooling, and were generally active in trying to understand the political and social issues of Washington, D.C. These kinds of active engagements with dominant political and social institutions disrupt a normative stereotype of impoverished African Americans as uneducated, isolated from mainstream issues and interests, and as needing access to middle-class norms and values. Beginning with post-segregation, such underclass theorizing is one that liberals and conservatives have sponsored politically in terms of shaping social services, welfare, and education policies (Lewis 1966; Moynihan 1968; NCEE 1983). On the contrary, being politically and socially active was critical to how people in Southeast understood their identities as Black Washingtonians. Indeed, many of the after school students were uncharacteristically familiar with local politics compared to my idea of the average preadolescent/teen. For example, in an essay titled, "The Mayor Election," ten-year-old Delonte wrote in September 2010, he details how he had a bet going with his mother that Vincent Gray, the 2010 challenger to incumbent Adrian Fenty, would be elected because he would do a better job improving the local neighborhoods in Wards 7 and 8 (see chapter 6). His perspective aligned with most of the adults I spoke with, who perceived Fenty to be neglectful of their community and Gray as a local man who would represent their interests and concerns (Gray lived in neighboring Ward 7).

When Kaya Henderson replaced Michelle Rhee as education chancellor in November 2010, thirteen-year-old Felisha threw open the door to the after school program, ran up to me, and gave me a bear hug, gasping, "Did you hear, Ms. Jennifer, we got a Black lady as Education Chancellor!" The American Dream for students, such as Delonte and Felisha, was for African Americans to achieve success and recognition within dominant social and political institutions that generally construct Blackness as incommensurate with achievement (Fordham 1996).

Privately, I was often frustrated by what I perceived as a general lack of critical consciousness among the community members I worked with in terms of their sponsoring of liberal democratic values that did not serve them. This is especially the case with how many students, after school staff, and community members I spoke to on a regular basis sponsored a meritocratic view of success. As I thought through my goals for critical language pedagogy with the students, I grappled with the notion that I would have to try and help students unlearn oppressive ideologies that did not serve them while also respecting their ways of participating in schooling on their own terms. For one, people from Southeast often expressed the view that one's hard work would eventually lead to inclusion in the form of social and economic mobility. Like the working-class "Brothers" of MacLeod's (1995) study, the families of Southeast accepted the dominant meritocratic achievement ideology and judged themselves by its criteria. But recalling the example of Obama's symbolic victory given before, their views of success also appeared to represent the integrationist ideal of seeking to transform one's stigmatized racial identity by way of achieving in the dominant society (DuBois 1995[1903]; Fordham 1996). As I eventually came to understand, the achievement ideology among families Southeast was not so much an uncritical sponsoring of normativity as much as it was a politics of disidentification constructed as anti-racism, specifically with respect to being able to achieve academically.

This kind of "uncritical resistance" (Fordham 1996) on the part of the families I worked with is neither arbitrary nor exceptional. Rather, I suggest that it is rooted in a longer history of Black Washingtonians' political and social identity (see Asch & Musgrove 2019). Fordham argues Black identity (in the singular) has been constructed in relation to the pursuit of achievement in the nation's capital. Fordham's claim is a rather abstract and unproblematized theorizing a unitary Black collective sense of self grounded in double consciousness, and she does not explain how Black Washingtonians' sense of identity and achievement is similar to or different from other African American urban communities who have experienced similar conditions of oppression and exclusion. However, Prince's (2014) ethnography, Asch and Musgrove's (2019) history of Black activism in Washington, D.C., and Roe's (2005) historical analysis of "dual" (segregated) schooling in Washington, D.C., provide some important insights about Black identities in relation to the pursuit of education as specific to the city's history and racial landscape.

First, as discussed earlier, Washington, D.C., provided unusual opportunities for African Americans' social and economic advancement beginning in the Emancipation period. This process was complicated by colorism, defined as "an outgrowth of racism whereby lighter-skinned Blacks gain increased social status and privilege" (Prince 2014, p. 43). African American social mobility depended, with some exceptions, on skin color as well as access to jobs provided by whites, "proper" comportment, and family connections. Prince notes that while colorism was not unique to D.C., the "light-skinned elite . . . have been singled out for their distinctive income-generating opportunities and lifestyles that, over the years, have differentiated life in D.C. from that of other nearby cities" (2014, pp. 43–44, citing Gatewood 1993). This included the formation of elite Black communities who were dedicated to social justice and anti-racism, particularly by way of the establishment of an education system for Black Washingtonians. W. E. B. DuBois, who theorized education's role in social justice, personal moral improvement, and racial uplift, is included among the Black elite scholars who shaped Black schooling early on. Moreover, the teaching profession in particular enabled African Americans to achieve middle-class status, and teachers became the largest African American professional class in the city (Prince 2014).

Schooling in the District has long been characterized by African Americans' efforts to secure equal access to the facilities and resources needed for quality schooling for its population. While efforts to establish Black schools in Washington, D.C., actually predate the Civil War and the creation of a public school system, the high quality of educational institutions for African Americans peaked in the 1860s and 1870s with the creation of several institutions, including Howard University, the M Street High School, and Dunbar High School. Federal oversight of Black schools began in 1862. After Emancipation, from 1867 until just before the second wave of African American migration in the 1940s, Washington, D.C., maintained a segregated public school system that shared a common curriculum but separate facilities and funding for African American and white students under a common Board of Education. Roe (2005) refers to this arrangement as the "dual school system" in Washington, D.C. Even though both waves of migration that followed the two World Wars produced large growth spurts in African American population, it was the second wave in particular that stressed the existing resources for Black schools and educators.

In the years prior to 1945, many of D.C.'s Black public schools had established a reputation for academic excellence nationally. However, these schools quickly declined academically as funding and building space became stretched. African American educators and parents fought to secure the proportional amount of monies and facilities needed to accommodate the population growth that followed World War II. But the D.C. Board of Education, which had a white majority, consistently refused to do so (Levy 2004; Roe 2005). In 1951, with the help of attorneys, the

parents who had consolidated the various Parent Teacher Associations (PTAs) into
the Consolidated Parent Group (CPG) brought suit against the Board of Education.
District Court judge Walter Bastian dismissed *Bolling v. Sharpe* (1951) by citing
another legal suit that had upheld the legality of segregated schools. *Bolling* was then
heard in the Supreme Court in 1954 as a companion case to others across the country that had been combined under a case in Topeka, Kansas, which we now know
as the one that legally desegregated Black and white public schools in the nation—
Brown v. Board of Education (1954).

Since schools were legally desegregated, the belief that the D.C. school system
has been in crisis has been pervasive among Washingtonians across lines of race
and class (Levy 2004). Though not part of my fieldwork, casual conversations with
various DCPS teachers, parents, and employees in the central office during the five
years I lived in D.C. confirmed this common discourse. Much of this sense of crisis
is due to the fact that differently positioned stakeholders have fought for different
kinds of school governance within the larger question of home rule administration.
Introduced in 1973, five years after the local civil rights riots and a few years after the
election of the city's first African American mayor, Walter Washington, home rule
was enacted along with the establishment of the local legislative body, the D.C. City
Council. Not only did home rule require that local governance, including budgets
and legislation, be overseen by Congress, it also means that D.C. lacks the revenue
offered by statehood to support city infrastructure, including schools. Politically,
it also constitutes a form of disenfranchisement for many, especially according to
African American residents, since D.C. has no voting representative in Congress[4]
(Manning 1996; Modan 2007; Prince 2014).

As Levy (2004) notes, struggles for control of schooling in the District have long
been racialized between African Americans and whites. While African Americans
have sought to achieve social equity via schooling in the post-Civil Rights period,
whites have feared loss of control over key city resources such as education (Fordham
1996; Levy 2004). Though home rule is generally limiting in the ways described
earlier, complicating this issue is that African American Washingtonians have actually sought quality schooling under the protection of home rule. This is because the
Supreme Court-elected D.C. Board of Education had consistently tried to avoid
their demands. Citing Diner's (1982) report on D.C. schooling, Levy describes this
process:

> After the Second World War, issues of home rule for the District, civil rights, and
> desegregation intensified already existing conflicts among the different actors in the
> school governance system and provided additional bases for demands for change. Home
> rule proposals included an elected school board as an important element. At the same
> time, as blacks became an increasingly large majority in the city, they sought increased
> political power, including power over the schools incompatible with the existence of a
> court-appointed board of education. The fact that the board tried to avoid addressing
> black demands for equity and desegregation, and that the actions it did take aroused acri-
> mony among both blacks and whites, intensified the quest for change. (Levy 2004, p. 2)

Home rule, then, was seen as an important resource for achieving de facto equality since desegregation had not improved the conditions of schools or the ameliorated the lack of resources for African Americans in Washington, D.C., or more widely throughout the nation's cities. In 1966, twelve years after the de jure segregation of the nation's public schools, the proliferation of classroom studies on the supposed academic failures of African American students were couched within competing perspectives. Pro-segregationists who wanted to prove that integration had not worked cited low test scores, low standards, and discipline problems as factors that had lowered the quality of schools. Proponents of desegregation, on the other hand, noted that factors related to structural inequality, such as inadequate facilities and budgeting, created the problem of a failing education system (Diner 1982; Levy 2004). As a result, the superintendent of schools and the Board of Education invited scholars from the Teacher's College of Columbia University to conduct a comprehensive study of the D.C. school system in the hopes of creating a model school system under integration. Within this fifteen-month research project, a total of thirty-three task forces investigated the conditions of the public schools and published its findings in 1967, the year following the study, under director A. Harry Passow. The nearly 600 pages of findings are impossible to summarize, but the major relevant finding was that the problem of poor schools was related to structural and administrative shortcomings:

> Despite some examples of good quality education . . . education in the District is in deep and probably worsening trouble. Unlike most large city systems which have a core of "slum" schools surrounded by a more affluent ring, the District has a predominance of so-called "inner-city" schools. These schools include large concentrations of economically disadvantaged children, a largely re-segregated pupil population, a predominantly Negro staff, a number of over-aged and inadequate school buildings and inappropriate materials and programs. (Passow 1967, p. 2)

In the 1967 Passow study, it is possible to see the early articulation of competing perspectives on the issue of racialized inequality. On the surface, these place scholars in two divided camps. While politically conservative scholars and policymakers are generally understood to hold "culture-blaming" perspectives, in which the morals and values of racialized groups are targeted as the cause of academic failure, liberal and progressive counterparts are understood as articulating "structure-blaming" perspectives, which point to factors that create an uneven playing field between African Americans and whites (Sperling & Vaughan 2009).

But from the Passow's study's perspective, the conditions of the schools and curriculum not only reflected but also helped to reproduce the wider conditions and, crucially, *culture* of poverty in the inner-cities of D.C. Citing the national Panel on Educational Research and Development, the study defined schooling purpose and the District schools' failure to meet it as follows: "Adolescents depart ill-prepared to lead a satisfying, useful life or to participate successfully in the community . . . the inability of large numbers of children to reverse the spiral of futility and break out of the poverty-stricken ghettos suggests that the schools are no more successful in attaining [non-academic] goals than they are in the more traditional academic objectives (Passow 1967, p. 2).

According to the Passow report, the goal of schooling was to correct the so-called "culture of poverty" among inner-city African American students, a perspective that essentializes and pathologizes the survival strategies of the poor despite the fact that structural conditions are recognized as the cause (Lewis 1966; see Bourgois 2003 and Naples 2004 for critique). From a structurally focused perspective, little has been done to ameliorate the poor conditions of schooling for African Americans in Washington, D.C. (Diner 1982; Levy 2004), and as urban school districts become increasingly "minority-majority" in terms of ethnic student make-up, schooling policies are increasingly focused on promoting culture-blaming while denying the lingering existence of racialized inequality (Bartlett et al. 2002; Lipman and Haines 2007).

Following the publication of the Passow report, the next few decades of school governance were, at best, inconsistent as the District sought a structure-focused solution for improving school and student performance. It identified federal (congressional) oversight as a major problem, so in 1968, a local education board was elected in the first expression of home rule (Meyer 1996).[5] But the school district continued to struggle and in 1996, President Clinton appointed a control board to oversee the locally elected board. But in 2001, the same year President Bush's NCLB Act debuted new national standards for achievement under rigorous teacher evaluation and high-stakes testing, the Control Board closed again, leaving school governance to the local school board, comprising a mix of appointed and elected members.

NEOLIBERALISM, CITIES, AND AFRICAN AMERICAN EXCLUSION

The same year I began graduate school in 2007, Adrian Fenty, an African American man in his late thirties, had been elected to the office of mayor. Fenty had run on a platform promising the revitalization of the poorest parts of D.C. The plan of so-called revitalization focused on creating privatized urban developments that would promote capital accumulation, primarily in the form of real estate and commercial businesses. In order to make room for these structures, parts of the city would have to be made over and attract people who could afford to invest in the kinds of private structures planned for development. Wards 5, 7, and 8, the areas with the highest number of African Americans with the lowest incomes in the city, were targeted for racialized gentrification, a process that was masked under the discourse of renewing neighborhoods that were, as I mentioned earlier, referred to as "vacant" or "blighted."

A big part of Fenty's campaign and plans was school reform that promised to make over what was widely perceived to be the nation's worst school district. Upon his election, he stripped the school board of its powers and handed near-sole decision-making authority over to a newly minted Education Chancellor, Michelle Rhee. For many Washingtonians, the three to four years following were a total disaster for the school system. After closing over twenty-three schools and firing 241 tenured DCPS teachers under a rigid accountability model that blamed individual schools and teachers for failing to meet the NCLB's achievement measure, called Adequate Yearly Progress (AYP), Rhee's education reform empire collapsed. In fall 2010, a series of cheating scandals were reported DCPS-wide (Turque 2010; Austermuhle 2013). Rhee was lauded nationally for her toughness, as made evident in the December 8, 2008, issue of *Time* magazine. Posing upright with a stern stare at the camera, Rhee holds a broom standing at the front of a classroom to symbolically indicate her sweeping reforms; accompanying her pose is the headline, "How to Fix America's Schools." Rhee is also depicted as a hero who stems the tide of backlash from a villainized teacher's union in the documentary film *Waiting for Superman* (Guggenheim 2010) and in news media reporting that retrospectively evaluates her impact as positive (Mead 2017). But locally, Rhee was a pariah who was perceived to consistently trivialize and silence the criticisms of parents, teachers, and activists, who pointed out that she ignored the structural facts of poverty and race in her "no excuses" approach to ensuring that DCPS would turn around low student performance (Turque 2010). It is widely believed that Adrian Fenty lost the 2010 mayor election to Vincent Gray due to the Rhee scandal, though he was also widely perceived among the city's African American communities to only represent the interests of whites and gentrification (Prince 2014; Mead 2017).

During Rhee's tenure, DCPS implemented a number of extremely detailed measures for evaluating student and teacher performance, relying on high-stakes testing outcomes and whether schools met AYP under the NCLB. Schools that did not meet AYP were closed and often reopened as privately funded and managed charter schools, which admitted students on either an application or lottery basis (Holland 2010). By 2008, DCPS enrollment had dropped dramatically, which fueled local and national perceptions of the school system as failing. Kaya Henderson continued as Education Chancellor after Rhee resigned and Fenty lost the 2010 mayor's election to Gray. She continued to close in Wards 7 and 8 along the lines of her predecessor, and in areas where a number of private charters had opened (Brown 2013; Mead 2017). Many in Southeast perceived this process to help pave the way for gentrification: in 2012, the local grassroots organization called Empower D.C. planned to bring suit against the District for Henderson's plan to close fifteen under-enrolled schools, citing racial discrimination. While Henderson remarked that DCPS was "paying too much and offering too little," Empower D.C. and local council members from Ward 7 noted that many families had left the DCPS schools in the area due to under-funding and poor conditions. Unfortunately, Empower D.C. eventually lost the lawsuit (Prince, personal communication).

As is evident in extra-local discourses about what Rhee did for the D.C. schooling system (e.g., Mead 2017), the schooling reforms introduced by the Fenty-Rhee administration struck many as a common-sense effort to rectify the problem of "bad teachers" and "bad schools." While African American students were rendered visible as a problem population within explicitly racializing discourses about the

"Black-white achievement gap," public and policy discourses avoided naming structural racism as the reason for African American students' so-called failures in school. Instead, colorblind discourses such as the "poverty gap," which argues that income level is more of a prediction of academic failure than race, and deficit discourses that pointed to linguistic and cultural difference, became common-sense explanations for why African American students were performing in school. One cultural difference theory was based on educational research that proposed African American students avoid academic success as a form of "acting white" (Fordham & Ogbu 1986; Fordham 1996). The idea of "resistant Black students" has been widely cited over and over again in national discourses on education and has even been supported by well-known African Americans in public remarks, including Bill Cosby and President Obama (Dyson 2003; Wildhagen 2011; McWhorter 2019).

Colorblind discourses that blame minorities while avoiding explicit references to "race" were neither exclusive to school reform in Washington, D.C., nor did they begin in the 2000s when school districts across the country enacted similar NCLB policy-driven reforms (Bartlett et al. 2002; Lipman and Haines 2007; Guggenheim 2010; Lipman 2011; Rosa 2019). This kind of school reform echoes *A Nation at Risk*, a report authored by the Reagan administration's education task force in the early 1980s. Grounded in neoliberal ideology, the report proposed a national crisis of minority underachievement. As Bartlett, Frederick, Gulbrandsen, and Murillo explain, the report framed schools as "exist[ing] to boost national economic performance, and proposed business people as those best qualified to craft education policy . . . . During the 1980s, conservatives framed the poor as a disreputable and underserving 'black underclass.' . . . Further, they claimed that social programs for the poor created a 'drag' on the economy" (2002, p. 10, citing Mickelson & Ray 1994). Similar language can be found in the DCPS Reform Priorities of the Fenty Administration report, which states, "Many of our students are challenged by circumstances outside of the schools' control, such as poverty and primary languages other than English. But there can be no excuses" (2007, p. 7). This language of neoliberal school reform, rather than directly identifying their referents, uses colorblind terms to refer to African Americans and Latinxs, recasting poverty and language as choices that are not only indexical of these groups but markers of failure to assimilate as well. Such a colorblind recasting of a long-standing meritocratic achievement ideology contradictorily holds entire racialized groups accountable for having "cultures of failure" while also asserting that individuals should "rise above race" by pursuing success on an uneven playing field.

It bears mentioning that Fenty and Rhee's schooling reforms of the late 2000s in Washington, D.C., also facilitated neoliberalism in a broader sense: they repositioned schools to be key resources for city developments that were aimed at capital accumulation (Lipman 2011). Neoliberalism is a political economic theory whose proponents argue that human well-being is best advanced through an unregulated market geared toward the accumulation of profit (Harvey 2005; Lipman 2011). In the process, infrastructure and social services are cleared for capital-generating entities, such as real estate and commercial businesses. In many U.S. cities, gentrification is not just an explicitly neoliberal project; it depends on racial exclusion to function (Goldberg 2009; Lipman 2011). Washington, D.C.'s emergence as a "neoliberal city" in the 2000s shares similarities to others, in which the poorest performing schools were turned over to become redeveloped, often private charters as part of gentrification (Bartlett et al. 2002; Lipman and Haines 2007; Goldberg 2009; Sackler 2010; Lipman 2011; Rosa 2019). School reform, which focused on the closure of so-called failing institutions in the poorest areas with the highest number of racialized minority students only to reopen as charters, should be seen as part of a neoliberal racial project that operates as accumulation by dispossession: cities' social resources are stripped from the poor and handed over to for-profit developers. Over the past ten years, the African American DCPS student population has decreased from 74 percent to 60 percent while the number of white students has increased by 5 percent (dcps.gov/node/966292). This may be a direct reflection of racialized gentrification and the exclusion of African Americans.

NEOLIBERAL MULTICULTURALISM, RACE, AND LANGUAGE

Even more broadly, Washington, D.C.'s structure and logic of schooling reform connects to a wider racialization process that I call "neoliberal multiculturalism." Following scholars who theorize the coproduction of race and language in relation to neoliberalism and multiculturalism as modes of governance, I argue that neoliberal multiculturalism is marked by the simultaneous appropriation and rejection of racial Otherness and that language is central to this process (Urciuoli 1996; Flores 2017; Roth-Gordon et al. 2020; Rosa 2019). Neoliberal multiculturalism promotes ideologies of difference and diversity that frame race as "not seen" (colorblindness) or as "no longer mattering" (postracialism) while constructing linguistic and cultural signifiers of essentialized difference in relation to the imagined norm of unmarked whiteness (Alim 2016a; Bonilla-Silva 2018). Contemporary constructions of white supremacy involve the cultural domination of racialized Others via linguistic appropriation and mocking (Hill 2008; Chun 2016), the indexical bleaching of racialized language (Bucholtz 2016), and the co-optation of ethnoracial minorities' social movements through the claiming of white allyship (Delfino, forthcoming). At the same time, language and other cultural practices that index racial difference reconstruct racialized minorities as unassimilable Others in relation to a U.S. nation that continually reimagines itself as white (Leeman 2004; Ocampo 2016; Rosa 2019). Thus, while white appropriations of AAL create an artifice of diversity and inclusion (Cutler 2003; Roth-Gordon et al. 2020), actual speakers of AAL are racially pathologized as inarticulate, incoherent, or unintelligent (Alim & Smitherman 2012; Rickford & King 2016). This process, I argue, sustains neoliberalism's colorblind racism and the postracial myth by presenting linguistic and cultural practices of "accumulation-by-dispossession" as diversity and inclusion (Flores 2017).

As a racial project that facilitates neoliberal colorblindness, schools are sites for the reproduction of racial difference and what Flores and Rosa (2015) call "raciolinguistic ideologies." As they explain, raciolinguistic ideologies "conflate certain racialized bodies with linguistic deficiency unrelated to any objective linguistic practices. That is, raciolinguistic ideologies produce racialized speaking subjects who are constructed as linguistically deviant even when engaging in linguistic practices positioned as normative or innovative when produced by privileged white subjects" (Flores & Rosa 2015, p. 150). Importantly, raciolinguistic ideologies are expressed through deracialized discourses about "appropriateness," "languagelessness," and "articulateness," which reproduce whiteness as an unmarked and invisible norm while indirectly construing racialized groups as deviant or disorderly in relation to an imagined "standard" language[6] (Alim & Smitherman 2012; Flores & Rosa 2015; Rosa 2016). The myth of postracialism is maintained, then, through colorblind discourses that characterize the linguistic practices of particular groups as deviant while reframing pathologizing or deficit ideologies as a matter of appropriateness. As Love-Nichols argues, "Colorblind discourses of language . . . focus on the supposed insufficient vocabulary (Avineri et al. 2015) and lack of formality of racialized varieties to explain their 'inappropriateness'" (2018, p. 93). The superficial nod to diversity and inclusion is thus predicated on the discursive construction of languages such as AAL as acceptable for private sphere interactions but completely inappropriate for public and institutional life (Urciuoli 1996; Hill 2009; Love 2018). Similarly, Rosa (2016, 2019) and Flores (2017) show how the institutional framing of Latinx[7] students as in need of "standard" or "academic" English offers the apparent possibility of inclusion within neoliberal multicultural discourses of diversity while paradoxically limiting this potential: Latinx students are always-already read by listening subjects as imperfect language speakers via pathologizing readings of their bilingual or translingual practices.

Rosa's (2019) study illustrates how multiculturalism requires the performance of cultural authenticity in ways that transform but also reproduce existing racial orders within contemporary contexts of (neo)liberal governance. Thus, a Chicago high school's efforts to make students into "Young Latino Professionals" requires what he theorizes as a contradictory navigation of cultural assimilation and difference: students are expected to maintain a Latino cultural identity, but in the service of a liberal multicultural state that is predicated on hegemonic ideologies of inclusion and diversity. That is to say, Latinx students need to display particular forms of linguistic and cultural difference to be construed as authentic racial subjects, and these performances are predicated on types of difference that do not threaten or disrupt white supremacy. Thus, since racialization is predicated on outsider status, particular groups can never fully assimilate in a neoliberal multicultural state. Moreover, their perceived failure to do so is projected as evidence of their essentialized outsider status, as indicated by linguistic and cultural markers of difference.

NAVIGATING RACE, LANGUAGE, AND ACHIEVEMENT:
AFTER SCHOOL IN RACIOLINGUISTIC PERSPECTIVE

As I mentioned in the beginning of the chapter, one of the greatest and saddest ironies to result from my teaching and research in the after school program was the reproduction of the deficit ideologies that some of us consciously sought to avoid and unlearn in the after school program. As I often perceived it, a majority of the staff and parents were not only on board with schooling's purpose, but with the idea that the program was in place to socialize students out of the culture and lifestyle of poverty. Some parents even sponsored deficit discourses by voicing racialized stereotypes of African Americans as unwilling to work hard. For instance, I caught up with the mother of a sibling duo one afternoon on our way walking to the program. She showed me a shortcut through a hole cut into a chain link fence that divided two building parking lots, and graciously held aside a hanging piece to let me and her children through before going through herself. When we started walking through the second parking lot, she pointed to an area that had just been cleared of building debris and piled into a dumpster. She explained to me that the job had just been completed.

"I hate to say it," she began, looking embarrassed and laughing lightly. "But the job was done by Spanish people, and it only took a few days. If it had been one of us, we'd still be looking at a mess for weeks on end!" Like her, many other parents and staff expressed, if not so baldly, the idea that "people" in Southeast were responsible for their lived circumstances due to laziness or, more commonly, because they chose to abide by the culture of poverty or street life rather than adopt the values and manners needed for mainstream success.

To briefly explain the staffing of the after school program, Urban Pathways hired a mix of young AmeriCorps volunteers in their twenties on a yearly basis (usually white), and also maintained a regular staff of people who were residents of the local neighborhood, all African American. The after school and summer programs were also staffed with various youth volunteers from one of the local high schools or Howard University, and they were also African American. For the 2010–2011 school year, Matt and I were the only regular after school staff who were understood to be racially white. Matt, a twenty-five-year-old Jewish American man from Los Angeles, was an AmeriCorps volunteer and was hired to direct the family literacy program for a year. In addition to Matt and myself, Shelley, another (white) AmeriCorps volunteer, and various Christian groups from across the country came on an infrequent basis to work and play with the students. Otherwise, the students had virtually no regular contact with white people: they attended all-African American schools and lived in an all-African American neighborhood, where one or two families were referred to as "mixed" (one African American and one white parent). Raymond and Mr. Morris, two African American men in their thirties who have become good friends of mine over the years, shored up the academic enrichment program across the street from family literacy, in the large community center that had been built a few years prior. Minnie, a former AmeriCorps volunteer who worked as part of the administrative staff in the church office, was an African American woman a few years younger than I and had also become a close friend. Finally Ms. Betty and Ms. Reeves staffed the family literacy and academic enrichment programs, respectively. Matt and I grew close with Ms. Betty and the four of her children who attended family literacy: Deandre (13, M), Joseph (10, M), Alisha (9, F), and Keri (8, F). For any neighborhood news, Ms. Betty was my (unsolicited) ears and eyes. Every afternoon that I went to the family literacy program, she gave me the run down on which students had acted up or gotten good grades at school, what the youth in the local area had been up to (usually no good), who was sick or well, fighting or making up and, crucially, how to contact other parents when I needed to.

It would be remiss to characterize any differences in educational perspective or purpose as a "Black-white" issue, or any sort of cultural tension that one would assume could result from a "cross-racial" situation like ours. Individually, we all had different ideas about language, literacy, and education but oriented toward the common goal of helping the after school students maintain or achieve academic excellence in school. Most of the progressive ideals about race and social justice that Victor and I discussed in his office the day I interviewed for the summer position were brought up in executive or administrative staff meetings; in the day-to-day business of after school, it would have been considered impolite and face-threatening to mention race at all in "mixed company." I even left the topic of racial identity out of my description of my research project to parents when reviewing consent and assent forms with them: to be studying race would only sharpen students' sense of being made out to be different. Based on pilot research and previous conversations with students, I perceived the students and their families to want to be treated unexceptionally in this matter. Even though I broached the topic a few times, the students would usually fold uncomfortably into silence if I was the one to initiate questions about "how Black people talk," for example. So I purposefully avoided pointing to race in questions and conversations to ask about "how kids from Southeast talk" as a matter of tact and research ethics.

Of the Urban Pathways' staff members, I aligned philosophically and politically closest with Minnie and Raymond. Each in our own way, we spurned the assimilatory project of schooling and consciously sought to make the students' language and identity practices heard, seen, and felt in an educational context. Like many of the Howard University volunteers and local teens, slightly older Minnie had been an accomplished student and was pursuing her Master's in Education. She explained to me that she had deliberately not chosen Howard because she felt that it "[taught] Black people to assimilate" and preferred the sense of Black cultural visibility at the school she did choose to attend. Raymond, who had also attended college at a local university, had "come up" from a working-poor background similar to the students, but in a different Washington, D.C., neighborhood. Similar to Minnie, he perceived Howard and a few of the volunteers to be "bougie" (stuck-up and overly proper) and went out of his way to teach me "the ropes" when it came to the students. Raymond was my key informant on *joning* and other types of "street talk," and explained to me how to use it as a way of relating to the students. And in a spring 2011 staff meeting, Raymond and I were the only ones in the room who vocalized the position that joning should not be prohibited as a form of bullying, as almost all of the other staff pathologized it as such.

Other staff and even the parents of the after school students sponsored school-normative views of language, literacy, and the purpose of learning much more so than Raymond, Minnie, and I. For instance, many parents interpreted my research as a means to better teach the students how to speak "proper" English so that they would do better in school and expressed their sincere gratitude at having me, the graduate student from American University, to teach them. Parents and staff also sponsored the practice of having students complete their homework no matter what, keeping them from play and other recreational activities as necessary. Since we were working in the era of "teach to the test," in which students would come to the program loaded with books and rote practice worksheets, many if not most of the students had to spend the whole time completing what they had been assigned at school. The holistic goal of intellectual and social growth that Victor, Minnie, Raymond, Matt, and I sought became folded back into educational goals that none of us were on board with: while Matt and others never openly critiqued the achievement gap or the high-stakes testing used to support deficit ideologies, we nevertheless saw and felt its futility as the after school program became restricted to a routine of worksheets, perhaps an hour of play, and then a hot meal at 5:30 p.m. before the program let out.

DISCUSSION

The chapters to follow document the push-and-pull of how differently positioned after school participants sought to make sense of race in relation to language. Specifically, they describe how the students were understood to be "succeeding" or "failing" in school in relation to how they were perceived to express themselves linguistically and discursively, against my ethnographic focus on how students participated in their own kinds of raciolinguistic transformation. In spite, or perhaps because of, the fact that everyone tried to comfortably avoid talking about race, privilege, and inequality out in the open, deficit ideologies related to students being willfully underprepared for school structured our efforts to help them succeed, even though nobody meant to participate in the reproduction of racial inequality (cf. Pollock 2004).

In providing a historical and ethnographic analysis of the wider process of racialization, this chapter seeks to disrupt the "common-sense" ideology and practices of exclusion that helped rationalize and drive school reform at local and more widely reaching levels. This chapter also critiques the achievement ideology of the families I worked with as a kind of "uncritical resistance" (Fordham 1996) to racial exclusion. I argue this ideology might be better conceptualized as "critical acceptance," or disidentification with the dominant framing of success as inclusion and mobility. The families and students themselves negotiated racial exclusion by seeking to overcome it rather than challenge the rules of the game. Even though they sponsored the American Dream, they did so as part of an alternative vision for racial equality in and beyond education. And as the students often reminded me in the way they responded to my questions and in conversations, language, life, and the meanings therein were about more than "just race," or not about race at all. It may be that students have partially internalized colorblind thinking, but such a view can also be interpreted as a statement that compels one to critically read beyond race in order to address lived experience and achieve equality.

NOTES

1. See (Reese 2019) for an ethnographic study of unequal food access in Southeast D.C.
2. See Prince (2014) for the historical impact of racism on redlining and wealth inequality.
3. See Chatman (2016) on pan-African identity in Washington, D.C.
4. Ted Kennedy remarked on this too.
5. For example, D.C. residents were not able to elect their own City mayor and City Council until 1973.
6. For critical analyses of standard language ideology in the United States, see Silverstein (1996), Urciuoli (2001), and Lippi-Green (2012). Note that ideologies of standardization are not the same as "English-Only" language ideologies, which maintain the idea of a purist monolingual English-speaking population and which racialize non-English-speaking immigrant populations as Other (Wiley & Lukes 1996; Leeman 2004).
7. "Latinx" is the nonbinary, gender-inclusive form that replaces "Latina/o."

2

Talking "Like a Race"

Language and Identity in Southeast

One afternoon in March as I was completing an art activity with four girls, Alisha called out her second-best friend Janice for "acting like a white girl." Perhaps to Alisha, Janice was putting on a show of being overly proper as she went about dabbing spots of glue on her paper while announcing that she "only glue[d] her four corners." Even before Alisha said anything, I noticed that Janice had uncharacteristically rhoticized her r's in "four corners" rather than vocalizing them as she normally did, all the while gluing in an overly delicate manner. Responding to Janice's affected mannerisms, Alisha responded dismissively, "Girl, you act like a white girl." Since I rarely (over)heard students having conversations about language and racial identity, I decided to try and steer the interaction toward an informal interview about what it means to talk and act "like a race."

"How do white girls act?" I asked no one in particular, eyes down toward my own paper, fearful that I was being too provocative with my question. But one of the girls gleefully performed a white girl voice ("Oh my gosh, I need the glue!") Following this performance, Mary, Alisha, and Janice produced a series of impressions, as shown in the transcript given further. Alisha's and Janice's voicing performances of talking Black and white are indicated by the use of quotation marks:[1]

1	Jen	What does talking Black mean?
2	Mary	((hollering sound))
3	Alisha	No no.
4		((lowered pitch)) "[H]ey. Sup?"
5		"Sup son? Sup?"
6	Jen	What's talking white mean?
7	Alisha	((raised pitch, softened volume)) "Oh, hello:, Janice."
8	Janice	Girl, you act like a white girl!

9	Alisha	((raised pitch)) "Oh, yes? Yes! It's wo:nderful!"
10	Janice	((lowered pitch, amplified volume)) "Son, don't talk
11		about me like [d]at!"
12	Multiple	((laughter))

To explain the girls' styling of voices (Bakhtin 1981; Hill 1995), Janice and Alisha use linguistic and prosodic features as well as differently styled greetings to indicate differences between talking Black and talking white. Here, talking Black is stylized through the use of lowered pitch and higher volume relative to the girls' normal speaking voices as well as the greeting, "Sup, son?" Together, these features index a Black male speaker who is greeting another casually, using what students would identify as "slang" words ("son") and pronunciation ("sup") in the local setting of their neighborhood. By contrast, in lines 7 and 9, Alisha performs talking white using raised pitch, softened volume, and a gratuitously formal manner that indicates one female speaker is addressing another ("Oh, hello:, Janice."). Playfully, Janice rebuffs Alisha's attempt to "talk white" to her with her version of talking Black: "Son, don't talk about me like [d]at!" (lines 10–11) using the same prosodic features and address term ("son") Alisha had recruited in her own performance.

It might be easy to dismiss these performances as children's play and the girls as simply impersonating individuals that they might have heard in their everyday lives. But I argue that the system of prosodic, linguistic, and pragmatic contrasts created in their parodies of talking white and Black index idealized speaker types that recruit wider ideologies about language as connected to racial and class difference. While talking Black is indexically associated with "street tough" urban Black men from the urban "ghetto" or "hood" (Anderson 1990), talking white is indexically linked to the opposite social type according to race, gender, and social face: a soft-spoken white woman who uses politeness forms typically associated with a "proper" middle class. These symbolic juxtapositions of talking "like a race," embodied in the performance of social types, is not arbitrary, but rather provides a metalinguistic illustration of how Black linguistic practices were racialized among students as slang while white linguistic practices were contrastively elevated to the status of being proper or correct speech. Yet Blake, the fifteen-year-old tutor, pointedly remarked at that moment that whites also speak slang: "Ms. [Researcher's name] it don't matter, because all of us, talk alike. Blacks, we have our own slang, and y'all have y'all's slang . . . y'all say, 'Dude.' We say 'Son.'"

What might explain the ways in which students such as Alisha, Janice, and Blake relate language to race? I describe this ethnographic encounter to anchor the focus of this chapter, which examines how the after school students constructed their own models of language, race, and identity in response to their raciolinguistic socialization as "problem students" and future street youth. Following Chaparro (2019), I define raciolinguistic socialization as the ways in which white, middle-class ideologies about race and class are used to evaluate children's linguistic practices, their language development, and what language means in terms of their futures. As I discuss in this chapter, the social construction of Black preadolescence, and more broadly, the social production of age within raciolinguistic chronotopes of anxiety and resistance, shaped how students constructed their own models of language, identity, and future success. Overwhelmingly, adults' fears that students would be read as "problem students" or become future street youth instead of upwardly mobile shaped the linguistic practices and language ideologies of the preadolescents. As I show through ethnographic description and analysis, I interpret students' language and identity practices as resistance to pathologized Blackness and as a projected hope into the present and future for the transformation of race.

RACIOLINGUISTIC SOCIALIZATION, ENREGISTERMENT, AND THE PRODUCTION OF IDENTITY

Recalling the introductory vignette where four girls are performing talking like a race, I want to note that both the girls' parodies and Blake's comments offer up the question of what it means to talk white or Black, the linking of speech styles with race and class, and whether there is any validity to the contrastive identity models of "polite white girl" versus "street tough gangsta." After all, as Blake pointedly remarked, white people speak slang too, and I believe his point was to say that white people are not considered "gangstas" for doing so. But why would the girls even choose these particular representational figures to begin with? Since all of them were laughing at the performances, something in the styling of voices registered as true in terms of being worthy of parody and perhaps to a certain degree, linguistic mocking.

To further unpack the process of raciolinguistic socialization, children learn what it means to "talk like a race" through routine everyday interaction in particular spaces. As Chaparro explains:

> Raciolinguistic socialization brings to the fore the way that, in classroom and educational spaces, and through everyday interaction, children are socialized in ways that reinforce perceptions of language use and ability that are intimately tied to racialization and class position. Indeed, part of understanding the work of raciolinguistic ideologies involves analyzing how race and class become important mediating factors in how children's language practices [are] perceived and evaluated by teachers and other students. (2019, p. 3)

As I explain in this chapter, raciolinguistic socialization goes beyond the walls of the school and classroom interactions to include how adults, older siblings, and peers oriented the after school students to what it means to speak *proper* versus *slang* and the racialized and class meanings of doing so. It is useful to introduce another term, *raciolinguistic enregisterment*, which describes the process by which language becomes linked to particular types of racialized bodies, which then constitute models of personhood (Rosa 2019).[2] Talking white and Black are not simply about "sounding like a race" because they carry meanings and consequences for social judgment (i.e., authenticity) and social mobility (i.e., getting a well-paying job). Like gender, raciolinguistic enregisterment becomes so common-sense over time that bodies that do not fit a hegemonic raciolinguistic identity model are policed as inauthentic, such as when Alisha called out Janice for "acting like a white girl." This kind of raciolinguistic assessment, called "linguistic policing," is discussed at length by Alim and Smitherman (2012), who explain that whites' characterizations of Barack Obama as articulate exceptionalize him against pathologizing stereotypes of African Americans as inarticulate and, by implication, less intelligent. As the concepts of raciolinguistic socialization and enregisterment suggest, any kind of perceived linguistic inauthenticity is institutionally measured against raciolinguistic ideologies that prioritize white perspectives on what language is, what it should be, and the value of particular kinds of language use when used by one kind of speaker versus another. Hence, the importance of Blake's point about the hypocrisy of associating slang only with Black people.

Raciolinguistic Enregisterment: The (Linguistic) Policing of Black Preadolescence

While school and the after school program were not the only sites of raciolinguistic socialization for the preadolescent students, these spaces were where they spent a majority of their day. Students' parents also played a significant role in orienting them to the linguistic practices they would need for school and future success, including speaking "proper" and learning how to styleshift as the situation would demand. Working from a position of anxiety about students' education and their futures, teachers and parents transmitted a common message: that it was inappropriate (at best) to speak slang in school-based settings. For parents and African American staff especially, slang and the street-based activities with which it was associated (i.e., gangbanging, gambling, and street youth culture) belonged in the public neighborhood space of the "street" and perhaps in private spaces such as the home among intimates and family members. All teachers and parents took up institutional listening subject positions rooted in a raciolinguistic chronotope of anxiety about how preadolescents' peer linguistic practices would be heard and policed as aggressive, threatening, inappropriate, or simply "incorrect" in school-based settings, even those who tried to validate AAL as integral for peer socializing.

Thus, not all adults pathologized the language and social activities typically associated with "street culture" (Hannerz 2003[1966]; Liebow 1967; Anderson 1990), but all were concerned that students might possibly be identified by either local youth or police as signaling some sort of gang or street culture affiliation in the way they walked, talked, or dressed in the local setting of the neighborhood. The following ethnographic example illustrates how the after school students were racially policed in relation to adult-centered anxieties that their bodies would signal social deviance or criminality, and early on in their lives. One afternoon, Minnie relayed to me how one of the five-year-old boys got into trouble with Raymond for turning the board game Monopoly into a game of street dice (gambling). The boy recruited other students who belonged to the "little kids" group (ages five to eight) and started rolling the Monopoly dice against a far wall in the gym behind a stack of bleachers. Given the location he chose, the young boy likely already knew that what he was doing would be considered misbehavior or deviant. I thought that Raymond might have stopped the activity perhaps because he shared Minnie's view that gambling was a morally bad social practice. I was therefore surprised, knowing that Raymond enjoyed betting in contexts such as Fantasy Football. At the same time, it was not the first time I had been surprised by Raymond's stringency, since he had also come up with the "no Facebook" rule for the older students when they were using the computers as part of their free activity hour, a rationale that I will also explain shortly following this example.

When I asked him why he decided to stop the game of dice, Raymond told me that he did not have any objection to gambling itself. Rather, he was disconcerted by the highly stylized manner in which the five-year-old boy was performing the activity. "Jen, he had the form and everything," Raymond told me, signaling disbelief in his tone and facial expression. "He looked just like one of the men on the [street] corner doing it," he continued while demonstrating a stereotypically stylized swagger taken up by an adult "street hustler" when rolling and throwing dice. I noticed that Raymond was unusually disturbed by this incident, since he usually only rolled his eyes and perhaps chuckled after stopping one of the older students in their tracks for exhibiting similar "inappropriate" behaviors that were indexically associated with street toughness.

Though he did not directly state his point, I knew Raymond's concern with this incident was that students might have been picking up street values much earlier than expected: in the preadolescent years. In my several years with Urban Pathways, I noticed in the after school program and out in the neighborhood that parents vigorously policed young children for behaviors that could potentially be read as criminal. For example, I would often stop by the local corner store or grocery store to pick up snacks or treats and noticed how angry and fearful caregivers would be with children as young as one or two when they curiously reached for something that caught their eye. In many instances, the adult would slap the child's hand or rip away the object and yell at him or her, and possibly even deliver a few spanks until the child cried in fear, explaining to the child that they were never to touch or even reach for anything that did not belong to them. Elementary schoolchildren interacting in large groups in public were often told by supervising adults to lower their voices, stop running and yelling, and generally to act as calm and deferential as possible, with more severe verbal threats and punitive measures named than I had ever encountered teaching or being a student myself in predominantly white or multi-ethnic schools in the suburbs. To summarize, I noticed that there were extreme disciplinary sanctions and restrictions on ways of acting that were normal for any children applied to African American children: running, yelling, excitement, displays of frustration and anger, and wanting to look at or touch things in public space. Since adults could not control the hegemonic gaze, which would read Black children's bodies as social threats in public space when displaying these behaviors, they controlled and policed the children to minimize their public and institutional visibility as social threats.

If Black children are racially policed so early on, then the racialized enregisterment of their bodies as socially deviant or possibly criminal in the preadolescent and teen years raises the stakes of local management strategies with respect to adults' policing of their language and identity practices. One only need recall how Trayvon Martin's hooded sweatshirt was claimed to signal to his shooter, George Zimmerman, that the seventeen-year-old boy was a violent criminal carrying a weapon even though he was in fact holding onto bag of Skittles in the front pocket of the garment. I heard of incidents involving hyperbolic policing occurred in Southeast. One thirteen-year-old boy was handcuffed by a white male police officer after he formed the shape of a gun with his hands and aimed it at him. When the police officer talked to his mother about the incident, she responded that he should "book" (process and charge) her son so that he would learn a lesson. According to Ms. Betty, who told me the story, the mother was frustrated because the boy often got into trouble at school and with police, and she felt her own disciplinary efforts were not enough to stem what she perceived to be increasingly troublesome behavior.

I myself was a participant in an incident of misrecognition one afternoon, when thirteen-year-old J.J. came dressed wearing a white tank top, baggy khaki pants, and a Black du-rag to the after school program rather than his usual school uniform. He walked up the empty parking lot to the community center doors with a limping swagger characteristic of teen boys and men in the neighborhood as well as in hip-hop and other arenas of Black popular culture (i.e., stand-up comedy), I wondered who the young man was and what he wanted, since he looked older than a student and too young to be an inquiring parent. J.J. was tall and muscled enough at thirteen years old for me to mistake him for an older teenager. When he reached the doors, my heart stopped as I realized it was him: his goofy, friendly grin and wave identified the J.J. I knew and contrasted sharply with the embodied signifiers of street toughness I had read on his body as he walked up. Before I could think about it, I said aloud, "Oh, my god. Is he really dressed like that?" Mr. Morris, whom I had been chatting with, said, "I'll talk to him," and pulled him aside once J.J. came inside. Even though I did not participate in or hear the conversation, I knew Mr. Morris was explaining to J.J. that his appearance could attract the attention of police or gang members, and that either scenario could put him in danger. By the surprised and shocked look on his face, I guessed that J.J. actually had no idea that his appearance would invoke such assumptions or consequences. Perhaps compared to Terrance or Deandre, two thirteen-year-old boys who regularly received sharp verbal reprobations from their mothers and teachers about their facial expressions, posture, tone, and overall "attitudes," J.J. had not been schooled in such matters.

Other kinds of socialization and disciplining intended in part to shield the preadolescent students from being seen and heard as social threats or criminals included restrictions on language use and discursive practice. At the beginning of this section, I mentioned Raymond's "no Facebook" rule, which he implemented out of fear that the preadolescents and early teens would create profiles listing ages in the teen to young adult range and use the platform to "talk shit" to youth who might or might not be gang members. As I discuss in more detail in chapter 4, adults worried that students were not yet mature enough to handle being competent in the art of ritual insults (Labov 1972; Mendoza-Denton 2008) and other AAL discourse styles, which indexed street toughness. Verbal displays of street toughness could misfire and incite a violent brawl.

It is important to note how the raciolinguistic enregisterment of the preadolescent children's bodies intersected with the social production of their age. African American children who are even younger than Trayvon were depicted in news media as adults with criminal intent, and they are policed and sentenced as adults in the legal system. But among adults in the after school program, the preadolescents and early teens were often treated as naïve but stubborn admirers of street culture, capable at any time of being swayed by the seeming public power commanded by older youth in the local neighborhood and, on a much larger scale, hip-hop artists who sponsored and displayed street toughness in their music. The contradictory production of their age as simultaneously criminal adults and naïve children bracketed how they navigated the production of their racialized bodies as actual or potential social threats. This age-inflected liminality was also shaped by the fact that many of the preadolescents and early teens were also managing household tasks in the absence of adult or youth caregivers while also being subject to the kinds of socialization and discipline typically reserved for children. Considering these factors, I want to suggest that much of the students' existential anxieties and displays of strong emotions such as anger, which are usually attributed to biological factors such as changing hormones or psychological states induced by living in a culture of poverty were in fact produced by raciolinguistic policing and further sharpened by contradictory ideologies about their maturity and age. The policing techniques of parents and teachers ultimately stemmed from a system that only recognizes them as always-already potential criminals or social threats, as a reinscription of governmental surveillance (Rosa 2019, p. 59).

Street Toughness and School Readiness as Binary Identity Models

The after school students experienced pressure to minimize their visibility as social threats, and they also had to navigate a choice the raciolinguistic tropes of being either "street tough" or "school ready." The following story illustrates how students had to negotiate a projected choice to be one or the other. One afternoon, I walked into the community center up the street to speak to Raymond about a delivery from the D.C. food pantry and noticed one of the staff members roundly chastising twelve-year-old Jamal for "having an attitude." As far as I could tell, Jamal had been arguing with Ms. Reeves, an African American woman in her fifties and appeared extremely flustered at not being able to explain himself. His head was down and to the side, brow furrowed as Ms. Reeves verbally dominated the exchange. I had not heard what Jamal had said, only Ms. Reeves' rebuking of his so-called attitude. "Don't come in here talking to me with that kind of language," she bellowed. "You want to talk street talk, then take that out into the streets. Don't bring it in here."

Such instances were not uncommon in the after school program or as students reported to me when they arrived from school: they were constantly policed for "having an attitude" either for using street register or for arguing with an adult. African American staff and students referred to particular discourse and lexical items associated with urban, youth-based uses of AAL as "talking street," a term that was synonymous with talking Black and slang. These particular linguistic forms were indexically linked to street tough identity models, such as the tough-talking Black man in the opening example, and they enregistered such linguistic practices as culturally Black. That is to say, what linguists broadly refer to as "African American Language" accreted racialized meaning in relation to idealized speaker types who simultaneously indexed cultural authenticity. As I explain further, cultural pathology was indexed vis-à-vis its contrastive positioning relative to the language and identity practices indexically associated with "school readiness," voiced in the form of a polite or deferential white woman in the opening example. The binary contrast is summarized in Table 2.1.

Table 2.1   Street-Tough and School-Ready Identity Models

	Street-Tough	*School-Ready*
Linguistic labels	Slang, talking Black, talking street, talking ghetto	Proper, polite, correct
Lexical items, phrases	Son, girl, nigga, dawg, guh	Please, excuse me, honorific titles (Ms. and Mr.)
Linguistic practices	Joning, trash talk	
Phonology and grammar (select, not complete)	Consonant cluster reduction ("missing letters in words")	Correction or hypercorrection of consonant clusters (e.g., past tense -ed, /sk/ to /st/) and double negatives
	Double negatives ("ain't got no")	
Social face wants and politeness	Fighting; ability to defend oneself in threatening situations	Doing homework
		Deferential to adults
		Sitting still
	Illicit activities (gangs, drugs)	Avoiding peer interactions during academic learning interactions (i.e., not joning or teasing)
	Hanging out on the street; dancing and listening to loud music	

Source: Image by Author.

"Street toughness" and "school readiness" are terms that I have chosen to gloss the ideological tension between cultural identity and academic success. For racially minoritized students, school readiness requires the performance of an assimilatory identity. As mentioned earlier, a binary logic organized linguistic and cultural practices according to these identity models such that students could not be street-tough and school-ready at the same time. Identity practices associated with street toughness were generally characterized as "inappropriate" for in the after school program and peer interactions even though the ability to appear tough was important to defending oneself and maintaining social face in the local neighborhood. As I discuss further in chapter 4, street toughness, and the styles of conflict talk associated with it, were also integral to peer interaction and peer practices of language socialization. But after school staff and instructors created an exclusionary space with respect to street toughness by characterizing students who took up its identity markers as "having an attitude." If students were fighting or joning, or reported to have been at school, they were predictively characterized as "problem students" who would not do well academically; the irony was that students were suspended from school when they engaged in such practices. Additionally, many parents of suspended students kept them out of after school as a disciplinary measure, primarily to keep them from being able to socialize with peers. If the students did their homework at home (which parents often required as part of their punishment), they were not able to receive the same kind of tutoring as in after school. Thus, even though school and after school absences contributed significantly to poor academic performance and advisory reporting (report cards), the students' behavior or attitudes were determined to be the cause of their academic failure in school, including being kept behind a grade level after repeated punitive measures were enforced.

Both institutional and community notions of street toughness were rooted in the hypervisibility of Southeast as a predominantly African American "ghetto" and contrastively positioned against school readiness as an idealized assimilatory identity model. This racialized distinction was symbolically marked by language and other communicative practices as well as a normative discourse of urban space, a place-based moral geography, which represents white gentrification as the idealized norm for socioeconomic success (Modan 2007; Prince 2014). Perceptions of AAL as aggressive, threatening, or inappropriate for the after school space because of its indexical link to street toughness were usually the grounds for characterizing students as having an attitude and policing their behavior.

These symbolic markers of raciolinguistic difference pathologized AAL as inappropriate language, not the use of phonology and morphosyntactic constructions such as zero copula, the absence of third person singular "s" marking, and final t/d deletion. After school instructors corrected such features in writing assignments, but students were not usually corrected toward using an idealized "standard" in their speech. Instead, the raciolinguistic enregisterment of AAL as "street talk" or "talking ghetto" in indexical relation to pathologized "street types," such as gangstas, hustlers, drug dealers, "hos," and teen mothers.

This overdetermination of students' identities as always-already academic failures created institutional disciplinary practices, which would actually determine their academic failures in reality, as I briefly described earlier. Every afternoon, I would greet students by asking them, "How was your day?" or "How was school?" only to find that they or a peer had been "put out of class" or suspended for some sort of behavioral infraction related to their "attitudes." Because students were determined not to want to be "school ready," they were effectively denied access to regular instruction and tutoring.

Using the concepts of raciolinguistic enregisterment and socialization to examine how particular linguistic forms come to be representative of particular types of people and processes of Othering helps foreground a raciolinguistic perspective. Recalling points I made in the introduction, a raciolinguistic perspective seeks to interrogate rather than reify notions of difference that appear to be self-evident rather than socially constructed, especially with respect to the sociolinguistic study of AAL as deviant or deficient in relation to an imagined Standard English. The ethnographic examples I have provided so far indicate that such a sociolinguistic model of linguistic difference is quite far removed from the everyday ideologies, perceptions, and practices that stigmatize uses of AAL as inappropriate for classroom interaction and academic learning; moreover, it reproduces the normative ideology of racialization against the unmarked norm of whiteness (Silverstein 1996; Urcuioli 2001; Flores & Rosa 2015).

Of particular concern to after school staff and parents was how language indicated attitudes symbolizing students' unwillingness to assimilate to school-based expectations for appropriate behavior and interactions. Discourses of school readiness demanded that students abandon street tough identity markers, including linguistic forms and practices that signaled affiliation with hip-hop and youth in Southeast, not AAL linguistic forms wholly or in the abstract. Accounting for participants' raciolinguistic ideologies and metalinguistic awareness is crucial for constructing a dynamic analysis of *both* race and language as co-constituted, and highlights different kinds of transformation, resistance, and change. As I discuss in the rest of the chapter, these processes were central to how students reconstructed race and language in their identity practices.

"WHAT IS THE CORRECT WAY TO SPEAK?": STYLESHIFTING AS LINGUISTIC PRACTICE AND LANGUAGE IDEOLOGY

Though it is important to account for ways in which the students were socialized into preexisting relationships between language and race via socialization and enregisterment, it is also crucial to explain and describe how students responded to these processes in constructing their own raciolinguistic models of identity. For one, the preadolescent students often challenged the binary opposition between street toughness and school readiness. One of the most memorable critical literacy activities I did with students was called, "What does a scientist look like?" I had learned about this activity in a teacher training program provided by another local nonprofit organization. This organization aimed to diversify student participation in science-based after school programs at elementary and middle school grade levels, focusing on statistically underrepresented populations, especially girls, ethnoracial minorities, and differently abled students. The very first activity trainees completed in the program was "What does a scientist look like?" We had poster boards and various art supplies and were told to get to work in groups. We all drew some version of an older white male wearing glasses and a lab coat—in other words, the expected stereotype of a person who does science. The program trainers assured the trainees that our students would all do the same and explained that the point of the lesson was to talk with our students about how and why we did not draw other figures. But when I saw the results among my after school students, not one of them drew a white man in a lab coat. Instead, all of the figures were African Americans producing some kind of science: rockets, chemicals, and solutions to social problems. More than a few figures looked strikingly similar to either Barack or Michelle Obama. One drawing, which is shown below in figure 2.1, displays a male figure wearing urban streetwear. He is handling a smoking beaker at a lab table, and the speech bubble reads, "WOW we made an experiment!"

Figure 2.1   Street Tough Scientist. *Source:* Photo by Author.

I was proud to see that all of my students drew African American scientists, but the particularly assertive out-of-placeness of this one figure moved me. All of the other students' figures were adults in professional attire such as suits, and their faces displayed bright smiles of accomplishment. This man's seemingly impassive expression, emphasized by sunglasses that conceal his eyes, and his streetwear are indicators of street toughness and ideologically juxtapose with the laboratory setting and his choice of words: "Wow we made an experiment!" We might compare this utterance to the styles of talking white and Black produced by Janice and Alisha in the opening example as well as the lexemes and phrases in figure 2.2: the street tough figure is using linguistic features commonly considered proper, polite, or standard, which for the students are indexically associated with talking white. Moreover, the exclamatory style of the utterance here is somewhat comparable to Alisha's performance of talking white, and if anything, it is certainly distant from Janice's contrastive performance of talking Black. The scientist, in other words, was linguistically styleshifting into speech normatively considered appropriate for the laboratory setting while otherwise retaining other key elements of street toughness, such as his expression and outfit.

In combining ideologically juxtaposing aspects of identity (language and dress), this figure disrupts a racializing trope of African Americans as inarticulate (Alim & Smitherman 2012) by taking up linguistic forms considered standard and appropriate for what Hill (2009) terms "white public space." Sociolinguistic research shows

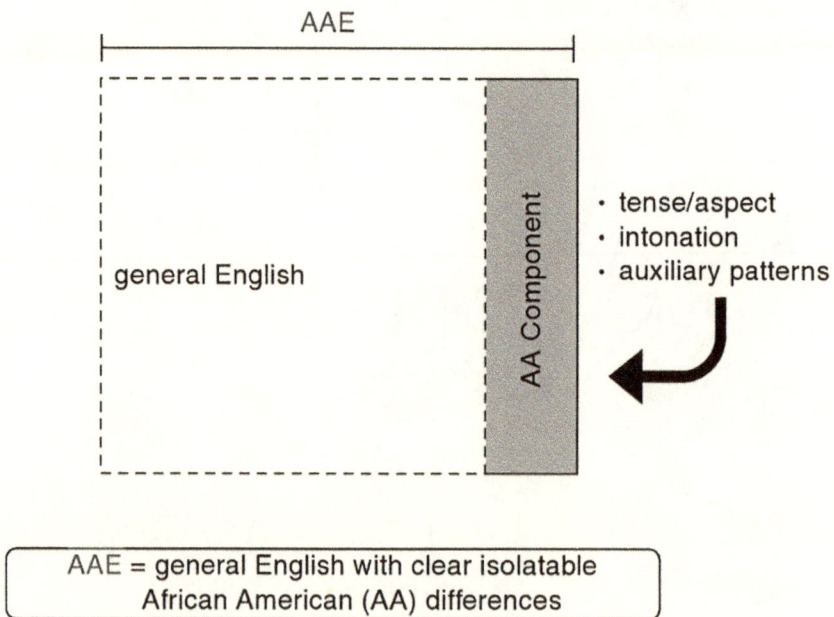

Figure 2.2 The Dual Component Model (Green 2011).

that AAL speakers are typically attentive not only to stylistic differences and their function, but also to how their speech is perceived by different interlocutors and overhearers and styleshift accordingly (Baugh 1983; Rickford & McNair-Knox 1994; Morgan 2002; Alim 2004; Alim & Smitherman 2012). Yet listening subjects often hold AAL speakers accountable for the ways in which they are perceived to fail to take up "proper" forms of speech according to white hegemonic norms, because of racialized stereotypes such as the belief that African Americans are uneducated (Alim & Smitherman 2012) or resistant (Fordham 1999; McWhorter 2000). Lay and research-based perspectives alike have contributed to the view that African Americans speak only AAL when in fact there are only some distinctive features that linguistically define AAL as non-Standard in relation to the idealized system referred to as Standard English. In reality, there are more similarities than differences between the two varieties, as suggested by Labov's (1998) dual component model (see also Green 2011). This dual component model is illustrated graphically in figure 2.2.

The students I interviewed in focus groups held expressed the view that African Americans speak both slang and proper and styleshift according to situation. According to their definitions, slang and proper are situational variations of the same language, or *registers*. Their notions of correct English involved attention to formal differences but more importantly, appropriate usage, defined by attention to context and audience. For instance, when I asked students what is "correct" English, Bianca and Shanae defined it as "polite words" and "correct pronunciation":

1	Jen	What is correct English?
2	Bianca	That you, speaking the words like, you not using slang words, you
3		use like, polite words.
4	Shanae	Correct, English is, when you pronounce something the correct
5		way instead of saying it . . .
6	Bianca	A different way?
7	Shanae	A slang way.

Shanae and Bianca's younger sister, Malia, further outlined for me when they ("kids") would speak slang as opposed to proper:

1	Shanae	We speak slang, like, half of the time, but when we talking to
2		teachers, the slang, we don't talk slang, we ask them a question
3		which, we say it right. When we talking to our peers, we talk slang.
4	Jen	Can you give me an example of how you would talk differently?
5	Shanae	"Brianna, can you help me with my homework, gi:rl. And "girl" is
6		spelled, "G-U-R-L."
7		((.<5)) And to a teacher, you would say, "Excuse me Ms. [name],
8		can you help me with my homework, please?"
9		Sometimes, because listen. The last time I asked[3] this girl for
10		something, she said, "I ain't GOT no more!" They way

11   they speak...
12   Jen   So what would be the right way to say that?
13   Malia   "I don't have."
14   Shanae   When they grow up, they don't want kids to speak slang and stuff,
15   they want them to speak properly.

Bianca and Shanae's definitions of the correct way to speak juxtapose polite words with slang. As suggested by their metapragmatic differentiation between the two, slang itself is not defined as incorrect speech relative to proper in the abstract; rather, what is correct and incorrect language is determined by the social face requirements for situation, setting, and addressee. In the same way that Shanae explained in the transcript given earlier, the twelve students who participated in focus groups explained that they spoke slang with their friends and proper to adult members of their households and to their teachers. Shanae's and Bianca's metapragmatic descriptions indicate how students' uses of each style indexed age hierarchies within the local community: while polite speech indicated deference toward an adult (i.e., formality), slang, which included "cussing" and "negative words," was reserved for peer socializing (i.e., informality). Shanae notes further that growing up involves speaking properly and abandoning the practice of speaking slang; other students such as Jamal noted that speaking correct English is important for getting hired for a job. The last comment I have shown from Shanae indicates that adults ("they") socialized children into speaking proper as a rite of passage into successful adulthood.

Recall that in the voicing performances I described at the beginning of this chapter, Alisha and Janice contrasted slang and proper by indexically associating each style with talking Black and talking white. Their performances plus Blake's commentary indicate students' awareness that slang was racially marked according to a hegemonic language ideology that pathologizes Black linguistic practices as slang, incorrect, or too impolite/informal for white public space. Moreover, students were aware of the need to assimilate by talking white in order to participate in school and get a job. In the transcript given earlier, Shanae glosses this process of assimilation as adults desiring children to grow up by way of achieving mainstream success; one of the ways of doing so is to linguistically pass in spaces dominated by white, middle-class perspectives and norms. As suggested by the focus group data, summarized in the chart and exemplified by Shanae and Bianca's commentary, students parsed language differences and learned to styleshift according to a raciolinguistic ideology of appropriateness (Flores & Rosa 2015) via the linguistic socialization and policing of adults. However, as suggested in the image of the street tough scientist, students often did so without wholly subscribing to the school-ready model of assimilating culturally and linguistically. The scientist, in other words, represents a transracial figure whose embodied style combines elements of street toughness and school readiness in a space that typically requires total assimilation to white cultural norms as a precondition for success. The students, in other words, did not necessarily see street toughness as incommensurate with academic or future achievements despite their explicit language ideologies. As I describe in the next section, they actually challenged the binary opposition between street tough and school-ready identity models by stylistically blending or combining elements of both in their linguistic and cultural practices as well as by expropriating race-based distinctions to other organizing principles of identity, including age, place/location, and gender.

IDENTITY AND STYLE: CONSTRUCTING BLACKNESS THROUGH CONSUMPTION AND HYBRIDITY

Like older teens and youth, the nine- to thirteen-year-old students constructed identity as part of peer-centered negotiations of style, in which the careful display of coolness was paramount (Bucholtz 2011; Nakassis 2016). In sociolinguistics, style has been defined as the selection of a linguistic or discursive form within a possible field of socially stratified choices (Irvine 2001; Coupland 2007), and this concept has been applied to examine how teens and youth modify or disrupt received models of language and race or ethnicity (Rampton 1995; Bucholtz 2011). For example, as in the opening example of this chapter, young people often recruit or appropriate linguistic stereotypes in order to dismantle the idea that particular language(s) (only) belong to particular groups; they might also otherwise defy raciolinguistic boundaries by crossing, blending, and sharing linguistic codes in multiethnic settings (Paris 2011). As I describe in chapters 3 and 4, the after school students code-mixed, style-shifted, and renamed their linguistic practices to disrupt raciolinguistic ideologies of appropriateness and articulateness. Here, I describe how they defined and practiced style in ways that challenge racialized stereotypes about identity, social class, and taste. Style, in other words, was an identity practice grounded in students' resistance to the street tough/school-ready binary and the raciolinguistic ideologies in which this opposition was grounded.

And as with older teens and youth, practices of consumption were central to how students displayed their stylistic orientations to coolness as a primary identity practice. Consumption, in the sense of buying items considered to be in style or cool, was inevitably limited by the fact of poverty. Nevertheless, many students often sported expensive sneakers or clothing items that trended among young people in Southeast, such as the latest style of Nike Foamposite sneakers, which cost around $140 a pair in 2010. At the same time, coolness was limited to being appropriately flashy: flaunting too many expensive items would not only be looked down upon and critiqued by students (and parents of other children), and doing so would make the student a target of theft at school or in the neighborhood.

Students drew from multiple sources in order to construct style within their ongoing and ever-changing discourses about what was cool. Major sources were hip-hop, influential Black musical artists in other genres, and go-go, a Washington,

D.C.,-style of funk developed by Chuck Brown in the 1970s. By 2010, students characterized go-go as a style of hip-hop exclusively associated with Southeast hip hop style and practiced dance steps such as "beat ya feet," which was stylistically modeled after breakdancing styles of foot shuffling. But students also drew from other sources of popular culture to construct style, including top-forty music, films, and TV shows that are generally packaged, sold, and discursively characterized as "mainstream." I was somewhat surprised to learn that students not only watched cartoons such as Sponge Bob but also films considered to be American pop culture classics. One boy, twelve-year-old Delonte, regularly quoted lines from the film *The Breakfast Club*, which he had watched at home after school on TV. Another boy, twelve-year-old Tyler, practiced his go-go dance steps to Lady Gaga songs. Some students listened to their parents' preferred music, including rap, R&B, soul, and go-go music from past generations. For instance, Ms. Betty's ten-year-old son Joseph made everyone laugh when, in a show of independence from peer-normative discourses of coolness, announced in a focus group that he didn't listen to hip-hop, but instead preferred to listen to "Green Al." Trendsetting and trend-following, then, bracketed how students navigated style and coolness, with the ideal state being able to successfully do both at once.

In constructing identity, the preadolescent students squarely characterized their orientations to coolness and trendiness as kids' practices while also emphasizing their local identities as being from ("repping") Southeast and displaying typical markers of Southeast trendiness. These place-based identity markers included particular hair styles, shape, cut, and fit of pants (usually jeans), sneaker brands and styles, slang words and discourse practices, and dance moves that accompanied go-go hip-hop. At the time of my research, the fit of pants for boys, teens, and youth versus adult men drew a sharp age-based distinction: the influence of skater style, via Lupe Fiasco's music videos,[4] produced a trend whereby preadolescent boys and teens would "sag" extremely tight jeans below the buttocks, often exposing brightly colored boxer briefs and patterned fabric belts with metal buckles. Men in their thirties, on the other hand, wore the baggier pants typically associated with the "gangsta" era of hip-hop (Kelley 1994). Young girls wore their hair beaded, braided, or with bows, whereas teenage girls and women often wore straightened short or long hairstyles or braids ("rows"), often using attachments with longer hairstyles and braids. Per my observations throughout the city, the way in which hair was braided or straightened was specific to Southeast, but also trended by neighborhood. The same could be said for brand of clothing and shoes worn.

Since the students came straight from school, I saw them in their public school or charter uniforms, which were either blue or red polo shirts (depending on the school), khaki pants or skirts, and black shoes. In figure 2.3, Paul models what students would typically wear to the after school program, and struck a "gangsta" pose after asking me to take a photo of him.

Figure 2.3   Paul Posing for Camera. *Source*: Photo by Author.

Researchers have noted that high school students who are required to wear uniforms try to modify them as a form of rebellion to conformity or policing (Garot 2010; Rosa 2019). Since I was not present at the students' school day, I cannot speak to what they did with their uniforms there, but they often untucked their shirts on the way to or during the after school program, which would not have been allowed at school. They often blithely went about activities with shoelaces untied, and girls individualized their looks with bright hair beads or bows and socks. My interpretation of this was less deliberate rebellion, but wearing their uniforms in a more relaxed and comfortable fashion while they played and moved around. But as Paul's posing illustrates, students would wear uniforms and adopt extralinguistic markers of street toughness in an identity act of hybridity, much like the scientist in figure 2.1.

Much of Southeast identity practices drew from the cultural logic of mainstream U.S. hip-hop, in which a major trope includes street toughness (Kelley 1994;

Cutler 2003; Alim et al. 2010). However, when I asked, students denied that some of the stylistic choices and organizing principles were more broadly symbolic of mainstream representations of Black urban life. Some students denied that African Americans from other cities shared similar affiliations to and styles derived from hip-hop, insisting that "people from Southeast" or 25th Street had their own way of doing things. This way of describing what they did was not necessarily due to any sort of objective misunderstanding or difference in perspective, but rather, might instead be interpreted as a localizing discourse aimed at appropriating Blackness for their own uses and meanings as kids.

Regional or territorial affiliation with particular city neighborhoods is another trope in hip-hop that the students drew from in order to claim their identities as being from or repping Southeast or 25th Street (Rose 1994). Yet students expressed notions about Black cultural differences that did not come from hip-hop, but from community-based discourses about what it means to be a Black Washingtonian. A strong discourse of belonging for students had to do with the perceived accents of Black staff who were not from Washington, D.C. For one, African American and Nigerian staff members who came to work with students over the summer were teased about the clothes they wore, their haircuts, and their speech. For instance, Alvin, a summer instructor who was originally from Houston and attending school at Howard, was teased for sounding "country" and for the shape of his fade haircut. And while students looked north to New York for sources of music, fashion, and dance steps, they usually found ways to integrate small pieces of extra-local cultural practice into an already-existing D.C.-style template rather than to copy them outright. When the science program instructor, a Nigerian graduate student at Howard, introduced himself to the students, they could barely contain their laughter at the sound of his speech and whispered to each other about his "funny accent." Shortly after he began the science program, one student explained to another who asked who he was that Mr. Keegan was "African, not Black." Similarly, not having tenure in the local community as one from Southeast, or even Washington, D.C., could render one an outsider. Terrance, who returned to the neighborhood with his mother after two years away in Virginia, was one of the few students to note that white people joned (teased) differently than Black people. In response, Joseph teased, "Yeah, he would know since he from Kentucky where the white people at." For the students, then, cultural Blackness, and to a significant degree, authenticity, was localized and particular to city and neighborhood even though they reached outward to hip-hop and other larger global tropes to construct their identities.

Students expropriated mainstream tropes of Blackness as street toughness to construct age- and place-specific identities. However, the question as to whether they were resisting or accommodating hegemonic ideologies about race and social class that intersect to produce Blackness-as-pathology is less straightforward. I discuss such ideological contradictions in more detail in chapters 3–5. Nevertheless, it can be said that the students sought to transform pathologizing discourses about Blackness by expressing different kinds of logic with respect to their linguistic and cultural practices as "kids from Southeast." One the one hand, all of the students I talked to insisted that all kids, regardless of race, participated in trend consumption and invented new slang words (even though much of their slang was actually derived from current hip-hop music). A possible interpretation of such stancetaking is the same I proposed with respect to Blake's comment in the opening to this chapter: the students were critiquing racial ideologies that mark out Black practices as not just as exceptional, but also socially deviant and corrupting.[5] The students, in other words, might be seen as destabilizing raciolinguistic stigma by globalizing their cultural practices in claiming to orient to mainstream trends in the same way that they claimed all kids do. Children and teens around the world appear to be similarly constructing global youth identities not just to avoid stigma, but to claim status among peers (Bucholtz 2001; Nakassis 2016; Morales 2020). Analysis of how African American children construct Blackness outside of the perceived limits on what they know culturally and linguistically by virtue of being isolated in racially homogenous and impoverished neighborhoods therefore merits further study (e.g., Labov 2010), especially when aimed toward the goal of providing "culturally sustaining pedagogies" (Paris & Alim 2017).

It is noteworthy that the students drew from multiple sources of popular culture, not just Black cultural forms and practices, in order to construct their local identities as kids from Southeast, which indirectly indexes a claim to Black identity. Participating in the consumption of mainstream trends and appropriating them to construct their own local styles did not challenge or disrupt for them any sense of Black cultural authenticity. This sense of authenticity is normatively constructed in opposition to white cultural practices by subjects within hegemonic ideologies of racial difference and known as the *Black-white binary* (Chun 2001; Bucholtz 2004; for critique see Rosa 2019). Moreover, Blackness is also often recursively appropriated by subjects who mean to resist hegemony by inverting the prestige value assigned to white versus Black language and culture (Fordham 1999). But the students' identity practices challenge the notion of a Black and white cultural dichotomy in the way they blend and claim multiple cultural influences in the making of their styles, and in the way in which they localize their identities as being (from) Southeast/25th Street, in this sense working against racializing generalizations about "what Black people do and don't do."

Finally, it is commonly assumed by researchers and layfolk alike that African Americans from impoverished urban neighborhoods have little exposure to culture outside of their neighborhoods, which then restricts awareness and opportunities. For example, while Labov (2010) acknowledges that impoverished African Americans from urban neighborhoods have knowledge of "mainstream" cultural and linguistic forms, he argues that it is not sufficient to change their circumstances of cultural isolation and linguistic divergence, which then causes students to fall behind in school. As I discussed in chapter 1, such a well-intended but assimilatory perspective was shared by the executive staff of Urban Pathways, who insisted on providing field trips for the primary purpose of exposing students to culture and forms of living assumed to benefit them in contrast to the limitations and restrictions of their neighborhood. But as we see from the consumption practices of the preadolescent students, they not only drew from generally popular style and trends to construct their own identities but also they used them to consciously reshape local understandings of Blackness. It is in these two ways, by globalizing and localizing Blackness through cultural hybridity, that students challenged and transformed dominant racial thinking about Blackness as stigma and/or pathology.

SCALED-DOWN STREET TOUGHNESS: GENDER AND LINGUISTIC PRACTICE

As mentioned in the first section of this chapter, adults feared that the preadolescent students were blindly modeling the lifestyle choices of older teens and youth who embodied street toughness, with negative consequences for their academic achievement and future successes. Much of these fears were structured according to gender and class-based stereotypes of boys as possibly violent and gang-affiliated and girls as possible teen mothers. For boys and girls, the term "ghetto" indexed these differential gender and class-based interpellations of street-youth-in-becoming, and the term "loudness" signaled the visibility of these particular gender stereotypes, especially for girls. By my ethnographic reading, preadolescent students often played with these stereotypes in order to provoke a reaction—for example, singing aloud lyrics to misogynistic or sexually explicit hip-hop songs—but they did not necessarily mean to model them as a serious orientation to street toughness. At the same time, staff members often confided concerns to me that particular students, usually twelve- or thirteen-year-olds, were being recruited into street life by older peers and, for some girls, boyfriends with whom they were said to be having sex.

It is important to note that while older teens who were understood to embody Southeast style and street toughness certainly influenced the preadolescents' and thirteen-year-olds' identity practices, they did not wholly determine the students' choices or stylistic practices as adults commonly believed. The students not only borrowed selectively from the styles of local youth; they often took a critical stance toward what they considered to be excessive displays of street toughness and tailored their own practices accordingly. One of the ways in which they scaled street toughness down was to minimize the use of "cussing" and "negative words," both of which constituted part of "street talk." Girls especially policed peers who were determined to be using foul or inappropriate language. Consider the following examples, when several girls were playing computer games in the lab and *joning*, or exchanging ritual insults, in the absence of adults. While joning was generally considered appropriate for peer socializing, some students tried to restrict others' use of expletives. In line 6, Bianca negatively evaluates Tanika's use of "shit" (line 2); in line 22, after sixteen more exchanges between Tanika and her Makaila, Bianca tells her to watch her mouth:

1	Makaila	Your family live in Haiti.
2	Tanika	Grandma in your (inaudible) shit!
3	Unidentified	Look at you! Look at you! Look at you!
4	Makaila	(inaudible) no food-having, with no parents, girl.
5	Bianca	((to Tanika)) Why you cussin?
6	Tanika	'Cos she tryin to jone!
22	Bianca	Tanika, watch your mouth!
23	Unidentified	Oh! And you know they recording you too!
24	Bianca	Oh, she about to get someone in trouble.
25	Tanika	She cussed at me first, I don't need to get in
26		trouble.

In lines 23 and 24, two girls bring forth a primary concern of the preadolescent students: getting in trouble with adults. But discourses about respectability and politeness, which Shanae had said some students learned at home from adults, influenced particular students' restrictions on the use of slang. As she explained to me, "Adults tell children to speak proper because, they taught them better home training to not talk slang like, 'Nigga, get out of my way!' Instead, you say, 'Excuse me, may you get out of my way, please . . . . Scoot over, please.' Instead of using slang."

While students generally spoke slang as part of their peer interactions, students recognized gender differences in use and intent. For one, boys were said to use the n-word and sexual themes in ritual insults. Shanae explained, "Slang means to me like, when you use negative words. Like, when you say, 'dawg' or call somebody a 'nigga', or, use a cuss word. That's slang . . . 'your mother was in my bed last night,' boys be sayin that." Jamal noted that he spoke slang to express anger or play around with someone: "I speak slang when I'm angry, or sometimes when I'm just playin. Mainly, I mumble it under my breath about the teachers, and sometimes, when I don't like somebody."

Such perceived gender distinctions in linguistic displays of street toughness ideologically scale up to the gender and race-based distinctions made between slang and proper, if we recall the voicing performances of talking Black and white in the opening of this chapter. It appears that the students perceived boys to be more likely to speak slang as displays of street toughness while girls are more likely to restrict use to peer contexts, and even to exercise more respectability and politeness when they use slang, at least in spaces requiring the performance of school readiness. But for either boys or girls, inappropriate uses of slang in the after school program were policed by peers as "acting ghetto" or being "too loud," which suggest complicity to some extent with raciolinguistic ideologies of appropriateness. At the same time, students also policed displays of being too proper, as we see in the opening ethnographic story with Janice and Alisha. The trick for students, then, was to have one foot in the community and one in the school in the sense of managing both street toughness and school readiness. Being able to scale down or adapt street toughness to academic settings was one strategy that girls appeared to use with more self-conscious frequency in order to meet these requirements. Chapter 4, which analyzes uses of joning in the after school program, indicates that girls were typically more successful not because of what they did differently from boys, but because of larger ideological contradictions that stigmatize particular displays of Blackness as inappropriate, and which point to the hypervisibility of figures such as street-tough Black men and sexually transgressive Black women in the form of "hos" or teenaged mothers.

DISCUSSION

This chapter presents possibilities for interpreting the preadolescents' and early teens' language and identity practices as a transracial project in response to raciolinguistic socialization and enregisterment, which were articulated in relation to a chronotope of anxiety, more so than resistance. In different ways, the students challenged the ideological contradiction between having to be either street tough or school ready, but not both at the same time. In this sense, they constructed their own raciolinguistic chronotope of resistance. As I have argued in this chapter, the identity models of street-tough and school-ready are more broadly indexical of a Black/white binary model of identity, which culturally pathologizes street tough forms of Blackness while understanding these to be authentic identity models of Otherness. Here, as part of a raciolinguistic perspective, it is important to note that it is not particular forms or practices that signal Black pathology, but the possibility of always being read as too "ghetto," "loud," or "having an attitude problem" in white public spaces that enregisters students' voices and bodies as racially Other. It is this possibility of being read as Other that students attempted to navigate in minimizing or scaling down street toughness while also not fully endorsing the assimilatory model of school readiness.

For much of this chapter, I describe students' cultural and linguistic practices as more broadly engaged with social processes and categories other than race and as intersectional with other ideologies of difference, such as age, place/location, and gender. While some critical race theorists are likely to disagree, not all of their lived experiences were about navigating racial Otherness in relation to white hegemony, but instead about creating their own systems of linguistic and cultural differentiation within a peer-centered world of identity exploration and play. As I learned in the course of my research, students would expropriate or recursively construct signifiers of Blackness to create other kinds of language and identity practices, such as what children do in contrast to adults. For many of them, growing up meant leaving behind the linguistic and cultural practices of children, such as "cussing" and using slang to navigate schooling, in favor of practices such as styleshifting. This way of thinking about future success is inevitably overshadowed by the requirement to assimilate according to the expectations of white public space, and it is easy to dismiss their way of interpreting growing up as a form of false consciousness about the wider process of racialized cultural assimilation. But another interpretive possibility that I have proposed in this chapter is that the students are engaging in acts of raciolinguistic transformation by grounding their versions of Blackness into existing structures of difference. As Rosa notes at the end of his monograph on Latinx youth, "The reimagining of [borders] . . . demonstrates that worlds beyond these borders are not just possible, but waiting to be recognized" (2019, p. 213). The next three chapters, which analyze students' linguistic practices, focus in depth on how students used language to transform discourses about race, identity, and academic success in the after school program.

NOTES

1. For clarity, I have left out the overlapping talk and transcribed only the turns that were relevant to the questions I was asking. In reality, the girls were answering my questions while verbally negotiating the task activity, giggling, and otherwise evaluating each other's impressions. Keri was present in the interaction but had no turns at talk during the part of the interaction represented here.

2. See Silverstein (2003) and Agha (2005) on the general theory of enregisterment.

3. "Asked" was pronounced with metathesis ("aksed").

4. I asked teenagers from pilot research I conducted in 2008–2009 and the after school students about the style of pants and many agreed that Lupe Fiasco was the originator of the style.

5. See Alim and Smitherman (2012) for a thorough analysis of raciolinguistic ideologies that pathologize AAL.

3

"He-Said-She-Said (Do This)"

Directives, Marking, and the Resemiotization of Authoritative Discourse

As I mentioned in the introduction, I was almost never able to leave aside my duties and identity as a teacher to simply observe the students and collect data. One of the things that I perceived to constantly interrupt my attempts to do so was students' apparent need to use me as a pawn in order to get what they wanted. I often found myself attempting to pacify their need to assert some sort of control or authority in a situation or to be right about something, such as the rules of a game. Quite frankly, at the time I thought of it as annoyingly preadolescent behavior. Consider the following excerpt, which documents Alisha's attempt to get her brother, Joseph, to give her back the seat she had been sitting in prior to her leaving it to help their younger sister, Keri, with her homework. Alisha's own attempts to get her seat back proved unsuccessful, so she recruited me to intervene on her behalf, while I was (angrily) trying to get all of the students to "find a seat" (line 2). Instead of heeding my decision, Joseph contested it, which produced the following dispute:

1	Alisha	Ms. Jennifer, tell Joseph to-
2	Jen	FIND A SEA:T!
3		I DON'T WANNA ASK AGAI:N!
		((1 s))
4	Alisha	Tell Joseph to get out my seat.
5	Jen	Who?
6	Alisha	Joseph.
7	Joseph	Blake was sitting here.
8	Jen	No,/
9	Alisha	/I was sitting right there.
10	Jen	She was.
11	Joseph	I saw Blake right here.

12	Alisha	I went to go help Keri.
13	Jen	Joseph, get out of her chair.
		((1 s))
14	Joseph	She ain't even a:s[k!]
15	Alisha	[He] always taking up my seat!
16	Jen	((to Joseph)) I'm asking Y[OU].
17	Joseph	((to Alisha)) [Shu]t up.
18	Jen	Joseph, get out of the chair.
19	Joseph	Mm. Nah.
		((2 seconds silence))
20	Jen	You know, it's better if you ask someone, "Hey,
21		are you still sitting in that seat?"
22		Is it really that difficult?
23	Joseph	Yea . . . .

As I mentioned before, disputes such as these initially proved incredibly frustrating for me because they were distractions from the kinds of talk and interaction that I wanted to document as a researcher. In my role as a teacher, they also distracted me from my attempts to "manage the classroom." However, it occurred to me several months into fieldwork that if these kinds of disputes occurred so frequently, I should probably take the opportunity to examine them a bit more closely. Upon initial analysis, I noticed that the highest frequency utterance type was *directives*, which are speech acts that are designed to get someone to do something (Searle 1970; Goodwin 1990). For example, three of the first four utterances in the transcript given earlier are all directives: "Tell Joseph to-" (Alisha, line 1), "Find a seat" (Researcher, line 2), and again, "Tell Joseph to get out my seat" (Alisha, line 4).

Second, I noticed that in addition to serving a purely instrumental purpose, such as Alisha trying to get her seat back, directives served at least three additional purposes for students. First, they used directives to evaluate and direct the behavior of their peers according to school-based disciplinary models for appropriate behavior. Second, they used directives to test or (re)appropriate the kinds of authoritative-institutional discourse typically afforded adults in their caregiving or teaching roles. As the examples in this chapter will show, the students were modeling, not resisting, the kinds of disciplinary frameworks we expected them to follow. Their disputes, in other words, reflected a wider process by which they were testing and, importantly, claiming, authoritative-institutional discourse for their own. Finally, the students frequently recruited directives to perform an AAL speech act known as *marking*, which is a parody or caricature of an individual's perceived mannerisms or attributes (Mitchell-Kernan 2001; Green 2002). For example, the preadolescent students often poked fun at or openly mocked teachers and parents, using imagined language varieties they called "talking white" and "talking Black" to evaluate particular adults' effectiveness in directing activities and performing disciplinary acts. Thus, while directives figured into students' attempts to control and define the after school "classroom" relative to other peers, marking helped them make sense of and challenge the kinds of raciolinguistic authority commanded by the different adults in their lives. Moreover, it helped them symbolically invert the social prestige value of language varieties they referred to as talking white and talking Black in the school-based setting of the after school space, a process which I refer to as *raciolinguistic resemiotization*.

Grounded in the aforementioned findings, this chapter examines how directives and marking helped students renegotiate the structure of classroom authority in the after school program. As reflected in marking speech acts, their renegotiations of the classroom disciplinary structure includes a critique of what is normatively defined as legitimate, articulate, or appropriate language in school-based settings. Drawing from theories of voicing as social-semiotic practice (Bakhtin 1980; Hill 1995; Reyes 2016, 2017), the chapter explores how students appropriated the authoritative-institutional discourse styles afforded caregivers and teachers to wield their own sense of classroom authority as well as fairness and justice.

First, I describe how directives function in classroom settings and provide examples of how students used them to recruit the authority of adults or appropriate their voices. Then, I describe the AAL speech act called *marking* and examine the raciolinguistic resemiotization of "articulate" and "appropriate" language when students parodied adults. In doing so, they inverted the prestige value of standard/academic English by performing imagined white and Black speech styles through the voicing of stereotypical figures such as "Valley Girl" and "surfer dude." As I illustrate in this section, gender was central to creating the iconic distinctions between white and Black language, and it functioned to destabilize the authority of white speech by feminizing it as weak and powerless. Through marking, students not only demonstrated a fine-grained awareness of raciolinguistic typification, but also of gendered language and stereotypical how it is linked to social power (i.e., women as weak, men as strong). Lastly, I conclude the chapter by looking at how voicing practices help us better understand how students attempt to reconstitute raciolinguistic ideologies.

"HE-SAID-SHE-SAID (DO THIS)": PREADOLESCENTS, CONFLICT TALK, AND DIRECTIVES

In Goodwin's (1990) study of African American children's peer groups, "he-said-she-said" refers to an elaborate dispute format in which girls, rather than simply "gossiping," are constructing their own moral/social order and roles, relations, and identities as they make sense of wider social frameworks for interaction. In my own fieldwork in a classroom setting, which is predicated on constant task activity, I found that the preadolescents' and early teens' disputes can be rather glossed as, "he-said-she-said-do-this," in which the students sought to make sense of the hows and whys of discipline, authority, and behavior according to the classroom logic established by schooling conventions and transmitted by teachers. As evident in their constant arguing, the students were constantly concerned with who was off-task, not following the rules, disrespecting someone, not sharing, not listening,

not letting someone take their turn, and the like. After school staff heard no end
to these kinds of arguments when students' directives to each other failed, and my
near-constant irritation with these types of disputes stemmed from the fact that I or
another staff member were expected to adjudicate students' commands and requests
when they failed. My irritation also stemmed from the belief that the students were
constantly distracting each other away from what Wortham (2007) describes as
the "primary business" of academic learning. Thus, despite my formal training in
anthropology and critical pedagogy, my personal annoyance stemmed, admittedly,
from the belief that the students were unwilling to behave in ways that would lead
them toward more effective forms of classroom participation and academic success.
My goal as a teacher was always to end disputes so we could move on to the things
we believed students needed to be doing in a classroom setting—learning and
becoming socialized toward "school-ready" behaviors such as listening to adults and
being fair to one another (i.e., learning how to share). Ironically, as the data in this
chapter will show, this is precisely often what they were trying to do when arguing
with one another.

Had I revisited Goodwin's ethnography earlier on in my fieldwork, I would have
realized that trying to stop task activity-based conflicts would be quite beside the
point. As she and other scholars have argued, preadolescents and teens, at least in
the United States and other European nations, often build and extend conflict rather
than stem it (see also Corsaro & Rizzo 1990; Eder 1990).[1] Moreover, it is common
for preadolescent children to use directives to test social face among peers (Mitchell-
Kernan & Kernan 1977), where *social face* is defined as any mode of self-presentation
in which a person aims to gain approval according to socially established lines (Goffman 1980). Thus, while adults typically seek to minimize face threat, children and
teens often do the opposite. For many young people, face-threatening acts (FTAs)
constitute a primary mode of peer socialization (Goodwin 1990; Tetreault 2010).
Conflict talk, or styles of speech used to negotiate disputes, arguments, and the like,
is therefore central to how most young people socialize with each other and, moreover, structure "politic" (rapport-building) interactions (Tetreault 2010).

Directives, then, often functioned among the students to build and sustain disputes, especially during task-based activities, whether the tasks assigned by teachers
or decided upon by the students in their learning and play. To recall my earlier
definition, directives are speech acts that are designed to get someone else to do
something and which impose some sort of obligatory action on the part of the recipient. Broadly speaking, they can take the form of commands, requests, hints, or pleas,
with various syntactic modifications aimed at meeting specific politeness and status
norms (Ervin-Tripp 1977; Goodwin 1990; Takano 2005). Thus, directives typically
vary in form according to status differences between individuals, politeness norms,
and speaking situation, and how speakers formulate and embed these speech acts in
wider contexts of activity thus presumes and entails, or *indexes* (Silverstein 2003),
wider assumptions about authority, status, and power relations between interlocutors. For example, in school classrooms, task activities and learning are typically
teacher-fronted, meaning that teachers use directives to instruct, guide activities, and

discipline students. Thus, teachers in using directives index their role as authority figures in the classroom in the act of using directives.

Importantly, teachers' directives perform moral as well as academic work: they orient students to the normative ethical stances, cultural values, and moral orders of the classroom and the wider, mainstream society. For example, as LeMaster (2006) shows in her ethnographic study of preschoolers, even very young children are not only highly attuned to how language is linked to positions of classroom authority; they also learn to use teacher-talk to steer other children's behavior toward a desired outcome, often in alignment with school-appropriate behavior. Interestingly, her findings suggest that children are often simply concerned with modeling or testing authority for themselves rather than gaining something from issuing a directive, such as a reward from a teacher for keeping a classmate on task. As the extracts in my study among older children will also suggest, there were instances in which students' directives were of secondary or no concern in terms of instrumental use or immediate benefit. Instead, directives often operated as part of wider evaluative strategies that students used to assess their peers in terms of what constituted appropriate behavior for after school and to participate in disciplinary activities usually reserved for teachers. I argue that it is in this capacity that they approached adults or used their voices to gain ground, assert status, and otherwise test authoritative discourse using same- to similar-age or younger peers as their primary targets.

Following Goodwin, I combine conversation and discourse analysis to explore a specific sort of constitutive relationship between directives and the wider context in which they occur: how the preadolescent students used directives to claim for themselves and attribute to others moral stances in relation to the kinds of social-academic disciplining to which they were subjected in after school. I argue that by analyzing how directives were used to help construct moral stances, it is possible to address how they attempted to make sense of and also to appropriate adults' voices as associated with institutional-authoritative discourse. The data in this chapter suggest that the after school students sought to make authoritative discourse "internally persuasive" (Bakhtin 1981) among peers, ultimately as part of the attempt to test and define kinds of authority to which they were made subject for themselves as well as make sense of the fundamentally moral project of schooling.

DIRECTIVES AND AUTHORITY IN THE AFTER SCHOOL CLASSROOM: STUDENTS' RECRUITMENT TACTICS

The extracts provided in this section illustrate three different ways in which students used directives and tied them to the authority of an adult: (1) authoring the directive and recruiting an adult to animate it; (2) reanimating a directive that has been initiated (authored) by an adult; and (3) animating adults as character figures (referees) in interaction. The analysis suggests that in using directives to build moral commentary on the actions and activities of their peers, students linguistically improvised within received models of authority to test its effectiveness for their own uses, neither wholly accepting nor resisting the kinds of moral authority they were subjected to in the classroom.

Recruitment Tactics: Student-Authored Directives

The first example given next is a transcript of an interaction that is typical of how the nine- to thirteen-year-old students used directives to shape their task activities and claim authoritative positions within it. Commonly, the students would be engaged in play and one of their own directives would fail to initiate the desired action from the recipient. At this point, the student who issued the failing speech act would call upon an adult to intervene. In extract 1, Deandre, Joseph, and Malcolm had been making "passes" for activities that the students needed permission for—namely, using the computers (lines 7, 11). Deandre and Malcolm tried to get Joseph to only make three based on the number of computers that were working at the time (lines 3, 5–6), but Joseph blew them off, saying "Blah blah blah" (line 4) and argued that they might need to make an additional number (line 8). It is at this point that Deandre called upon me, the nearest teacher, to intervene (line 9):

1. "Tell Joseph to make three passes"

1 →	Deandre	It's only four. So all you gotta do is make, four
2		passes.
		((5 s))
3		Actually, three.
4	Joseph	Blah blah blah.
5 →	Deandre	You only gotta make thr[ee]!
6	Malcolm	[Three]!
7		'Cos, it's only, three computers.
8	Joseph	You might need some more passes.
9	Deandre	Ms. Jennifer, tell Joseph to make three passes.
10	Jen	To make what?
11	Deandre	Three. 'Cos it's only three computers that work.
12	Joseph	A:nd more stuff.
13	Jen	There's only three?
14		((to Joseph)) Do you wanna let some other
15		people make passes, too?
16 →	Deandre	Yeah. Pick "Girl Boy."
17		For the bathroom.
18	Jen	((to Joseph)) You make three, and then someone
19		else makes three. 'Kay?
20	Deandre	Nah he already made his!
21	Jen	Okay, switch off with somebody, Joseph.
		((1 s))
22	Deandre	Come on.

23	Joseph	All right, gimme the p[asses].
24	Deandre	[Come o:n!]
25 →		Gimme that.
26	Joseph	What? Oh.

Here, I want to highlight how Deandre used two interactional strategies to attempt to claim authority within the task: (1) issuing directives that I have marked with arrows (lines 1–2, 5, 16, 25), and (2) using an adult as an authoritative resource when Joseph ignored him (line 9). In initially attempting to direct Joseph, Deandre simply provides information that tells him what number of passes he needs to make based on the number of working computers (lines 1–3, 5). But after I am called upon to mediate the boys' dispute, Deandre begins to use bald imperatives: "Pick 'Girl Boy'" (line 16) and "Gimme that" (line 25).

Lines 9 forward suggest that my role as mediator initiated a shift in how Deandre formulated his directives and, therein, his stance in the interaction: he displayed a more commanding role once I, the after school instructor, had decided that Joseph was to share task responsibilities and resources with the other two participants. In deciding in favor of what Deandre had wanted, I authorized his use of directly formulated commands. In other words, Deandre was not simply using imperatives to direct Joseph in his task: he was also displaying his right to tell Joseph what to do based on how I had mediated the task activity.

As in the opening vignette, where Alisha asks me to "tell Joseph" to get out of her seat, extract 1 shows how students often solicited adults to participate in their interactions directly as a source of decision-making authority. As this sequence illustrates, the student typically broke topic in asking an adult to intervene on his/her behalf when a dispute arose over ownership of objects or decision-making control in a task activity.

In contrast to asking a teacher to "tell so-and-so to (desired action)," the students also recruited adults to their interactions using a speech act they called *snitching* or *ratting* (also commonly known as *tattling*). Snitching varied in form: it could be formulated as a directive, as in extract 1, or it could simply report what the target had said or done. Unlike instances where students asked adults to mediate disputes, snitching had no obvious purpose other than to point out that the target was doing something he or she was not supposed to be doing, either in the immediate or general sense of what the rules for appropriate behavior were. Snitching was therefore not a problem-solving solution; instead, students initiated a moral claim about the target's behavior and then offered their peer up to the disciplinary authority of an adult. In other words, snitching constituted "discipline for discipline's sake." Perhaps for this reason, the older students looked down upon individuals who snitched: a common saying among them went, "Snitches get stitches." This was a mock warning that meant the party who snitched would have to face bullying from other children. Nevertheless, snitching was common and the following several examples highlight how students used it to lend power to their moral claims about who followed rules and who did not.

Extract 2 illustrates snitching. In this example, Ms. Betty and I had been attempt-ing to get several students to put away the Lego pieces they had been playing with. Five-year-old Ronald was bouncing a basketball while Deandre, Rashid, Malcolm, and Joseph tidied up. I directed the four boys' attention to a Lego piece that is lying on the floor (line 4). Deandre announced that Ronald is (still) bouncing the bas-ketball: "Look. Bouncing" (line 5), but then quickly reshifted focus to the clean-up activity, directing Malcolm to pick up a car (line 6):

2. "Look. Bouncing."

1	Ms. Betty	There go a piece up under the table.
		((Ronald is bouncing a basketball))
2	Jen	Ronald, not in here.
3	Joseph	Who threw my wheel in?
4	Jen	There's a Lego piece on that carpet, guys.
5 →	Deandre	Look. Bouncing.
6		Malcolm, get the car-
7	Ms. Betty	Ronald. You still bouncing that ball?
8		That's all flat.
9	Ronald	((negation)) Mm mm!

In calling for an adult, Deandre implicates the actions of both the target, Ronald, on the one hand, and the rest of the boys, on the other: Ronald is not helping to clean up like everybody else who had been playing with the Legos and asked to perform the task. Presumably, a motivating factor was that Deandre found this to be unfair and wanted to draw Ronald into the task. But in other instances of snitching, the student who initiated the adult to interaction had no such motive. In some cases, students would simply call to the adult and denote the prohibited action, as in extracts 3 and 4:

3. "Mom. Joseph keep running in the closet"

1 →	Deandre	Mom. Joseph keep running in the closet.
2	Ms. Betty	Hey Joseph.
3		I told y'all to get over here and sit down.
4		You go in that closet, and you watch what I do.
5		Cos I to:ld you don't go in there.

4. "There go Deandre!"

1 →	Lenny	There go Deandre, [Ms. Jennifer]!
2	Deandre	Boy, I didn't even do that!
3	Lenny	Yes you di:d!

In both sequences, the speaker provides no specification as to what is wrong about the act or the person or even assumes the specification to be necessary. In extract 4, Ms. Betty addresses Joseph's actions immediately. But in extract 4, Deandre chal-lenges Lenny, negating his claim that Lenny had seen him do something wrong.

Deandre could have denied to me directly that he had been engaged in whatever Lenny had seen him doing; instead, he addresses Lenny using the term "Boy," countering the initial snitching move by hailing Lenny as a subordinate (extract 4, line 2). Deandre implies that Lenny is either wrong or lying, but rather than accusing Lenny outright, he makes reference to his own activity: "I didn't even do that!" As Coupland and Coupland (2009) argue, accusations such as "You're lying!" attribute morally negative epistemic stances to addressees and are usually characteristic of conflict talk. Lenny and Deandre were friends, which perhaps explains why Deandre selected a mitigated strategy of characterizing his peer's claim.

At other times, students constructed more elaborate depictions of participants when they snitched on one another, ones that extended beyond the point at which an adult became involved. In extract 5, Makila solicits my attention after making several unsuccessful attempts to help Janelle with her math homework. I am sitting at the same table with the two girls, helping Alisha with her social studies assignment as Makila and Janelle argue about the right answer (lines 1–11). Makila makes several bids for my attention (lines 3, 5–6, 8) before the fourth attempt is successful (lines 12–16). Here, Makila reports not that Janelle is doing her homework incorrectly, but that Janelle is not accepting Makila's tutoring. Knowing that Makila excelled in math and could help Janelle, who was a grade below her and typically struggled, I encouraged Janelle to let Makila tutor her (lines 17–18):

5. "Ms. Jennifer, she ain't want me to help her"

1	Janelle	That's not supposed to go that way.
2	Makila	Yes you do-
3 →		Nah. All right. Ms. Jennifer!
4	Jen	((to Alisha, who I am helping)) What's your next
5		date?
5 →	Makila	Ms. J? Ms. J, she said she wasn't
6		going nowhere, she don't want me to help her.
7	Jen	((helping Alisha))
8 →	Makila	[Ms. Jennifer]
9	Jen	((to Alisha)) Yeah. Put the date, on your line, and
10		then you can write abo:ve it, instead of belo:w it,
11		and then that saves you sp[ace].
12 →	Makila	[Ms. Jennifer],
13		She says she-she ain't want me to help her, she
14		said I'm not writing it right.
15		She not-she not doing it.
16		((inaudible)) ain't want me to help her.
17	Jen	((inaudible)) She knows what she's doing, she
18		can help you.
19	Makila	She wanna do it by herself, I'll let her.
20	Jen	Okay.
21	Makila	But Mr. Raymond gonna check it.

After I encourage Janelle to let Makila help her (lines 17–18), Makila continues to depict Janelle as stubborn, stating that she had tried to help her and was giving up on her efforts (line 19). Makila then notes that Raymond would check the assignment for correctness (line 21). It is here, at the end of the sequence, that she establishes the appropriateness of her characterization of Janelle. If the work had been completed incorrectly, the students not only had to redo it, but they also faced verbal disciplining if it was discovered that they had been messing around or refusing to complete the work.

The majority of Makila's talk is devoted to describing Janelle's behavior, though she could have simply reported her refusal and noted the consequences in a few turns. Janelle's behavior is the explicit subject of talk, but Makila is also displaying a moral characterization of herself, as a good citizen who is trying to help her peer with her homework. As Goffman (1980) and Goodwin (1990) argue, speakers embed in their talk portrayals of self in the process of characterizing others. Throughout the text, Makila draws attention to the act of helping Janelle (lines 6, 13–14, 16), implying that she is not only capable of doing so, but also that she is acting altruistically, concerned with acting as a buffer should Raymond later check Janelle's work (line 21). Thus, Makila reporting on Janelle's refusal to accept help functions not just to highlight her peer's misbehavior, but also to display, contrastively, her ability and willingness to help her peer. She is, in other words, making a hierarchical status distinction based on the implicit moral claim that she is being a "good student" and Janelle is being a "bad student."

In sum, the preadolescent students often authored or coauthored such moral claims about themselves and others according to classroom norms for appropriate behavior, voicing their own positions, but outsourcing the work of discipline to an adult when they were readily available. Students initiated directive utterance and the intent behind it: directive authorship belonged to the student, but it was the adult who animated the subsequent moves. Extracts 1 and 2 involved seeking an adult in situations where the petitioning student has failed to initiate a change in the state of affairs. In other words, there was usually a dispute preceding an adult's involvement and there was an immediately practical goal such as claiming objects or task-based authority. Snitching, on the other hand, did not necessarily involve addressing a prior dispute and could simply function to call attention to what a participant was doing wrong, as in extracts 2–5. Students used the disciplinary authority of adults in a similar fashion here, in the sense that the adult would issue directives to correct or change the behavior of the target. But the primary purpose of snitching involved students characterizing participants as doing right or wrong absent of any apparent personal benefit to the speaker. Students often produced elaborate depictions of selves and others into wider frames of reference for what constituted appropriate behavior in after school, often seeking, as I suggest Makila did in extract 5, institutional-authoritative recognition for acts such as being helpful to another. Unlike other ways in which students could and did seek this type of recognition, such as offering to help an instructor tidy up, a target was animated as a particular type of figure in interaction. The target's actions and behavior served to contrast with that of the speaker, whose self-display was implied in the way he or she claimed the right to evaluate his or her peer, using the adult as the recipient of talk.

Adults as Authors: Reanimating Authoritative-Institutional Discourse

In this section, I analyze a different participation framework that involved students using adults who were present in interaction. These are examples where adults issue a topic-initial directive to a student and then another student chimes in with his or her own immediately following. The student's directive at times reinforced the authorial intent of the adult and at others, constituted instances of "double-voicing" (Bakhtin 1981) in which students reanimated the directive to accomplish some other interactional purpose.

When adults issued directives, another student would often issue his or her own in a subsequent turn. The student's directive usually took the form of a bald imperative even though it could have been formulated using reported speech (i.e., "Ms. Jennifer said"). In some cases, the student who issued the directive was simply repeating what an adult had said, such that the original intent behind the adult's request was maintained. In extract 6, Malcolm tells Keri to get her homework, several minutes after I had first asked her. Keri had been conversing with another peer and Malcolm tried to get her attention:

6. "Get your homework"
1	Malcolm	Keri. Keri. KERI!
2	Jen	((to Deandre)) 'Kay. Gimme a second, Deandre.
3→	Malcolm	((to Keri)) Get your ho:mework!
4	Jen	Sweetie what did you do with your homework?
5	Malcolm	Her mother gonna help her.

Repeating an adult's directive as an assistive move was especially common when a preadolescent student's younger sibling was the recipient. Most of the preadolescents and early teens had brothers or sisters enrolled in the younger age group (five to eight years) and were charged with the task of reporting back to their parents or main caregivers regarding the younger child's behavior. In this sense, it was not just after school staff who were sources of decision-making authority and discipline for the students. Many times, students cited their parents and other caregivers in issuing directives to their peers and younger counterparts as well as to support directives that instructors issued to students. In extract 7, I told five-year-old Ronald to put away his basketball; Janice, his ten-year-old sister, overheard me and threatened to call their mother:

7. "Don't let nobody talk to you or Imma call mommy."
1	Jen	Ronald. Put that away.
2	Janice	Ronald. Don't let nobody talk to you or Imma
3		((I'm going to)) call mommy.

Thus, in many instances, students used a bald imperative with same-/similar-age or younger peers when the directive's authorship could be attributed to an adult who was already involved in disciplining students. As the section to follow shows, students mitigated their directives when they were authorizing them.

In contrast to the examples in the previous, where the student approaches an adult to author the directive themselves, in these examples, the adult both authors and animates the directive. In a follow-up turn, students reanimate the request, but directive authorship and intent remains with the adult. Quite the opposite from the previous section, in which the student is the author of the directive and the adult the animator, in these examples, the adult is the author and the student is the animator; the student, then, is engaged in an act of revoicing an adult's authority.

Disaligning with Authoritative-Institutional Discourse

In extracts 6 and 7, the student aligns his or her stance in interaction with that of the adult: both work toward the same directive goal. And most directive goals were tied to the primary purpose of after school: socializing children into behaving as necessary for their academic success in a school classroom. Such uses of directives, in other words, can be said to support the moral project of disciplining students into their expected roles. At other times, students revoiced adults' directives in a way that disaligned with the original directive goal and the disciplinary role assumed by an adult, even though on the surface, the utterance suggested otherwise. The student's directive was usually more aggravated in form than what the adult had produced and linked to hyperbolic, subordinating depictions of the recipient. The "character ties" (Goodwin 1990) created in these directives suggest that students were testing status claims with their peers and also that they were satirizing authoritative discourse. The recipient of the directive, in other words, was not the only target of evaluative commentary: the adult, construed as the principal figure in such interactions, was too.

Satirical evaluations of authoritative discourse sometimes occurred when students did not want to perform the tasks requested by an adult. A common situation was when adults instructed students to clean up their play areas. Perhaps unsurprisingly, "clean-up time" was always antagonistic: adults repeated their directives, impatiently, raising their voices, commanding students, and issuing threats to take away free time privileges as the students argued with each other about who had made what mess and who was to clean up what, always attempting to defer the task activity on to another participant. Issuing directives allowed students to claim a different role within the clean-up task: instead of cleaning up, they co-participated in directing it. But as discussed earlier, their directives also intensified the social aggravation already at hand, both in terms of how the directive itself was formulated, and also more broadly in shaping the interaction. Such uses could prove disruptive rather than collaborative, as the next two sequences suggest.

In extract 8, I tell several boys to pick up Lego pieces that had been scattered around the floor, using a neutral address term, "guys" (lines 1–2). J.J. then commands Ronald to pick up the pieces I had pointed to, addressing him as a subordinate, "boy" (lines 3):

8. "Pick that stuff up off of there, boy!"

1	Jen	Guys, pick up the Legos, there's more under that
2		table over there.
3→	J.J.	Ronald, pick that stuff up off of there, boy!
4→	Deandre	Pick that stuff up! Off the ground,
5	Ronald.	
6	Ronald	What'd I do?
7→	Deandre	[You pick that stuff up off the floor!]
8→	Joseph	[All that stuff Ronald, you]
9		gotta pick that up!
10	Jen	Ronald, p[ick it up ((inaudible))]
11	Ronald	[I ain't do that!]
12	Deandre	Yes you [di:d!]
13	Joseph	[di:d!]
14	Deandre	I saw you, Roger ((inaudible))
15	Joseph	You just bust up your car part, boy!
16→		All right now, get down, pick that up/
17→	J.J.	/And
18		=beg for Jesus.
19	Multiple	((laugh))

Deandre and Joseph chime in (lines 8–10) and I tell Ronald to participate in the task (line 10). Ronald denies that he had made the mess (line 11) and Deandre and Joseph counter (lines 12–15). Joseph also addresses Ronald as "boy" (line 15), reinforcing the subordinate position he has been assigned by J.J. in a prior turn. Joseph then again commands Ronald to get down and pick up the Legos; J.J. latches on to instruct Ronald to assume a suppliant position: "And beg for Jesus" (lines 16–17). At this point, multiple students recognize the boys' task activity direction as a game and laugh (line 19).

Here the three older boys—J.J., Deandre, and Joseph—have used my original directive as an opportunity to play a status game with their younger peer, Ronald, as the target of their bullying. The directives they use are aggravated relative to how I formulated mine (line 1–2): as discussed earlier, J.J. and Joseph address him as "boy," tying their imperatives to a subordinate characterization of Ronald. I had first asked all of the participants to clean up, assigning equal responsibility to all of them for performing the task; here, the older boys reposition themselves so that they are codirecting Ronald rather than cleaning up. But unlike my original instruction, these directives are double-voiced: the older boys are not simply attempting to get Ronald to clean up (so that they don't have to do it themselves), they are being domineering toward a younger boy.

This example suggests that the intensification and rechanneling of my original directive to aggressively subordinate Ronald satirized the disciplinary discourse used by instructors and other after school adults. The older boys' directives mockingly echo the authorial intent of the adult's, which is suggested in how they so explicitly command Ronald into literally assuming a position of subservience. Additionally, as noted earlier, the directive goal is not aligned with that of the adult: it disrupts the original purpose of getting all of the students to clean up after themselves in a coordinated fashion.

Extract 9 is taken from another interaction in which Ms. Betty and I are directing the students to clean up. I begin at a point after Denise and another student had become involved in some horseplay while arguing about who was to pick up which items. Denise tells the other student to get his "bitch self up" (line 1); I exclaim her name aloud (line 2), and Joseph tells her, "Watch your mouth, young lady!" (line 3). Denise apologizes and Ms. Betty continues to direct the clean up task (lines 5–8). Joseph then begins to sing aloud that he told Denise to listen but she did not (lines 9–10), and then tells another student not to put away the car he had been playing with:

9. "Watch your mouth, young lady!"

1	Denise	Get your bitch self up, no I'm not.
2	Jen	Denise!
3→	Joseph	Watch your mouth, young lady!
4	Denise	Oh, I'm sorry.
5	Joseph	I warned her!
6	Ms. Betty	Deandre, put those up!
7		I see two pieces down here. Come on, get them
8		pieces up. Now one, two, three, four, five
9	Joseph	((singing)) I told her to listen!
10		She ain't wanna listen!

Here, the goal of adults is to get the students to put away their playthings. Joseph does not issue a directive for this purpose, but instead capitalizes on the topical break I introduce in reproaching Denise and shifts the focus to her cursing. He elaborates on my reproach by issuing an imperative, addressing her as "young lady" and lending additional disciplinary weight to my original utterance. Joseph, in other words, evaluates the original utterance in his subsequent directive as much as he aims to provoke his peer and the situation: he intensifies what has already been said by using an address term that adults commonly use to mark a child's subordinate status when they are engaged in disciplining the recipient. Yet in lines 9–10, he crows at the end of the sequence. Similar to extract 10, Joseph adopts a multivoiced stance in this interaction, one that is somewhat contradictory: he claims disciplinary authority relative to his peer Denise, but by formulating a directive that also appears to mock the authoritative-institutional voice he uses it to provoke her and distract away from what Ms. Betty and I were actually trying to accomplish in that interaction.

The students repeated or intensified adults' directives in subsequent turns, to either align or disalign with the disciplinary intent underlying the adult's original request. In other words, students used aggravated forms to reanimate the original directive from the adult, but channeled them to different uses. Thus, in extracts 7 and 8, Malcolm and Janice collaborate with the adult speaker to get their peers to perform the requested action while in the last two, speakers apply the adult's voice to a directive purpose that in some ways contradicts what was intended in the original utterance. In extracts 9 and 10, students claimed the type of disciplinary authority accorded adults and not only used it to assert status over their peers, but also to furnish evaluative commentary on the act of disciplining students into appropriate behavior. The exaggerated tone of domination found evident in these uses—for example, as tied to subordinating characterizations of the recipient—sequentially followed and elaborated on the adult's directive as critical meta-commentary on authoritative institutional discourse itself. Here, students could claim to be codirecting task activities; however, such uses typically occurred when students did not want to perform the requested task and allowed participants to introduce (further) disruption into an already agonistically toned activity such as cleaning up at the end of the afternoon. Adults' directives thus provided occasion for the older students to improvise status claims among peers by reanimating a directive that had already been authored, but students' own directives did not always simply function to socialize peers into appropriate classroom behavior. At times, their directives were multivoiced in terms of how they used authoritative-institutional discourse among peers.

Citing Power: Animating Adults as Characters in Interaction

In this section, I explore how students linked their directives to adult figures to make sense of and apply different authoritative voices to their peer-based interactions. When students directed the activities and behaviors of peers on their own, they often used modal directives, which are syntactically modified commands, and animated adults as figures in interaction. A student would commonly use a directive as follows: "You gotta" or "You can + [command]." Adults were subsequently animated in different ways: students cited them using indirect or direct constructed dialogue, voiced them as characters, or used them in threats, such as when Janice told Ronald, "Don't let nobody talk to you or Imma call mommy." Especially when students disciplined each other, they animated the recipient's parents or caregivers. Many students were close kin if not siblings; caregiving responsibility was often shared among the families participating in after school and a student could easily claim one of the adults in their kin network as a disciplining authority as well as one to whom they could/should report back.

Animating an adult's voice to direct the actions of or discipline another peer positioned the student as an intermediary authority figure. Students sometimes used the authoritative voices of parents/caregivers to create their own moral situation in the interactional moment, which extract 11 illustrates. Here, J.J. had arrived to after school after his younger brother, Rashid did (seven years). Both boys had stopped by home first. Where line 1 begins, J.J. had just entered the room and immediately told Rashid that he was to report home in order to do the homework that he had left there, on instruction from their father. Rashid did not want to do his homework; he wanted to stay in after school (line 6). Rashid had told Ms. Betty (Deandre's mother) and I that he did not have any school assignments for the day, which Deandre had overheard (lines 9, 11, 12–13):

10.	"He said you gotta do your homework!"		
	1	J.J.	Rashid. You gotta go home.
	2	Rashid	((protests, inaudible))
	3	J.J.	((inaudible)) yuh huh, he trying to come and get
	4		you.
	5	Deandre	You gotta go ho[me]
	6	Rashid	[I'm staying.]
	7		=You lyin!
	8→	J.J.	He said you gotta do your homework!
	9	Deandre	He just said he ain't had none.
	10	J.J.	I don't want him- to get him in trouble.
	11	Deandre	Why he just lie then?
	12		((amplified volume)) He just lied to my mother
	13		a:nd Ms. Jennifer, talking bout some he ain't have
	14		no homework.
	15	Rashid	I d:o got homewo:rk.
	16	J.J.	But he gotta go home or you gonna get, in
	17		trouble.
	18	Deandre	Andre gonna get in trouble too then.
	19	Andre	No I'm not!
	20	Deandre	Yes you is! Little boy.

J.J. issues the first directive (line 1), and then explains that their father would come down to retrieve Rashid if he did not return home (lines 3–4). Given the information in line 1, where J.J. tells Rashid to go home, his next turn in which he tells Rashid that their father was "trying to come" and collect Rashid was not a propositional statement of fact, but rather a warning: Rashid had verbally protested (lines 2). If their father would have had to come get Rashid himself rather than Rashid returning home on their father's instruction, it meant that Rashid had disobeyed and would be in trouble. At this point, Deandre also intervenes to tell Rashid he has to go home (line 5). Rashid continues to protest, accusing J.J. of lying about what their father said (lines 5–7). J.J. then counters the epistemic accusation using indirect reported speech: their father said Rashid had to do his homework (line 8). Deandre "snitches" on Rashid, addressing J.J. but amplifying his volume to announce, within hearing range of Ms. Betty and myself, that Rashid had lied about not having any homework (lines 9, 11, 12–13).

It is at this point that the boys who had told Rashid to go home, J.J. and Deandre, take up different stances in terms of what they are doing with their directive utterances and which adults they invoke in the interaction. J.J. claims that he does not want Rashid to get in trouble with their father (lines 10, 16–17). Deandre, for his part, is primarily concerned with reporting for all to hear Rashid's misbehavior, announcing to J.J. but in a loud volume the transgression for which Ms. Betty or I could discipline him: having lied to both of us. In short, J.J. wants to comply with the directive originally authored by his father. By contrast, Deandre concerns himself with detailing the moral parameters of another act of misbehavior that Rashid has committed: lying. Deandre, then, is attempting to recruit one of the adults who are present in the room. Directive authorship comes from Rashid's father, who wants Rashid to complete his homework. Deandre at first participates in trying to get Rashid to go home, in alignment with J.J. and the boys' father. But then Deandre diverts the directive aim, depicting Rashid in moral terms: Rashid has lied and needs to be disciplined by one of the adults in the room. Rashid, for his part, is now stuck between a rock and a hard place as J.J. and Deandre animate the issue using moral voices that address different aspects of misbehavior: Rashid not only needs to go home and answer to his father, but he also needs to answer to Ms. Betty and me for lying about not having any homework.

In extract 10, J.J. and Deandre are bringing different authoritative voices to bear on a moral issue that acquires divergent meanings in the middle of the interaction: it is not just about what Rashid needs to do, but about to whom he needs to answer. From an adult's perspective, the solution here is delayed: all that needs to happen is for Rashid to go home and either get or do his homework. The boys, on the other hand, are preoccupied not with the solution, but instead debate the nature of Rashid's disobedience. Invoking adults through their reported directives and actions was key to how they were not only making sense of authoritative discourse, but animating versus appropriating it to claim disciplinary authority with their younger peer.

As I mean to show by analyzing this set of examples, students sometimes served as intermediaries to adults' directives, but also insourced them as character figures. Adults' voices were not merely instrumental in attempting to get peers to do something, but instead allowed the students to independently make sense of and test how to use authoritative discourse on their own. When adults were not present in the interaction, directives were more commonly formulated indirectly. This does not mean that students necessarily attempted to mitigate face threat or minimize conflict: it simply suggests, perhaps, that they sought to modify their strategies for claiming status and moral authority on their own, without having to involve an adult as a participant to their interactions.

MARKING AND THE RESEMIOTIZATION OF ARTICULATE LANGUAGE

At times, the students (re)voiced adults' directives in a parodying or mocking manner, using an African American discourse practice called *marking* to perform and reconfigure raciolinguistic ideologies of "appropriate" and "articulate" language in the after school space. According to scholars of AAL, *marking* involves quoting a speaker while styling their individual mannerism and comportment in a pejorative and ridiculing manner (Rickford & Rickford 2000; Green 2002; Morgan 2002). No adult, whether white or African American, was exempt from this practice, though the focus in this presentation is how students indexed these ethnoracial identity categories in their marking performances of adults "doing discipline."

Marking is commonly discussed in the literature on AAL as a form of verbal art that functions simultaneously as humor and critique. Specifically, it socially characterizes individuals as members of particular groups by drawing out and exaggerating specific linguistic forms and general mannerisms indexically associated with those groups—for example, whites as high-pitched, nasal, and overly proper or stilted (Mitchell-Kernan 1972; Rickford & Rickford 2001; Green 2002). But marking performances in the after school program were not simply evaluative statements about the individual adults who were academically supervising and directing or disciplining students. Here, I want to shift the focus away from the interactional work marking can do as verbal performance, including but not limited to humor, teasing, and critique of particular individuals, to explore the process by which students' marking inverted a dominant language ideology in the after school program that assigns positive value to white linguistic practices and negative value to African American linguistic practices. This language ideology was transmitted via a general discourse of what was considered to be linguistically "appropriate" for academic learning and general comportment in the after school space, and it sponsored the belief that students needed to shift away from AAL and acquire what many call "Standard" or "academic" English. Drawing from Silverstein's discussion of monoglot Standard, Flores and Rosa (2015) note that in current language education efforts, a raciolinguistic ideology of "appropriateness" represents Standard English as a unified set of linguistic practices that are orderly, proper, and needed for academic success, compared to racially minoritized languages such as AAL. AAL, on the other hand, is characterized as disorderly, deficient, and inappropriate language, especially for academic learning and school-based norms for appropriate behavior. When using AAL discourse practices, for example, ritual insults, the students in the after school program were deemed to be aggressive and as having bad attitudes, and therefore unprepared for and resistant to learning (Delfino 2016). The school-based discourse of appropriateness, then, projects onto racially minoritized students qualities of lack or deficiency, by claiming that they need to acquire and use so-called Standard English for school and future socioeconomic advancement. Students' marking performances not only inverted this discourse of appropriateness; they also challenged the idea that whites speak a unitary kind of English by employing a range of various race and gender stereotypes in their voicing of white adults.

Feminizing Talking "White"

As discussed earlier, several students generally depicted white instructors as ineffective in trying to recruit students into tasks while representing African American instructors and parents as comparatively more adept at doing discipline. On top of changing directive formulation (e.g., commands vs. requests), students deployed prosodic, phonological, and lexical features to create contrasts between gendered Black and white voices. As Reyes (2016) notes, voicing is the process by which identifiable features of language become linked to socially recognizable figure-types. In marking instructors, students drew on contrastive schemas depicting linguistic and social differences between whites and Blacks that are well established in African American popular culture and everyday life (Rickford & Rickford 2000; Fought 2006; Delfino 2020). In the stand-up routines of African American comedians, for example, talking white is feminized as "proper" and formal speech, while talking Black is masculinized as informal, cool, and tough urban street talk. As the extracts to follow show, this binary race/gender/class schema formed the basis for students marking adults performing acts of verbal discipline, and it symbolically inverted school-based language ideologies of appropriateness and articulateness.

In addition to performing hyper-standard pronunciation with consonants such as postvocalic /r/, white instructors were commonly depicted as having nasal, high-pitched, and shrill voices. Deandre often liked to mock me when I was trying to gain the attention of the preadolescent students, represented in extract 12.

Extract 12: "Can you please be on your best behavior?"

1	Multiple	((talking))
2	Jen	I have something to say,
3		Can you-
4		Guys,
5	Deandre	((nasal)) Can you please be on your best
6		beha:vior,
7	Jen	No, that's not what I have to say,

To explain, in lines 4 and 5, Deandre follows up on my unsuccessful attempt to get students' attention by marking me: he makes an imaginary request for "best behavior." He frames it as an overly polite or formal request, riffing on my apparent hesitancy to impose on the students as indicated in my turns at talk, by repeating and intensifying the modal construction I attempted in line 3: "Can you please be on your best behavior?" My overly polite and proper manner is also indexed in the way Deandre produces an exaggerated "standard" final /r/ in the word "behavior": it is elongated and firmly rhotic, which for AAL speakers is generally a well established variant of "standard" or "proper" speech (citations). These grammatical and phonological features, coupled with the high pitch and nasal voice quality, indicate that Deandre is marking me not just as hesitant, but perhaps also as pleading and shrill, and therefore taking a negative stance toward how I make a bid for attention.

In extract 13, Deandre again uses raised pitch and an aggressively nasal voice quality to mimic the way I pronounce a student's name, intervening in my attempt to assist another student with a task to draw attention to his marking speech act. He keys this performance by loudly asserting, "Ms. Jennifer, everybody know how YOU speak." What you hear in lines 3 and again in 8 is the end of that name, which I have edited to protect that student's confidentiality:

13. "Ms. Jennifer, everybody know how you speak"

1	Jen	Wait it's-
2	Deandre	[Ms. Researcher] everybody know how YOU speak,
3		((nazalized)) [i:]
4	Jen	Is that how I talk?
5	Deandre	((volume reduction)) Yah.
6	Jen	((laughter)) tssss h
		((>.5 pause))
7	Deandre	((soft)) That's how I talk?
8		((loud)) [i:]

In addition to parodying how I say that particular student's name, Deandre also revoices my question, "Is that how I talk?", in an extremely soft voice and high pitch. This voice registers as childlike, indexing my helplessness and inarticulateness when confronted by a face-threatening impersonation. Among the children and adults in the local neighborhood, a more common and appropriate verbal tactic for handling face threat was to respond with a counter-impression or insult, both strong markers of an "articulate" speaker (Rickford & Rickford 2000; Alim & Smitherman 2012). Assuming that this exchange functioned at least in part as a verbal duel, I failed to produce a matching response: in this situation, Deandre was the articulate speaker, and I was not.

I want to extend my interpretation of these examples further: they illustrate how Deandre's marking often depicted me as taking a hesitant, overly polite, or pleading stance toward the students, perhaps often to the point of being shrill. These stances indexed negative qualities stereotypically associated with white women: namely, being weak, childlike, and powerless or helpless in defending themselves. My verbal inarticulateness, then, functioned as linguistic icons of these wider racial and gender stereotypes, and contrasted dramatically with the articulate power of African American verbal styles of discipline.

Students feminized white speech whether the individual being marked was female-identifying. Three of the girls, Janice, Alisha, and Keri, often impersonated Matt, the twenty-five-year-old Jewish American instructor from Los Angeles, by indexically associating him with the "surfer dude" stereotype. Note that in performing a collaborative series of impersonations, there is an overly gratuitous use of lexical markers stereotypically associated with California speech: "dude" and "totally," both pronounced with hyper-fronted vowels:

14. "DUDE!"

1	Alisha	"DU:DE!"
2	Anon.	"Totally, totally, totally!"
3		["Du:de"]

4	Alisha	["Why would] you do that, du:de?"
		((1.5s))
5	Janice	"Du:de, du:de, to you,"
6	Alisha	"Du:de."
7	Anon.	"Dude."
8		((<.5s)) That's – he be like, "DU:DE! What are you
9		doing?"=
10		="Du:de,"
11	Janice	h h h
12		"Stop playing, dude."
		((<.5 s))
13	Resear.	h h h
14	Alisha	"You just dont-
15		not to hurt the- guy,"
16		"Stop hit- h h
17	Janice	"Hey dude! Why you don't listen to me, dude?"
18		"You don't get it."

While the lexical marker "dude" indicates the kind of casual stance-taking habitu-ally taken up by young white men to display "cool" masculinity (Kiesling 2004), there is an implicit emasculation of Matt's disciplinary style in lines 12–16. Note that in these lines, Matt is represented as unsuccessfully attempting to break up a play fight between boys, using only his words to try and intervene. Additionally, Alisha is attempting to suppress her giggling, raising the quoted language to a higher pitch and softer volume compared with Janice's deeper voicing of Matt, which to my ears was pretty representative of his actual speaking voice. Alisha's impression, in other words, depicts Matt as uselessly standing by while the boys are engaged in the pretty normal peer business of fighting. Play fighting and real fighting were not uncommon among either boys or girls, and African American instructors and staff would not hesitate to physically intervene in such instances when a fight was determined to get too serious, pulling students apart. Thus, Alisha's voicing of Matt is quite possibly a double-voiced evaluation of his lack of masculine toughness in hanging back and only verbally trying to break up the fight that was underway; she is effectively emasculating him.

In all three extracts, Matt and myself were racialized as white via the voicing of corny or stereotypical figure-types who, according to African American cultural per-spectives, lack toughness or authority. In all three examples, talking white is depicted as lacking in disciplinary power. Among African Americans and other minoritized groups, whiteness is indexed through linguistic forms signaling hesitancy, formal-ity, and "empty" politeness expressions, and thereby stereotypically associated with "unmasculinity," if not femininity (Fought 2006). Analysis of these extracts confirm that students hear and voice whiteness in alignment with patriarchal or sexist ideolo-gies of language and power—that is to say, feminized language lacks public author-ity. Such language ideologies privilege direct and forceful language as authoritative or as appropriately and only belonging to men (Eckert & McConnell-Ginnett 2013). Thus, by linguistically emasculating whiteness and the persons construed as embodying those qualities, students were subverting a raciolinguistic ideology of appropriateness by depicting white instructors as weak classroom authorities.

Resemiotizing AAL as Articulate Language

As the next two examples show, students positively aligned with Black styles of discipline in styling African American adults' voices as appropriately tough and serious. In such marking performances, students tended to use forceful and direct language, phonological and grammatical features of AAL, and deployed a relatively lower pitch range compared with how they voiced white instructors. Interactionally, African American adults' voices were used to support or facilitate disciplinary actions, rather than to critique or undermine them. Thus, while students aligned negatively with white instructors' disciplinary efforts, they aligned positively with African American instructors, staff, and parents.

Consider extract 15, where Joseph is using an AAL discourse style called "loud talk" (Paris 2011) to let everyone know during homework hour that twelve-year-old Malcolm got a "talking to" the other day for not doing his homework. He caps off his story by impersonating Malcolm's father, who evidently threatened to whip Malcolm's butt:

> 15. Mock threat (Joseph)
> 1   So that's why he got a talking ((to)) yesterday.
> 2   "I'm supposed to whip your butt for not doin
> 3   your homework!"

Linguistically, the story abstract in line 1 and the marking speech act that follows are delivered in AAL, most characteristically in the use of vocalized r's and the syllable stress pattern in the marking performance. In the marking performance, the father's voice is performed in a dramatically lowered pitch, helping to style the utterance as a forcefully delivered mock threat. In his story abstract in the first line, Joseph summarizes closes the story by stating, "So that's why." Rather than being just a summary of the story, this tag functions as an evaluative statement that justifies the talking-to as much as it explains what happened. Joseph thus appears to be displaying positive alignment with Malcolm's father: the point of the story, which took place during homework hour, was to announce loudly enough for all to hear that Malcolm had already been "talked to" about not doing his homework.

Lastly, extract 16 is taken from an interaction where CeCe, a charismatic thirteen-year-old who often exchanged mock insults and threats with African American instructors and staff, asks her peers to "get back to work" under threat of Raymond, the site director's, watchful eye. She marks him by quoting a line he used often with the students to indicate that they were not behaving according to expectations, "Cheese and crackers!":

Extract 16: "Cheese and crackers!"

1	Cece	I just wanna know, can we get back to work
2		now/
3	Multiple	Ohhhh!
4		h h h h
5	Cece	I'm just asking, I got work to do.
6		I'm not trying to be funny,
7		He lookin at me like,
8		"Cheese and crackers!" man!
9	Multiple	((laughter))

The quoted utterance itself is not overtly stylized because CeCe does not deviate from her normal speaking voice when she says it. In fact, the utterance alone is silly enough to the students that she may not have had to do anything else other than say it: as you can hear, her peers laugh quite animatedly, or as they would have characterized it "bust up," at the quoted line. The marking speech act appears to function not as critique, but as an interpersonal verbal duel that CeCe starts to manage competing demands in the interaction: socializing with her peers on the one hand, and recruiting everyone back to work. While "Cheese and crackers!" is a neutral, cutesy statement that disaligns with the stereotypical image of an adult male AAL speaker, the withering look CeCe is suggesting Raymond is delivering at that moment is not: it conveys that he is about to "get tough" on the students. The marking speech act, then, is produced in compliance with the threat of further discipline on Raymond's part. It also bears mentioning that this example indicates the co-naturalization of race, gender, and language: Raymond is an "iconic speaker" (Mendoza-Denton 2008) in the sense that he literally embodies street toughness simply by virtue of how is body and language is read as authentically Black. This example proves the durability of race and gender as a social fact: Raymond can say something like "Cheese and crackers!" and still command authority/be considered articulate while a white instructor who might try to "talk tough" would not necessarily be able to discipline the students.

In students' marking of Black authority figures, race, class, and gender were co-indexed with references to "street tough" masculinity, qualities which are negatively appraised from the perspective of hegemonic whiteness but valued as the prestige norm in hip-hop and in urban African American communities (Kelley 1994; Cutler 2003; Alim et al. 2010). The after school students routinely listened to popular and local styles of hip-hop and modeled much of their identity practices after teens and youth in the neighborhood, including the ways in which they positively appraised the ability to talk "slang," "ghetto," or "street" as part of their displays of street toughness (Delfino 2016). The resemiotization of street toughness as masculine prestige has its origins in a hip-hop style called *gangsta rap* (Kelley 1994) and has influenced following styles.

As Kelley argues, gangsta rap initially offered a way for young Black men to symbolically empower themselves through language and discourse. Stylistically, gangsta rap indexes tough or hyperviolent Black masculinity, but recontextualizes it as a form of social power rather than as social pathology. Notably, gangsta rap draws on Black linguistic ideologies of articulateness for its social-semiotic effect of empowerment: African American discourse practices such as boasting, roasting, word play, and other language games are indications of verbosity and a quick wit, and they furnish the ability for participants to assess and invert power relations between interlocutors (Labov 1972; Morgan 2002; Alim et al. 2010). Gangsta rap's style, which involve the performance of mock threats or boasts to symbolically dominate an opponent, imagined or real, continues to thematically structure much of hip-hop even as the participant pool grows ethnically (Alim et al. 2010) and with women emcees. Gangsta stancetaking is thus endemic to hip-hop and can hypothetically be taken up by anyone, but it is nevertheless still indexically associated with "street tough" Black masculinity.

DISCUSSION

In this chapter, I illustrate the different ways in which students used directives and tied them to the authority of adults in order to test their own capacity for wielding power in the after school program: (1) authoring a directive and recruiting an adult to support it; (2) reanimating a directive that an adult had already authored; (3) citing adults as character figures in interaction. The chapter shows that even though the students oriented each other to "appropriate" modes of behavior in ways that reaffirmed wider expectations for recognizing authority and showing deference in a classroom setting, they often repurposed the language of authority and responsibility. With respect to both form and use, the students were appropriating institutional-authoritative discourse, not resisting the system of classroom discipline itself. In other words, the students were not challenging a voice system that morally authorized adults to direct children's activities, behavior, and interactions and to characterize participants as acting appropriately (or not). Students did challenge, put off, or refuse to carry out the actual modes of action proscribed by adults; however, these constituted responses that reaffirmed the disciplinary structure that was always-already in place—in particular, the asymmetrical subject positions of adults relative to children. And when satirizing adults' disciplinary discourse, the students performed the kinds of disciplinary language they heard from adults, modeling it to agonistic extremes to see what would result in terms of influencing their peers.

That the nine- to thirteen-year-old students modeled adults to claim authority, status, and independence in their peer interactions brings into question minority preteen and youth peer groups as colluding in the construction of rebellious, anti-authoritarian "(linguistic) cultures of opposition" (Fordham 1996; Ogbu 2003) to schooling and the kinds of behaviors it sponsors as normative and necessary for being appropriately socialized. Instead, the data in this chapter show that the students often attempted to discipline each other according to models they learned from adults.

Thus, directives indicate that the students were following school-appropriateness but, at times, trying to gain control within school-sponsored types of authority, working within the system, so to speak, to channel authority away from adults and claim it for themselves. Marking, on the other hand, tells us in what ways the students were critical of authoritative-institutional discourse, aka the system itself: toward the racialization of white speech as "articulate" language and AAL as disorderly or inappropriate. In forming a double-voiced system of critique about race, language, and discipline, the students effectively resemiotized the symbolic value of racialized languages in the after school space. AAL-speaking adults were depicted as articulate, capable, and effective, and white instructors as the opposite: inarticulate, hesitant, and weak.

By way of marking white speakers as out of place, silly, and ineffective while normalizing African American linguistic practices as appropriate for asymmetrical interactions between children and adults, the students transformed the dominant raciolinguistic ideology of white speech as orderly, proper, and appropriate in the after school space. Recruiting race and gender stereotypes, the students created both broad and narrow categories of distinction between white and African American language: broadly, white language as weak and feminine, and African American language as tough and masculine. Gender stereotypes, then, were central to the broader resemiotization of AAL as articulate speech and white language as inarticulate. And on a narrower plane of stylistic distinction, students also quite perceptively deployed more specific speaker stereotypes to parse and differentiate between particular ways of talking white and talking Black: the Valley Girl, helpless female, and surfer dude as styles of talking white, and tough men as the iconic speaker associated with talking Black. Undoubtedly, the students enjoyed playing on popular stereotypes that they encountered in their consumption of popular media. However, analyzing students' marking speech acts points to one way in which they played on received models and meanings of "appropriate" and "articulate" speech in order to lend power and prestige to Black language in a school-based setting.

I hope that scholars and practitioners of education learn from this chapter that African American students are not challenging or mocking white teachers per se. I suggest instead that minoritized students often critique the ways in which white teachers hear and characterize their language and that this process is misheard or misread as "resistance" to behaving or speaking respectfully. Voicing whiteness as Other helps racialized groups establish identity against the cultural and linguistic normativity of whiteness (Basso 1979; Fought 2006); thus, examining how minoritized groups voice white people points to an important process of linguistic *resemiotization*: how racialized minorities reposition themselves within a raciolinguistic field in which their linguistic practices are understood to index or symbolize their threatening or disorderly subjectivity. Perhaps the raciolinguistic perspective I offer in this chapter will afford a new opportunity for educators and schools oriented to hegemonic whiteness to question whether the teaching of "appropriate" and "articulate" language really serves racially minoritized students, and perhaps this chapter offers new possibilities for truly valuing the linguistic and cultural practices students bring with them to navigate schooling.

NOTE

1. These studies deal with children and youth in the United States and Europe. Thus, rather than presupposing a universal model of (pre)adolescence as a psychological or biological life stage in which conflict is "natural" to the preadolescent/youth condition, my argument is built on a cross-cultural comparison of young people who broadly experience race, gender, and class culture in complex industrial societies, and who would therefore share similar youth cultural practices of relating to one another thus (cf. Bucholtz 2002).

4

"You about to Get Cooked!"

Joning and Raciolinguistic Chronotopes of Policing and Survival

On the occasional Saturday, Urban Pathways' staff would take some of the family literacy students on a field trip. In November 2010, Raymond, Matt, and I took a group of eight children to the zoo—Ms. Betty's four children plus J.J., Janice, Lenny, and another boy. We met them at the Garden Park recreation room and hustled them into "Big Blue," our nickname for the blue passenger van that we used for such trips. Raymond drove off, taking an off-the-beaten-path route up from Southeast to Northwest. Matt, who sat in the back on one of the bench seats with the students, chatted with them. Raymond and I, up front, talked to each other, glad for the respite of some adult conversation after the morning hustle getting the excited children ready to go. We soon approached the northwest quadrant. As we did so, the change in the urban landscape was dramatically visible as soon as we hit the quadrant boundary. The streets suddenly boasted well-maintained row houses, and pedestrians, who were predominantly white, were going about their morning business.

At almost precisely the moment we turned onto the street that officially defined our crossover into northwest, I noticed some of the students' chatter grow unusually animated, so much so that Raymond and I could no longer hear or talk each other. The collective air of excitement seemed to be newly layered with anxiety or nerves. The children's talk and behavior was vibrant but unfocused and rambling, as if they had suddenly ingested a large dose of caffeine. I peeked behind me to see what was going on: the students seemed not to know what to do with themselves. Alisha and Keri giggled and wrung their hands, bouncing up and down in the bench seat directly behind me; the boys grew especially loud and animated in their chatter as they peered out of the van's back windows, the boys in the middle seats leaning across Joseph and Lenny, who were sitting nearest the windows. Joseph started a game of ritual insults, locally referred to as joning. He pointed to an elderly man on the street, walking with a limp and a cane, and loudly called out, "There go Mr. Matt." The other students screamed with delight. Lenny went next, picking out a woman with messy hair: "There go Alisha." Each child took his or her turn, picking out someone on the street, calling out a funny or strange characteristic or manner-ism, and implying that someone in the van, or someone we all knew from the after school program had a similar, freakish way about them. Because the game played on sociocultural understandings of particular types of bodies, mannerisms, or abilities as culturally non-normative (e.g., elderly age, obesity, limping), and also because all of us in the van were well aware that joning involves exaggerating physical character-istics of the person being insulted, everyone got the joke as we drove along and the students picked out features of persons we could presume the target also shared: the implicit messages from the examples above were thus, "Matt has a limp," "Alisha has messy hair." Raymond, Matt, and I tolerated the students' joning session while roll-ing our eyes at each other or giving each other side glances ("Here they go again").

Joseph, who had started the game, ended it by making the other students abso-lutely lose it and the three of us adults sharply suck in our breath in the attempt to hide our laughter: he picked out a woman in sweatpants who actually closely resembled an Urban Pathways' staff member, and stated, "There go Ms. Tina." The resemblance was uncanny, but this woman on the street was extremely overweight, wearing sweats, no makeup, and tottered from side to side as she walked. According to the insult frame, she was essentially a beta copy of Ms. Tina. Joseph's comparison showed the mastery involved joning: an insult is funny when its outrageous exag-gerations highlight or play on something conceivable or real. But, as this chapter dis-cusses, mastery of ritual insults, like most forms of teasing or humor in general, also involves successfully negotiating shared metacommunicative frames—for example, participants' understanding of what makes a joke a joke and an insult an insult.

Though the earlier-given story indicates that everyone in the van understood the joning session to be a language game, joning was usually a much more socially risky linguistic practice, both interpersonally and cross-culturally, in the after school pro-gram. Among students, as much as it led to laughter and clever returns, joning also created hurt feelings and provoked the need to save one's face by "fighting back," as students had explained to me, with words. Among staff members and teachers, jon-ing was generally policed as inappropriate, threatening, or aggressive language, even among the individuals who understood its importance for maintaining social face on the neighborhood blocks. Recalling that most students had described joning to me earlier that year as a defensive move ("I only do it back to people"), I could not help but note that the joning session in the van began shortly following the students' displays of jittery nerves, right when the van traversed the urban borderland that separated impoverished Southeast from the gentrified portion of the city.

Across the Anacostia River, into the central parts of the city with predominantly white and middle or upper-class neighborhoods, is where the after school students were especially likely to experience cultural, racial, and linguistic marginalization and erasure. I also could not help but note that students aimed their voices out the window, loud enough for passersby to hear them out of the van's open windows as they mocked pedestrians. They used clear markers of AAL, such as third-person singular -s absence: "There go" versus "There goes." For these reasons, the joning session struck me as a particularly assertive display of communicative agency: students were using precisely the kind of talk and behavior that provoked negative stereotypes of African American children as loud, aggressive, and threatening in order to claim their presence on the scene. Perhaps joning in this scenario was simply what the students were used to doing, either for peer solidarity and pleasure or to manage face-threatening situations. But I argue that joning also served to transform the students' anxieties about how they would be perceived: it allowed them to gain a form of symbolic and linguistic agency in mocking passersby by claiming a "Black linguistic space" (Alim 2004; Blackburn 2005) for themselves against the kinds of disapproval and erasure they were likely to encounter in settings such as northwest Washington, D.C.

I provide this ethnographic sketch to introduce the focus of this chapter, which explores how the preadolescent students used joning to manage their identities in relation to the goal of preparing them for success in school and beyond. Here, I elaborate on the concept of *raciolinguistic chronotopes* (Flores et al. 2018; Rosa 2019). I examine how chronotopes of policing and survival shaped to explore how students used joning to negotiate academic learning and resist institutionalized anxieties about their possible futures as street youth. Thus, while adults were concerned that joning would render the students vulnerable to raciolinguistic policing beyond the local neighborhood where joning was widely practiced, it allowed the students to simultaneously display positive, or even competitive, orientations toward academic learning and street toughness simultaneously.

WHAT IS JONING?

The linguistic practice African American Washingtonians call *joning* is a language game that can take the form of either obvious or indirect insults. Joning can be formulated as a ritual exchange in which participants compete in front of an audience using "yo mamma" and other explicit markers of language gaming (Labov 1972), or it can be styled more subtly, such as in the opening vignette. To explain, in this chapter's introductory example, the person-to-person comparison, "There go (name)" does not directly or overtly state anything derogatory, but rather needs to be inferred by context. This indirect style of insult is typically referred to as *signifying* (Roberts 1982; Mitchell-Kernan 2001). The linguistic practice linguists call *ritual insults*, in which participants challenge each other to a game of verbal dueling, is much more frequently documented in the existing literature on AAL. The reason joning was so interesting to me is because it took on multiple forms and functions beyond what scholars of AAL have typically documented, especially among children.

In sociolinguistics, ritual insults have garnered much attention due to their provocative nature, as they are formulated as mock threats and boasts. But ritual insults are even more noteworthy because of the elaborate verbal and analogical skills displayed by competent practitioners, especially teens and youth (Labov 1972; Heath 1983; Blackburn 2005; Mendoza-Denton 2008; Tetreault 2016). Moreover, ritual insults and other language games provide an important socializing function: as is the case for many racialized minorities living in impoverished urban neighborhoods, these kinds of linguistic skills helped the after school students to be tough and resilient in situations where language is considered essential for self-defense. For them, much of this included learning to appear tough in the local neighborhood so that no one, such as a bully or gang member, would "mess with them," as they explained to me.

A common type of joning took the form of ritual insults, which have a recognizable linguistic structure. As Labov (1972) explains, this structure can be expressed by the following rule: "*T (target) is so X (pejorative attribute) that P (exaggerated proposition).*" The speaker selects a target (T), assigns him/her a pejorative attribute (X), and modifies that attribute using hyperbole or exaggeration (P). The following two examples of joning illustrate such a formula:

1.   Linguistic structure of joning
    1a.   Joseph   Boy, you ugly boy, you look like a rabbit!
    1b.   Tai   Hey look y'all, his head look like burnt broccoli!

Labov argues that such a structure typically creates a protective bubble around the speech event: insults are not taken as insults, but rather indicate that a language game is occurring. In terms of the verbal artistic component, the point is not just to mirror the formula, but to create a better analogy by building on prior turns and themes. Hence, the structure invites repeated turns and responses between duelers.

Yet even when doing "joning contests," as thirteen-year-old Terrance called it, the students did not necessarily always engage in extended competitive sequences. I wondered why, having studied literature that documents these elaborate speech events. More commonly, the students sparred for one or two turns, at which point, someone got upset due to feeling personally insulted. I recognized that age might be a factor, since it takes time and experience to move from the rote formulas young children tend to practice (i.e., "yo mamma" sequences) to the improvised and more grammatically complex sequences displayed by teenagers and young men in particular (Abrahams 1968; Kochman 1972; Labov 1972). I also knew from reflecting on my own childhood experiences and from having taught children for several years that it also takes time and experience for many to recognize and to be able to emotionally weather teasing's function as humor beyond the immediate social embarrassment it causes when one is the target.

As a matter of fact, the students often engaged in joning to deliberately provoke social embarrassment: the point was to upset somebody in front of everyone else. For them, provoking anger and other emotional outbursts appeared to be an equal if not greater interactional priority than being creative with words. For example, one evening, about ten students were waiting around the front desk of the community center to be picked up by a parent or sibling. I was sitting at the desk while students flanked the sides and front and milled about chatting. Deandre, Joseph, and Alisha, Ms. Betty's children, and twins Makila and Makaila, were included in the group and were known to not get along. Appearing to pick a fight, Deandre called Makaila "bald-headed." Makaila's reaction was clearly angry. She fired back in her especially strident voice: "Your mother cook cold hot dogs, boy!" To explain, Makaila was implying that Deandre's mother, Ms. Betty, was too stupid to cook hot dogs properly. The insult also had a possible second meaning: the family was too poor to afford the gas needed for cooking. Perhaps it implied both. Either way, the insult enraged Deandre and his two younger siblings, who stood on one side of the community center welcome desk. Makaila and her twin sister Makila stood on the other. The rest of the students began to position themselves for a fight: they gathered around the two sets of dueling siblings and began to participate in insulting individuals on the opposing side. Instead of intervening, I had decided to watch and keep my audio recorder going in order to see what would happen. But Mr. Morris came running over to break up the now near fight: students were shouting back and forth and the two groups were leaning in toward each other. He shot me a bewildered look as if to say, "Jen, are you nuts letting this go on?"

I immediately felt terrible and incompetent: I was clearly unable to distinguish between children's verbal play and an actual fight, perhaps almost risking the students' physical safety in the process. But that is the hazard of teasing and other socially risky linguistic practices such as joning: the whole point is for children to eventually learn the social functions of humor. In the process, they have fun and get upset trying to breach the limits of socially acceptable language (Tetreault 2010; Delfino 2016). Thus, joning helped the after school students learn what the socially acceptable limits were on teasing, insults, and ribald language as well as the limits on displaying street tough stances. Any misfire in talking tough could put the students in harm's way, whether they decided to do it with a teen gang member from the neighborhood or with a teacher at school. This is the reason teachers and parents policed joning even if some recognized its importance for language learning and socialization.

JONING AND RACIOLINGUISTIC CHRONOTOPES

Because joning indexed a street tough identity and, by extension, the social figures likely to engage in street tough behaviors and activities, it was actively discouraged by some after school staff, such as the site director who took over Raymond's role in the spring. A former church minister, the new site director felt that the purpose of after-schooling was to socialize the students out of "negative behaviors" they learned at home and on the streets. She once glossed joning as "bullying" in a staff meeting. Shortly after this meeting, the new site director drew up a community pledges poster that listed the kinds of talk and behavior considered unacceptable in the after school program, including fighting and bullying. As indicated in figure 4.1, "Absolutely NO JONING!" was listed as the sixth item students needed to pledge not to engage

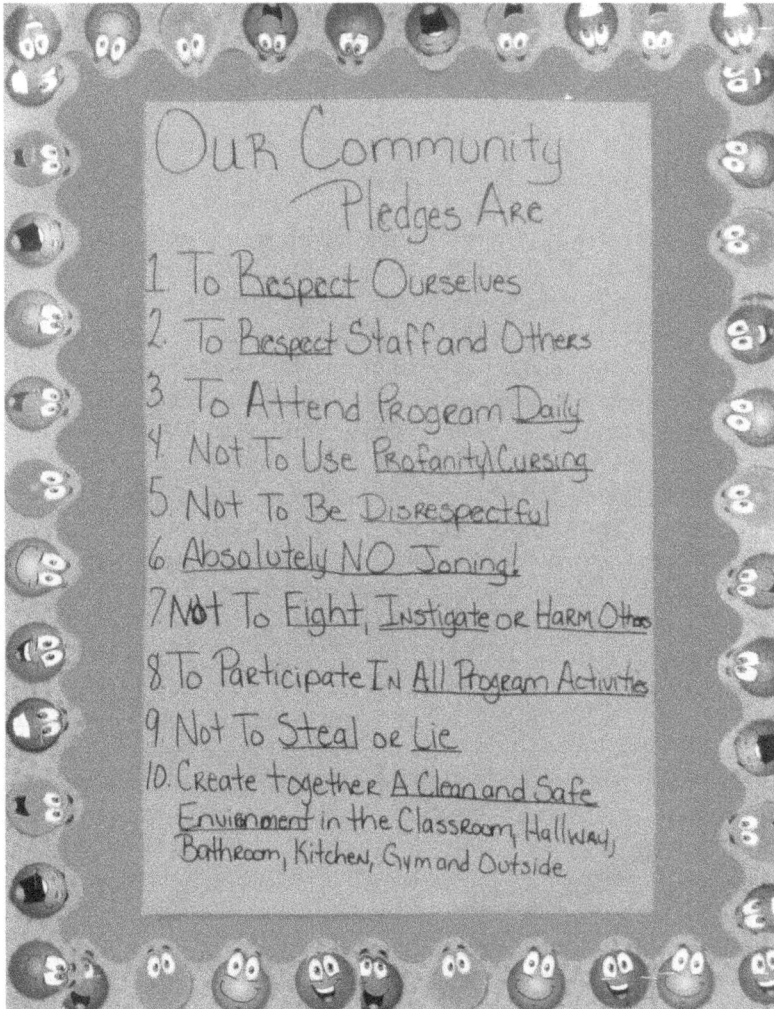

Figure 4.1 "Absolutely NO JONING!"

in: in contrast to all of the other items, "NO JONING!" was written in bold capital letters and finished with an exclamation mark.

Unlike the site director, most staff and teachers recognized that students would jone anyway and that they derived humor and pleasure from it. Individually, they used their judgment to determine whether joning crossed any lines into verbal bullying or fighting. A few adults, such as Raymond and Morris, both African American men in their thirties, used their own experience to spar with the students. As I frequently observed in the academic enrichment program, Raymond not only playfully encouraged the preadolescents and early teens to try and meet his skill level (something he regularly boasted they could never do), he also used joning sessions to model appropriate exchanges and discourage ones that would possibly provoke fights.

According to the adults who viewed it as a positive cultural activity, being able to handle longer exchanges indicated the emotional maturity characteristic of adults. For Raymond, joning involved, first and foremost, being able to read the room appropriately and produce clever insults. Bragging about his own skills, Raymond asserted, "You could have a million-dollar outfit on and by the time I'm done with you, make you feel like you just bought something at Marshall's."[1] Thus, in contrast to the after school students, who often joned to "start stuff" or "joned back" defend themselves against personal insult, Raymond and his buddies considered it first and foremost to be a game of verbal art. That is to say, while the primary function for students was to threaten social face (no one who has read the preceding chapters should be surprised in this regard), the primary function of joning for Raymond and his friends, at least, was the performance of verbal art—again, in the same way a rap battle is.

Despite the fact that most adults in the after school program understood that joning was integral to how students communicated with one another and a Black linguistic practice, they worried about how it would be perceived outside of the space of the neighborhood and the after school program. As a matter of fact, Terrance and I occasionally sparred, until his mother, who came by to participate in family literacy one afternoon, overheard Terrance taking a turn with me. Pointing her finger sternly at his face, she took him to task: "You playin with the wrong people." I learned later in an informal interview I conducted with Terrance that a schoolteacher in Virginia, where he had been living for several months prior to joining the after school program, had overheard him saying he was going to cut another student. Not understanding that "cutting someone up" referred to the verbal activity of ritual insult, the teacher inferred that thirteen-year-old Terrance had a knife and was going to physically harm the student. She reported him to the school administration.

Since Terrance's mother had grown up in the local neighborhood (along with Ms. Betty, who was her best friend), she certainly understood what joning meant to the children herself. Historically, joning is an AAL discourse practice, which speakers ground in the need to learn to survive and appear resilient: for this reason, joning and related styles are referred to as "verbal strategies" aimed at manipulating or transforming interactional outcomes (Green 2002; see also Rose 1994; Rickford & Rickford 2000; Mitchell-Kernan 2001; Morgan 2002). But Terrance's mother, like other parents and teachers, was forced to confront the reality that this kind of language would be criminalized as threatening or aggressive activity outside of the particular boundaries of the after school program and Southeast. In these spaces, joning was widely practiced as a language game that helped young people grow tough and to learn to laugh about lived experiences of poverty and stereotypes of Blackness. It is no accident that major themes include calling someone dumb, lazy, poor, "Black" (dark), bald-headed, being on welfare, and the like, as well as introduced by metaphors of fighting with weapons.

Raciolinguistic chronotopes of policing, policing and survival help explicate teachers' and students' ambivalence about joning's meaning and uses and why students continued to do it despite adults' policing of it. As conceptualized by Rosa (2016) and Flores et al. (2018), *raciolinguistic chronotopes* are cultural narratives that connect racialized bodies and voices to imagined pasts, presents, and futures. For Flores et al. (2018), anxiety and resistance are the raciolinguistic chronotopes that bracket the wider society's ambivalent stance toward Latinxs. On the one hand, a chronotope of anxiety positions Spanish as the past and English as the future of the Latinx community. On the other, bilingual education is part of a chronotope of resistance that affirms Spanish as part of the continued heritage of Latinxs. Raciolinguistic chronotopes of anxiety and resistance certainly shape narratives about who African American students are and who they should be, but they must be rendered specific to longer histories of the criminalization of Black bodies and voices. To acknowledge the historical specificity of anti-Blackness and its effects on language and other embodied practices, I will describe the raciolinguistic chronotopes of anxiety and resistance as *policing* and *survival*, respectively. As will become clear through my description and analysis of joning in the after school program, policing and survival anchored how joning was viewed simultaneously as detrimental to the students' present and future success yet also necessary for them to culturally and linguistically survive and thrive as members of an "imagined" Black community (Anderson 1990; Fordham 1996).

Joning as Conflict Talk and Verbal Art

As discussed in chapter 3, preadolescent children have their own interactional priorities, and conflict talk is integral to peer socializing. For the after school students, joning was part of a broader range of conflict talk styles that students used to maintain and threaten social face. In describing joning to me, several students felt that its primary purpose was to "start stuff" (start a fight), and some associated it with bullies. For example, Bianca glossed joning as "teasing" for me. To clarify what she meant by teasing, I asked, "Is it about being funny? Like, with the words you use?" In response, she shook her head, said that it was mean, and that people who joned intended to start fights.

Extract 2 illustrates how joning was linked to a type of person who intended to "start stuff." During this exchange, several of the preadolescent girls are playing games in the computer lab with no adults present. Tanika calls Janelle "ugly" (line 3) when Rachelle asks the group what level Janelle is on. In a responding insult, Janelle tells Tanika to be quiet with her "big self," and characterizes Tanika's joning as follows: "[You] always starting stuff" (lines 5–6):

2. Joning as "starting stuff" (initiating face threat)
    1   Rachelle   ((talking about Janelle)) What level she at?
    2   Makila   On th[ree].
    3   Tanika   [She ugly].
    4   Multiple   ((laughter))

5	Janelle	You need to be quiet with your big self.
6		Always starting stuff.

Though some students individually characterized others as ones who were "always starting stuff," every single student in the after school program initiated joning at some point or another. Peers often found such insults to be funny, as indicated by the laughter in the example above (line 4). However, as exemplified by Janelle's response to Tanika's joning (lines 5–6), the majority of students felt that initiating, viewed as a form of picking on someone, was inappropriate.

By contrast, joning back on somebody, or producing an insult to respond to face threat, was unanimously considered appropriate by all of the students. Extract 3 illustrates this logic of self-defense:

3. Joning as "fighting back" (defending against face threat)

1	Makaila	Rachelle got a grandma neck.
2		((laughter))
3		((small child requests help from older
4		student with opening juice box))
5	Makaila	Girl, your e:ars are old.
6	Bianca	Makaila, why you say that?
7	Makaila	'Cos she keep over here,
8		joning on, somebody too!
		((<.5s pause))
9	Bianca	O:h,
10	Makaila	((robot voicing)) I forgot how
		you jone.
11	Rachelle	What?
12	Makaila	I CA:N fight you back.

According to the turns at talk, Makaila appears to initiate joning; the first line, in which Makaila asserts, "Rachelle got a grandma neck," is a spontaneous utterance that followed several seconds of silence. A few students laugh, but Bianca negatively evaluates her linguistic performance: "Makaila, why you say that?" (line 6). Makaila responds that she is actually joning because Rachelle is doing it to "somebody too" (lines 7–8). Then, Bianca changes her evaluative stance to a neutral one after Makaila explains that she was not the one to start joning. She accepts Makaila's reasoning by simply stating, "Oh" (line 9) rather than furnishing additional commentary.

Before the exchange in extract 3 gave way to another topical focus, Makaila stated that she could fight Rachelle back (line 12). Her commentary about her intention, to fight back, is key for understanding how the students viewed appropriate versus inappropriate uses of joning: to defend against, not to provoke, face threat and social embarrassment. For the students, then, the point of joning, then, was to appear tough, not to start fights. Thus, on top of the sheer pleasure, students got out of embarrassing each other in front of an audience of peers, joning also helped them defend themselves against bullying or getting picked on for being soft. Appearing tough so that one would not be "messed with" was a key skill the students needed to learn in order to ward off threats to their physical safety, as physical fights and brawls were common at school and among children, teens, and youth the neighborhood. But joning, like most forms of teasing (cf. Lytra 2007), is inherently a socially risky practice in that intentions are never clear; there is always the possibility of offense. Thus, even though the students had their own definition of appropriate joning, in practice, there were inevitably competing interpretations and feelings, and language games or light teasing could always give way to more serious verbal or physical conflicts.

In addition to provoking and managing face threat, some students practiced joning as a verbal contest akin to Labov's (1972) description of ritual insults. Terrance and Alisha, for example, described joning as a language game and practiced it as such. In terms of speech event structure, two opponents verbally compete in front of an audience, whose laughter and commentary indicate a winner. Extract 4, which documents my meeting Terrance for the first time, illustrates. (Recall from an earlier example that Terrance and I joned on each other until his mother deemed it inappropriate.) After learning that I wanted to study the students' language, Terrance asked if I was going to study "25th Street language" and specifically named joning as an example of 25th Street language. He then proposed to have a joning contest, an attempt that fails because his interlocutors, Malcolm and J.J., did not want to participate:

4.   Terrance proposes a joning contest
   1   Terrance   All right, let's jone on each other.
   2   Malcolm   O:h! (inaudible) me, son.
   3   Jen   ((laughs)) All right, go ahead.
   4   Malcolm   Na:h, I ain't tryin to (inaudible), dog.
   5   Terrance   ((heightened pitch)) HE:Y, he have them
   6   ze:bra   shoes ((h h))
   7   Unidentified   Who?
   8   Terrance   It look like zebras.
   9   Done.
   10   Marcus   No you didn't, with them pa:nts!
                           ((>1s silence))
   11   Terrance   Huh?
   12   ((muttering))
   13   Andre   Hey, they better than the shoes YOU got on!

Terrance first attempts to draw in Malcolm as a target (line 2), but Malcolm declines to respond (line 4). Terrance quickly moves on to mock Marcus's shoes (lines 5–6, 8), and draws responses from Marcus (line 9) as well as Andre (line (12). Terrance relies on absurdity to jone, likening Marcus's shoes to a zebra (lines 5–6, 8), and then notes the end of his turn (line 9). Marcus and Andre appear to respond with personal insults, as they are plausible rather than hyperbolic claims: Marcus implies the poor quality of Terrance's pants (line 9), and Andre simply states that Marcus's shoes are better than Terrance's (line 12). In this case, then, the insult responses indicate that the joning contest folded into personal insult, and that the attempt to have a contest failed.

Alisha, Deandre and Joseph's nine year-old sister, was another student who described joning as verbal art. As I observed, she was particularly skilled at joning contests. As I describe later in this chapter, she also used joning to negotiate learning activities as well as to compete academically with other students. Alisha explained to me in a focus group that joning was about coming up with something good and "not corny" to "say to somebody." I asked Alisha for an example of a corny jone. She thought for a minute and said, "You yellow like a banana!" I paused myself, thinking, and responded, "That doesn't make any sense." "See?" she responded, eyes lighting up and smiling, presumably at the success of her corny example. "That's why it's a corny jone!"

In that moment, I did not understand the larger point Alisha offered in her example of a corny jone, but my subsequent reflections have made me realize how sophisticated her explanation was. The banana analogy denotes a simplistic, unoriginal picture: a banana is yellow, and it's relatively difficult, or perhaps unfunny, to visualize a person looking like one. Rather, the point of joning is to make a hyperbolic analogy that, when visualized, makes the insult recipient particularly ridiculous. For example, I had to stifle my own laughter when I once witnessed Bianca shout to her peers about a boy at another table, "His head look like a Boston Baked bean!" Thus, when Alisha first offered the banana example to me, I did not pick up on how precocious her attempt to explain to me what corny joning was simply by inventing the banana example on the spot. The banana jone indicates that she was not only skilled at improvising good jones, but also bad ones, though is possible that Alisha heard that corny jone herself and relayed it to me after recalling it from memory.

Despite the fact that students used joning for peer socializing and to verbally spar for fun, Bianca and a few others, such as Michael and CeCe, all thirteen years olds and considered academically accomplished because they diligently completed their homework and achieved high grades at school, that it distracted them from their schoolwork. These three students often ignored joning, even when it was done to them and generally tried to stop it when it was occurring among other students. Thus, unlike many other students, who expressed negative evaluations of joning but who regularly did it anyway, Bianca, Michael, and CeCe's views did not contradict their communicative habits. Yet even though CeCe had stopped joning the year I began fieldwork, she occasionally embedded joning into learning activities to project a stance of tough irreverence toward her academic learning.

To explain, in the two years prior to my fieldwork, both CeCe and Michael socialized with the other students, but began to distance themselves from most of the social interactions among the preadolescents by the time I started my research. Michael only spoke to other students when he played basketball and other games with them in the community center gym. CeCe and Michael made a point of buckling down on their homework during the allotted time, each sitting alone at their own table. CeCe's transformation in particular was, for me, a stark contrast to the persona she often displayed in my first few years of knowing her and which staff and other students described as "loud." The first two years I had known her, CeCe had led a pack of the academic enrichment students with her "ghetto girl" antics, joining on and "talking back" to instructors to the delight of the group. But over the course of my fieldwork, she became a model of the serious student, remaining quiet and shuttling her two younger siblings from school to after school, and then from after school to home. While she did not stop joning or being social entirely, I could not help but notice that she was no longer part of the core group of girls in the academic enrichment program. Moreover, she started to receive all A's and remarks on her "good citizenship" on her report cards from school, whereas before, she had been marked for behavior problems.

Thus, from about ten to twelve years old, CeCe had been known to jone aggressively with both peers and instructors. However, she began to make a point of saying that she was not going to jone on anyone the year that I started fieldwork, when she turned thirteen. That January, when the new science instructor introduced himself and his voluntary program, the students started to giggle and whisper about his Nigerian English "accent." To curb the students' laughter, Raymond playfully noted that the instructor had plenty to learn about himself, including joning. At the mention of joning, all of the students burst out laughing. CeCe covered her mouth and raised her hand. "If I do decide to do science," she offered, stifling her own laughter, "You won't see me do any joning."

Bianca, Michael, and CeCe appeared to refrain from and stop joning because they saw themselves as growing out of childish habits. By their assessments, joning was, in a certain sense, "kids' talk" or "something that kids do," and they ideologically aligned social maturation with the process of abandoning street toughness in favor of academic success. A few older teens and adults I spoke to perceived themselves to have succeeded in school and in their jobs because they chose to abandon the language and cultural practices of Southeast, first and foremost joning. Such a language ideology affirms the raciolinguistic distinction between street toughness and academic success as well as a meritocratic success ideology, as it implies that those who are wise enough to choose to assimilate are the ones who achieve success in the mainstream.

Students expressing the idea of choosing to engage in joning or not and what it means in terms of their future successes is not simply a personal choice, but rather an ideological position grounded in broader raciolinguistic chronotopes of policing and survival. For the students, joning was not simply integral to peer socializing, but necessary for navigating tough or threatening situations that involved face threat or situations that might involve physical violence. For this reason, I interpret joning as part of a longer Black cultural narrative of linguistic and cultural survival, literally and in the immediate sense, but also more broadly in terms of students maintaining a Black linguistic space and becoming competent members of an imagined Black community.

Nevertheless, many students realized that they would have to learn to negotiate belonging differently in the pursuit of academic success because of how joning and other styles of conflict talk were policed and criminalized as signs of violence and aggression. Thus, they adapted their linguistic practices accordingly. As I describe in the following section, many students used joning to negotiate academic learning.

Joning and the Linguistic Negotiation of Academic Learning

While a few of the near- and early teens reported that they stopped joning to focus on academic work, a few students joned on each other during academic learning activities and interactions. Joning was part of their competitive academic talk, but they also displayed identities that indexed street tough identities, such as "ghetto girl" or "street hustler." These identity performances sometimes deliberately played on stereotypes of Black students as aggressive, threatening, or disruptive. I suggest that these identity performances actually helped students challenge or poke fun at their raciolinguistic typing as "problem students."

Specifically, prosodic features such as vowel stress/lengthening, amplified volume, and dramatic contrasts in intonation and pitch, combined with other linguistic and discourse features, anchored identity performances in recognizable AAL speaker types, keying participants' attention to the fact that a verbal performance was occurring. In addition to prosody, discourse features and lexical items typically associated with joning and other AAL styles of verbal performance were styled with an exaggerated quality to mark off verbal play from the sequential environment of the conversations in which they occurred. Thus, joning and related styles of verbal art were salient as identity performances, if not subversive satires of street toughness, because of the way students styled these features to parody the cultural context and models of personhood associated with being "ghetto" or street tough.

Students often used joning was to compete academically with one another—for example, to start "smartness contests." For students such as Alisha and Mary, being considered dumb was extremely face-threatening, and such accusations were often used competitively get the right answer first when answering homework questions. This is shown in extract 5, in which Alisha and Mary are completing their homework together:

5. Alisha and Mary compete academically

1	Alisha	*I ain't put* no THREE right there!
2	Mary	((laughs))
3		I did that.
4	Alisha	I put the two, and I put the three.
5	Mary	O:h!
6	Alisha	The two is right here where that [a]t.
7	Mary	[OKA:Y,
8		okay].
9	Alisha	I'm sma:rt.
10	Mary	You're dumb.
11	Alisha	Girl shut up.

In line 9, Alisha claims "I'm sma:rt," lending jocularity to "smart" by lengthening the vowel, displaying a playfully competitive stance. But this boast follows Alisha's denial that she put the wrong answer, produced in falsetto (italics): "*I ain't put no THREE right there!*" (line 1), and an explanation of what she did write. AAL speakers use falsetto for a range of expressive purposes (Tarone 1972; Alim 2004). For example, falsetto can be used to convey indignation or frustration, especially when the speaker is responding to an interlocutor whom they perceive to have made a face-threatening claim (Rasmusen 2010). Here, Alisha appears to be jokingly boasting about being smart, but her initial stance of indignation and her response to Mary's mock insult, "Girl, shut up," indicate that being perceived as dumb was face-threatening.

Some of the girls also used joning to project a stance of tough irreverence when encouraging others to complete their homework. In extract 6, which comes from a larger interaction I had observed and took detailed field notes on, CeCe calls out in the middle of her peers' loud chatter to ask, "I just wanna know, can we get back to work now?" (lines 2–3), and then jones on Raymond (line 8) after several participants in the interaction react with the exclamation, "Ohhhh!" (line 4):

6. CeCe performs tough irreverence
    1   Multiple   ((talking and laughing))
    2   Cece   ((calls from across the room))
    3   I just wanna know, can we get back to
    4   work now?
    5   Multiple   Ohhhh!
    6   CeCe   I'm just asking, I got work to do.
    7   I'm not trying to be funny
                     ((playfully smacks peer))
    8   He ((Raymond)) lookin at me like,   9
    9   "Cheese and crackers!" man!
    10   Multiple   ((laughter))

Following her peers' response in line 4, CeCe mitigates her request that everyone "get back to work," asserting that she is not trying to be funny. But she simultaneously engages in mock physical conflict by swatting at her peer (lines 5–6). By joning on Raymond, the authority figure who had been watching the group from a short distance away, CeCe outsources the request for order, adding an impersonation of Raymond by citing a phrase he often exclaimed when his disciplinary attempts failed: "Cheese and crackers!" (lines 8–9). Cece's body language (mock fighting), as well as the joning speech act, helps her in constructing a stance of "tough" irreverence. This example, recorded in January 2011, is one of the few times I observed CeCe jone that year, and it was applied to spur on the productive completion of homework rather than to engage socially with peers.

Extracts 5 and 6 both illustrate how students used joning to display different stances toward academic learning—competitiveness and "tough irreverence." These stances could be laminated to style a stance that I call "competitive irreverence," which I explore in extract 7, using Alisha as the example speaker. In these extracts, the prosodic features, discourse markers, and lexical items typically associated with joning and other AAL verbal performance styles achieved an especially exaggerated quality based on how Alisha used them contrastively to mark off verbal play from the sequential environment of the conversations in which they occurred. In using such features to key her verbal performances, Alisha displayed stances or personae that students had described to me in focus groups as "tough," "street," or "ghetto," terms, which they also used synonymously with "talking Black." Specifically, I explore how Alisha used prosody, combined with lexical items such as "Girl" and body language showing toughness to help her anchor her verbal performances in the raciolinguistic identity model of "ghetto girl"—that is, an African American working-class female who is pejoratively deemed to be "loud" or confrontational (Fordham 1993; Chun 2009; Alim & Goodwin 2010).

In extract 7, Alisha recruits competitive irreverence by way of making fun of Mary's handwriting. Her pitch and intonation contours, as well as her mock disapproval ("suck teeth," line 9) contrast in the utterances to produce a playful critique:

7. Alisha teases Mary about her handwriting
    1   Alisha   You is there _
    2   It's seventy-five? _
    3   Mary   What?   4
    4   O:h!
    5   Alisha   That's seventy [fi:ve?/]
    6   Mary   [No!]
    7   Alisha   That don't look/like no one
    8   to me\
    9   ((sucks teeth)) That look like a S/
    10   and a seven.
    11   Mary   It's a tw:o/
    12   That is,
    13   a fif-TEEN,
    14   and a el-E-ven _

In her first two turns at talk, Alisha transitions from using level final intonation, an AAL prosodic feature that speakers commonly used to ask yes/no questions in requesting information, to increasing her final pitch and intonation contours, which peak when she repeats her question in line 5. This dramatizes Alisha's performance of incredulity and sets her up for her joning performance (lines 7–10), in which she critiques Mary's answer as not a number at all. Alisha's evenly applied stress and lowered pitch in line 7 and her use of suck teeth in line 9 juxtapose with her characterization of Mary's written answer ("S7") as contextualization cues that create a play of intentions. Thus, while the prosodic features signal serious or emphatic disapproval, Alisha's absurd claim about Mary's handwriting that she is also trying to be funny about it. I suggest that here Alisha's use of pitch and intonation contrasts key competitive playacting. That is to say, Alisha's pejoration of Mary's handwriting dialectically implies a mildly aggressive boast about her own.

Moreover, the playful exaggeration and humor established in Alisha's use of intonation and pitch key the speech act as an AAL verbal performance. I suggest that this creates room for Alisha to boast and critique her friend's schoolwork while avoiding a linguistic modeling of high achievement that might mark her as too arrogant, and possibly construed as "acting white" (Fordham 1996). There is a particular irony to this identity performance: while the joning speech act suggests mild aggression in terms of how Alisha uses it to display a competitive academic persona, she in fact uses it to mitigate what could have otherwise been perceived by Mary as an institutional-authoritative form of face threat to her skills and abilities as a student.

Linguistically, verbal performances such as Alisha's and CeCe's rely on indirect devices for cueing identity performances. For example, the uses of prosody, lexemes, and discourse markers we see in Alisha's talk indirectly indexed the mock aggression typically associated with other AAL styles of verbal play and competitiveness, and which may provoke stereotypes of AAL speakers as threatening or loud. In this regard, Alisha often performed a competitive irreverence, effectively laminating the performance of a "ghetto girl" identity onto her academically competitive approach to learning interactions.

Alisha anchored her social-academic status as a high achiever in a local identity model of acting/talking Black, which enabled her to achieve multiple goals in interaction: she could challenge the normative roles and relationships of classroom learning, playfully boast about her academic achievements, or take the lead on homework assignments without being perceived as acting white among her peers, enact social intimacy with her friends by provoking their laughter, and adopt a style of talking typically associated with African American teens and young women to explore local youth-based models of Black female identity. Finally, using joning and other AAL verbal performance styles to display socially risky identities such as "ghetto girl" also indexes the out of place or inappropriate uses of talking Black in academic settings. This indexicality allows for a styling of verbal play that contrasts with joning as conflict talk that so-called "unprepared" or "resistant" students used to detract from learning or to "start stuff."

Alisha and CeCe could get away with joning because both girls were considered to be model students: they achieved high grades at school and got their homework done in the after school program. This was not necessarily the case with other students such as Makaila and Makila, twelve-year-old twins who were very verbally gifted and "loud," but who did not achieve high grades or buckle down to do their homework. When the nine- to thirteen-year-old boys who attended the family literacy program joned, they were policed especially for being off task.

Extract 8 illustrates how the family literacy peer group of boys was typically policed as not engaging in learning by virtue of their joning. To explain the context, the fifteen-year-old volunteer tutor Blake had just opened the door to the family literacy classroom space as Lenny and seven-year-old Rashid sat down to read aloud, with me leading the activity. Though only seven years old, Rashid was unofficially part of the preadolescent peer group. Here, the two boys greeted Blake by remarking on his grown-out but newly trimmed hairstyle. Ms. Betty quickly intervened to put Rashid back on task (lines 3–4):

8. Lenny and Rashid jone on Blake
    1 Lenny   You need to CUT THAT!
    2 Rashid   You look like, George Bush!
    3 Ms. Betty   Hey Rashid, you need to ((inaudible)) and pay attention
    4 to that book.

Personally, I found Rashid's joning to be especially clever, since it relies on word play: Blake was growing out a "bush," or "Afro" hairstyle, and Rashid used the name of the recent ex-president to poke fun at Blake's hair. In terms of the insult's meaning, George Bush was white, known to be dumb, and much less of a desirable president to the students and their families as Barack Obama. There are several layers of meaning to explore, but at the very least, it was clever of Rashid to invert the symbolic meaning of his haircut—in other words, implying that Blake looked like a stock white guy when he was in fact growing out a hairstyle considered "natural" and symbolic of Black pride. Nevertheless, Ms. Betty quickly stifled the insult and told Rashid to focus on his reading.

Though Ms. Betty certainly appreciated and encouraged joning, she was first and foremost insistent that students focus on their homework or reading during the allotted times. Additionally, since one jone typically led to extended verbal contests where the boys tried to "top" each other, Ms. Betty may have wanted at that time to stop that from happening so that they would not collectively get distracted making fun of Blake's hair. Indeed, among this group of boys, joning took the form of verbal character contests in which they played with stereotypes of "ghetto" persona. Extract 9 illustrates. Here, I had just recruited J.J., Andre, and a few of the other boys into participating in a reading group for the afternoon. Andre had been engrossed with a game on his cellular phone as we sat around the table, while the others engaged in a jocular tête-à-tête routine themed around a street hustler trying to "sell stuff" and a crackhead who "talks to himself":

9. Street hustlers and crackheads
    1 Ms. Betty   (to Andre) Turn that off! Put that up.
    2 J.J.   Huh, Andre, before I sell it.
    3 Andre   Shut up! You're always talking about selling
    4   somebody's stuff.
    5   Want me to sell-sell your forehead for you, get
    6   you a smaller one _
    7   ((boys laugh))
    8 J.J.   ((laughs)) At least I don't talk to myself.
    9 Andre   Shut up, boy.

10	J.J.	He talk to himself.
11	Alisha	((laughs))
12	Ms. Betty	Alisha, be quiet.
13		'Cos you know.
14		((ventriloquizing, lowers volume)) J.J. does not play.
15	J.J.	[((laughs))]
16	Deandre	[Ohhhh!]

At the beginning of the sequence, Ms. Betty attempts to help me organize the start of the activity by directing Andre to turn off his phone, which had been producing loud noises. J.J. capitalizes on this verbal disciplining to draw attention to his identity display of a fast-talking street hustler, a metalinguistic typification that was literally modeled in his quick cadence (not represented in transcript) as he threatens to steal and sell the phone (line 2). This hustler persona was a character display that J.J. had been using frequently in the few weeks preceding this interaction and, moreover, wearing it out as Andre's quick response indicates (lines 3–6). J.J. laughs and jones back by picking up the crackhead theme from earlier in the interaction (lines 8, 10). Alisha overhears the interaction from a short distance and laughs (line 11). Ms. Betty verbally disciplines her for laughing and thereby intensifying the distracting joning session. But then, Ms. Betty participates in the joning speech event by noting that J.J. "does not play" (line 13)—in other words, she is suggesting that her daughter might be the next target of his jokes and would not be able to verbally keep up or might get "cooked" (publicly shamed).

The boys who participated in the family literacy program constituted a tight-knit peer group that children and adults alike perceived to cause trouble both in the program and in the neighborhood more widely. In their absence, other after school participants consistently described the boys as "always starting stuff," using stories of the verbal and physical fights they were involved in at school and on 25th Street to explain how bad they were. But these characterizations only told part of the story: the boys were ultimately friendly and on good terms with many of the other students; they commonly visited each other's houses to play and socialize after program time had ended. Additionally, a few of the boys, such as Deandre, his brother Joseph, Andre, and J.J. helped younger children with their schoolwork, particularly siblings for whom they served as caregivers and disciplining authorities in the absence of adults. And while the older boys often resisted completing schoolwork and verbally challenged instructors and other adults themselves, they disciplined their younger siblings, who were typically between the ages of five and seven years, into compliant behaviors.

This peer group included Ms. Betty's boys, Joseph and Deandre, and Lenny, Andre, Malcolm, and Marcus. In March, Terrance joined family literacy in the spring, approximately five months into this dissertation study. Matt, the lead instructor for family literacy, and I typically arranged oral reading practice groups with four to five of the boys at a time, to last for a minimum of twenty minutes each day. This was the primary focus of academic learning activity for the older boys, whereas instructors typically focused on homework completion with other students in the program. Lenny and Joseph read at a very basic introductory level; most of the other boys were not reading at grade level assessment. Deandre, for his part, was a fluent reader orally and in terms of comprehension. However, he had been placed in a special education class a grade level behind most of his peers. In terms of how he participated in after school learning activities, Deandre brought his homework twice in the course of the academic school year. One of these times, I observed him complete a reading, math, and science worksheet each in less than thirty minutes (on which he had produced entirely correct answers). Another time, I pointed out that he made a small mistake in spelling while checking over his work. In response, Deandre tore and crumpled up the sheet of paper, with tears in his eyes as he threw it in the trashcan. Most days, Deandre claimed that his teacher had not assigned any homework. Ms. Betty, Matt, and I spent much time negotiating, and even aggressively arguing at times, with Deandre and several of the other boys about practicing reading aloud before letting them have time to use the computers that were installed in the classroom.

Despite differences in the boys' reading and other academically assessed areas of knowledge, their school progress and records of performance (i.e., advisory reports and teachers' comments) as well as talk about their social behavior overdetermined their identification as problem or failing students. I argue that this overdetermination of their identities as street tough shaped perceptions of their joning as disruptive during their participation in reading groups and other after school learning activities, in contrast to how students identified as school-ready (Alisha, CeCe, and Mary) were viewed as "loud." The boys joned on to build their verbal art skills, always looking to see who could produce the funniest insult. I suggest that at least in part, doing so allowed them to display verbosity as resistance to their characterization as problem students: they could display an alternative set of language skills. I did notice that when the boys joned, it was often to embarrass students when they were positively appraised for being smart, on task, or otherwise academically accomplished.

As I have described using several examples, joning among the family literacy boys often involved invoking pathologized stereotypes of "ghetto" persona. They used such character contests as comic relief in relation to the raciolinguistic chronotope of policing, which predicted their futures as undesirable street types in advance of anything they were actually doing.

Ultimately, considering differences in how students were construed as disruptive or resistant when joning lends further insight into the raciolinguistic processes of socialization, policing, and enregisterment (see chapter 2). Though perceptions of some students being more disruptive than others appeared to be tied to how they performed in school, it also appears that there were also gendered patterns in the policing of joning as inappropriate to academic learning: girls who did not achieve good grades in school were typed as "loud" when they joned, and boys were routinely characterized as troublemakers. I could not help but notice that patterns of policing girls and boys for joning match closely how Wortham (2007) describes the emergence of "loud Black girls" and "resistant Black boys" as identity types in his ethnographic study of a Chicago high school classroom. As Wortham shows, it is especially noteworthy how these locally produced identities index and recreate more widely circulating identity models of African American students as resistant to academic learning over time (cf. Fordham 1993; Noguera 2008).

DISCUSSION

For the nine- to thirteen-year-old students, joning was a peer linguistic practice that students used to navigate broader raciolinguistic chronotopes of policing and survival. Adults wanted to help students find ways to be "appropriately" Black in light of the fact that linguistic practices such as joning would be criminalized as aggressive or threatening outside of the after school program and the Southeast neighborhood in which they lived. For this reason, they policed joning in order to prepare the students for academic success. While some adults, such as Terrance's mother and Raymond, were more concerned about potential interactional misfires, other adults, such as Ms. Betty, believed joning to be a distraction from academic learning. The students, for their part, navigated policing and survival differently: while many students showed restraint in using particular kinds of language considered inappropriate, such as cussing, many also used joning to provoke anxiety-based stereotypes of African Americans as social threats, gang members, or violent criminals.

Often, adults were concerned that with joning, the students were passively modeling what they saw and heard from street youth and "gangsta" hip-hop, thereby possibly propelling themselves into a continued future of raciolinguistic policing. However, my analysis suggests instead students' joning was grounded in a raciolinguistic chronotope of survival: it helped them to learn to appear, and to eventually be, tough in situations where they felt threatened, marginalized, erased, or disrespected. For them, learning how to "talk back" in different spaces was essential to their survival in the neighborhood and in school.

Over time, cultural and linguistic survival strategies would look different for different students. For Alisha, this meant adapting joning to the immediate task and goals of academic learning—in other words, carefully embedding it into a school-sanctioned activity. For Michael and CeCe, this meant no longer participating in joning: instead, cultural and linguistic survival meant moving away from "childish" language (i.e., conflict talk) to pursue academic success. A good number of students, however, continued to take up joning as a way of claiming a Black linguistic space against the assimilatory demand for schooling, as I initially illustrated with the example at the beginning of this chapter. While joning ultimately afforded these students some transformative power in the moment, it was always read and policed against wider anxieties that they were not yet school-ready and possibly making a choice to reject schooling to become street youth.

Joning, then, helps explain the ambivalence of students' and teachers' institutionalized subject positions within the wider "choices" laid out for their cultural and linguistic survival: students needed to find ways to be "appropriately" and perhaps even authentically Black while also pursuing academic success. As this and prior chapters document, students had their own ways of navigating and transforming Blackness against the raciolinguistic policing of adults, but had little success being heard and seen outside of their overdetermined identities as resistant "problem students." The next chapter, which explores the translingual sensibilities students brought to their writing and art projects, offers some critical pedagogical perspectives on how to recognize and better support the kinds of transformative work students are already doing in disrupting pathologizing raciolinguistic ideologies.

NOTE

1. Marshall's is a discount department store that is known to sell name-brand goods at bargain prices.

5

"You Don't Know How to Read!"

Racializing Discourses about Literacy

This chapter explores how the nine- to thirteen-year-old students used school-based discourses about academic achievement to construct their own identity models of "good" and "bad" students. In doing so, they often used racial stereotypes of African Americans to construe peers as illiterate or resistant Others. As a teacher-researcher, I found this especially troubling, as I was concerned about the possibility that they had internalized deficit discourses about their intelligence or were constructing a "culture of opposition" to schooling (Willis 1977; Fordham & Ogbu 1986; MacLeod 1995). Consider the interchange given next, which follows after twelve-year-old Jay asked Brandi, also twelve, and her ten-year-old sister, Janelle if Donna was going to join us for a game of Uno. The girls responded as follows:

1	Brandi	Nah, she do all educated stuff.
2	Janelle	She do all work.
3	Brandi	That's why she could be smart, cos she not gonna be dumb like the rest of us.

Brandi and Janelle do not just note that Donna has chosen to do her work (homework), but instead respond to the question by creating an identity distinction that is predicated on being smart and doing work on the one hand and dumb on the other, an academic identity position that the rest of the students are implied to inhabit by personal choice. In other words, Brandi appears to sponsor the idea that the after school students were collectively dumb because they chose not to do their work. On top of the fact that Brandi voiced a meritocratic ideology of achievement, which in the context of education policy and discourse, collectively blames racialized minorities for choosing failure. I was troubled that she, and other students as I knew from teaching them for three years, came to associate learning with work, which was a direct result of how they were taught at school and, to a certain degree, in the after school program. But I knew Brandi and many other students to take issue with the racialized achievement discourses presented to them at school, as this next ethnographic story illustrates. On the Martin Luther King, Jr. holiday in January 2011, Urban Pathways decided to host a day of educational and recreational activities for the students. The day's activities included listening to a live audio recording of Dr. King's "I Have a Dream" speech, followed by a few short presentations by some of the older children and small discussion groups, each led by a staff member. My discussion group comprised several research participants: twins Brandi and Bianca, their younger sisters Janelle and Marnie, another set of twin sisters, Makaila and Makila, and then Jay and Tanika. All were nine to twelve years old, on friendly terms, and attended the same middle school. A conversation about the achievement gap started when I decided to challenge the students on the idea of racial inequality disappearing with Dr. King's work: many students expressed the postracial view that the end of de jure segregation marked the end of racism. In response, I asked them if they thought Black students and white students attended the same kinds of schools. All of the students in the group expressed awareness of the fact that African American students attended worse schools than whites. Brandi shifted the topic toward how African American students were treated by their teachers, noting that she and her classmates were often told that "Black kids are not as smart as white kids." In this conversation, I discovered that some teachers used deficit discourses to collectively blame students for their so-called attitudes. Brandi gave me an example of what one of their teachers said to the whole classroom one day after Makila had angered him with some sort of behavioral transgression.

"He told us that we don't do as well in school as white people because we still run around in the field with bows and beads in our hair acting violent," Brandi recalled. To explain, Makila wore her hair in twists that were decorated with beads or bows; the teacher, an African American man, had used a respectability discourse to not only criticize her appearance and to suggest that she, like the other students in the class, acted wild, recruiting the racist trope of a field slave.[1] The anger and distress on Brandi's face, as well as the following remarks of her and other students, indicated to me that they at least partially comprehended the racist implications of the teacher's statement.

"We are just as smart as white people," Brandi continued. "No, we're smarter!" Jay chimed in. The students began to chatter animatedly, naming reasons why it was true that Black people were just as smart or smarter than whites. Brandi broke through the others' excited talk and asked me directly, "How would YOU feel if you had to go to school every day and be told that you were not as smart as white people?" I maintained eye contact with her and nodded with a pained look on my face. I felt that here was no way I could provide an appropriate verbal response, and at this point, Brandi and the other students looked devastated. Everyone had stopped talking. We sat in heavy silence until the whole group was called back together.

These two ethnographic examples illustrate how the after school students actively resisted their interpellation as failing Black students while also sponsoring schooling's meritocratic ideology, especially with respect to what it means to be smart and achieve academically. Students often used this meritocratic discourse of achievement to negatively characterize peers as not smart, illiterate, or resistant. I argue that instead of seeing this as evidence of having partially internalized commonsense thinking about race and academic achievement, such practices were, in part, a tactic that allowed students to escape the stereotype threat of embodying such racialized identity characteristics themselves. In other words, students used the school-normative individualization of achievement to defy racializing stereotypes that collectively characterize African Americans within discourses of deficit or lack. They disidentified with this form of symbolic domination while also reconstituting it in a fractally recursive configuration, as a form of "internal" domination (Irvine & Gal 2000; Reyes 2017). Such tactics were especially common in learning interactions that actively worked to students' disadvantage. Thus, in the last portion of this chapter, I focus on how students adopted this strategy to construct fractally recursive distinctions between literate selves and illiterate Others in reading-aloud groups, which was a commonly used learning activity that proved incredibly face-threatening for most of the students in the after school program.

CHALLENGING STEREOTYPES OF AFRICAN AMERICAN RESISTANCE TO SCHOOLING

Ethnographies that document how minoritized students resist schooling have shown that these students often perceive schooling for what it is: a disciplinary institution that is meant to sort them into their designated strata in a capitalist society characterized by racial and class inequality (Willis 1977; MacLeod 1995; Fordham 1996). This research has shed light on the fact that minoritized students' oppositional stances toward schooling are not a result of preexisting cultural and linguistic differences that cause a communicative mismatch in the classroom (e.g., Heath 1983; Phillips 2009), but rather constitute locally constructed responses to how they are institutionally policed and disciplined as bad or, as was often said in the after school program, "having an attitude." I both observed and heard stories of many of the same tactics of resistance among the preadolescents and early teens as the ones documented in Willis's (1977) study of the working-class, teenaged *lads* in northern England, which included work avoidance, pretending not to hear instructors, taking more time than needed to follow a disciplinary directive, and "talking back" to teachers when they chastised the students, almost always collectively, for their attitudes. As I knew from the studies of older youth, such practices of refusal tend to confirm the institutional stereotype of minoritized students as culturally uninterested, disengaged, and resistant to schooling rather than compel further questions about what caused students to behave in this way. And because white normativity is rarely challenged, students such as the lads or Fordham's (1996) low achievers often end up becoming complicit in their own oppression even though they might tell themselves they made the conscious choice to avoid or reject schooling.[2]

More often than not, students' practices of resistance become folded into the production of racial and class difference such that resistance to the school-institutional
management of these subjectivities will eventually come to index and confirm students'
status as unassimilable Others. As I mean to demonstrate shortly using examples, racialized minorities often resist the assimilatory aims of schooling, but selectively. Moreover,
their participation in schooling gets misrecognized as disruptive behavior, a process
that presumes and entails essentializing claims about racialized groups in general (Leap
1993; Wortham 2007). That is to say, students often participate in school-normative
practices critically or uncritically, but their ways of engaging are subsumed back into
hegemonic notions of "Black lack" and other deficit discourses (Rampton 1995; Fordham 1996; Wortham 2007; Mendoza-Denton 2008; Flores & Rosa 2015; Rosa 2019).
In the case of this study, the preadolescents and early teens were often seen and heard
by staff as collectively not wanting to participate in school, not valuing learning, and as
having attitudes. This was most often the case even though the students were actually
responding to local instances of discipline that they found unfair or unjustified.

Over time, instances of misrecognition end up confirming the stereotype that African American students construct oppositional cultures to schooling and academic
achievement (Fordham & Ogbu 1986; see Hubbard 1999 and Carter 2003 for
critique). As Wortham (2007) argues, attending to situated productions of identity
not only shows how racialized meanings can be applied to students in distinctive or
unpredictable ways; doing so reveals the tacit ways in which racial stereotypes can be
applied to students and reproduced or transformed over longer time scales.

The following examples illustrate instances in which staff collectively hailed the
whole group of preadolescents and early teens as "off task" even though each interaction began with a directive to a single recipient:

1. "And you ain't doin nothin"
1	Raymond	Don't laugh, is yours correct?
2	Unidentified	[No,]
3	Raymond	[Right.]
4		And you ain't doin nothin. Y'all ((inaudible))
5		stuff, when you're doing your stuff? When it's
6		your time to go the gym or computer? That's
7		gonna be my time.

2. "I'll have you all in trouble"
1	Ms. Reeves	Scuse me. Turn the computer back the way it
2		was. Do not move it again.
3	Unidentified	Look what she did to ((inaudible)) my shoes off!
4	Ms. Reeves	Next time I'll have you all in trouble. In here
5		((inaudible)) yourself.
6		I got some work you can do.
7	Bianca	((low volume)) I don't wanna do it.

8	Brandi	((low volume)) I ain't doing no work, I'm staying right
9		here.
10		We do enough of that in school.

It is telling that the entire group becomes subject to the moral characterization of being off task or misbehaving: more often than not, the students were collectively interpellated as colluding in bad behavior. Individual students often found themselves involved in the futile task of denying that they had done anything or, like Brandi and Bianca, they refused to comply with the forms of discipline staff threatened them with.

As shown in the second example, students would often refuse to do "work" when it was assigned as a disciplinary measure or as punishment for bad behavior. Assigning work and keeping students from play activities was a common disciplinary practice in the after school program, especially among African American staff who were said to be "old school" when it came to correcting students' behavior. Such figures included Ms. Reeves and, to a lesser degree, Raymond. According to several students and one of the teenaged tutors Marcus, teachers at the local middle school were also in the habit of assigning homework as punishment. In the following interaction, Marcus queries Felisha about why she does not have any homework, which leads into a conversation about how one teacher, who had also taught Marcus when he attended the school, assigned work "when you make her mad":

3. "When you make her mad, she'll give you homework!"

1	Marcus	Where your homework?
2	Felisha	Huh?
3		I ain't get no homework.
4	Marcus	((suspicious)) You ain't get no homework today?
5	Felisha	It's Tuesday-
6		She ain't give us no homework!
7	Marcus	What's today?
8	Multiple	Friday.
9	Marcus	Fri-Yeah, she don't give out homework Friday.
10	Felisha	We gotta get it, though.
11	Marcus	Huh?
12	Felisha	We get homework Monday through Friday.
13	Jen	Felisha's good, she does her homework.
14	Marcus	But y'all-y'all don't get homework Fridays.
15	Joseph	No we ain't get homework today cos we got our report
16		card/
17	Marcus	/She ain't give you-give us homework on, on, on
18		=Thursdays,
19		Thursdays or some Fridays, she ain't used to give us
20		homework.

21	Felisha	We gotta get homework EVERY day.
22	Joseph	We can't even get out the gate with no homework.
23	Felisha	Yeah but uh,
24	Joseph	But I go through the FRONT door.
25	Marcus	Nah nah nah h h h
26		y'all now, we ain't used to get homework like that.
27	Marcus	They gave us homework, but we ain't-
28	Felisha	That's probably cos our-
29		That's was probably cos our behavior last year.
30		Used to go home ((laughs)).
31	Joseph	We ain't had homework today.
32	Felisha	But, I got in trouble-
33		We used to go home,
		((trails off, 3s))
34		Ms. H ain't give us homework ONE day.
35		She ain't give us homework one day.
36		She said cos-
37	Marcus	When you make her mad she'll give you homework!

Felisha's and Marcus's speculations about why teachers assign them work is telling, as is Joseph's avoidance strategy of exiting out building doors that were not guarded by teachers loaded with homework. As with the first two extracts, the students are not spurning academic achievement; they are refusing to accept the punitive structure of learning that was made compulsory for their scholastic success. Felisha, who regularly got A's and B's on her report card, speculated that the reason for more homework was due to students' (bad) behavior. She may have personalized the interpretation, as her schoolteacher often determined her in-class behavior to be a problem. For example, her teachers' written narrative on her March 2011 report card was, "Felisha completes homework and classwork. I have seen improvement in her attitude. However, I need you to speak to her about her giggling and her wish to wear coats in class." Like CeCe, Denise, and a few other students in the after school program, Felisha was policed for her "attitude" while being able to achieve high grades. Many other students were not so lucky and suffered punitive consequences that kept them out of class and unable to continue the learning that would produce even passing grades.

While the majority of the students tried to avoid or openly refuse discipline, they never argued that what they were punished for (joning, fighting, talking back) was not in fact bad behavior. What they said is that other students were bad and caused them to act bad in return, much like the defensive logic students used with respect to *joning*, the local linguistic practice of ritual insults (see chapter 4). The following extract, which involves Felisha explaining why she got an uncharacteristic "D" grade on her report card to her peers, helps explain:

4. Felisha's spring report card
    1   Joseph   That say D?

2	Alisha	Yeah.
		((several seconds))
3	Felisha	Oh no, but I been gettin in trouble for something I ain't
4		do!
5		They be snitching on me!
6	Jen	What do you mean?
7	Felisha	Ms. ((Teacher's name)) gonna believe it too, they be lyin on
8		me!
9	Jen	About what?
10	Felisha	What I be doing up there. And then,
11		When I ((inaudible)) them they get mad and gonna start
12		jonin.
13		h h h h
14		They all be funny, though.
15	Jen	What, your teachers or your friends?
16	Felisha	The people that sit at my table!
17		They ain't my friends.
		((several seconds silence))
18		I'm about to fight.
19		A boy named Aaron.
20		He get on my nerves.
21		All day.
22	Jen	He fights?
23	Felisha	Mm hm.
24	Alisha	Yeah, he bad.
25	Felisha	He do too much!
26		He do too much!
27		He about to rat.
28	Felisha	((laughs)) He about to rat!
29	Jen	About what?
30	Felisha	I blast him. I hit him in his face. His glasses flew off his
31		face.

As it turns out, both Felisha and Aaron, a twelve-year-old boy who did not attend the after school program but who had attended the previous year's summer program, were accomplished students and rarely got "talked to" in the after school program. Recently, Ms. Betty had been singing Aaron's praises for making the regional spelling bee. I was therefore surprised at the altercation Felisha described, as well as her and Alisha's characterization of Aaron as bad. But according to Felisha, and other reports from Bianca and others, students who fought and tried to "mess with" them at school kept them from doing their work.

For the purposes of my analysis, it is not important to determine which students fought and who did not and whether it impacted their academic performance at school. Rather, I want to draw attention to the recursive creation of a figure which students imagine as an undesirable Other in contrast to their own identities as students trying to make it through school. As Irvine and Gal (2000) explain, *fractal recursivity* is the semiotic process by which a large-scale oppositional relationship gets projected onto a smaller scale of ideological distinction. That is to say, schools sponsor the idea that the linguistic and cultural practices of whites are normative and desirable and Blackness as the opposite. Students took this large-scale ideological distinction and recursively applied it to create new sets of contrastive academic identities, such as good/bad, smart/not smart, and literate/illiterate, to characterize each other individually as types of students.

This process inevitably involved the creation of an undesirable Other; the "problem student." The problem student fought, joned, talked back to teachers and staff, and deliberately messed with other students. In this sense, students were recursively drawing upon normative stereotypes of resistant African Americans and projecting that type onto others in order to constitute themselves as desirable or perhaps model students. At one point or another, I observed each and every student I worked with in the after school program provoke some sort of conflict, whether playful or serious. For this reason, I interpret their moral characterizations of good and bad students were a discursive invention rooted in the overdetermination of African American students as unwilling to achieve. Students like Felisha and Bianca, who were very insistent with me on how bad both students and teachers were at school, constructed a sort of uncritical resistance by seeking to avoid the racial stereotype rather than challenge its foundational logic (cf. Fordham 1996). Even though they were constructing a politics of resistance to being characterized as bad, such students also recursively constructed wider discourses that distinguish between a desirable African American figure such as Barack Obama, who is viewed as articulate by whites (Alim & Smitherman 2012), and those who are determined not to have linguistically and culturally assimilated from the perspective of hegemonic whiteness.

As Reyes argues in her study of Filipino elite university students, the construction of such desirable figures "is the product of a careful orchestration that positions it 'beside that which it critiques,' but never outside of a recursively constituted coloniality" (2017, p. 212). Such identity practices, then, are evidence not just of how people try to make sense of race, but also of how normative hierarches continue to act, ideologically and practically, to limit their agency—that is, what people believe to be true and what they do. Or, perhaps students such as Felisha and Bianca developed such identity models as a strategy that allowed them to at least temporarily try to cope with their inevitable racialization as resistant students regardless of what they did or did not do.

THE RECURSIVE CONSTRUCTION OF
INTELLIGENCE AND ACHIEVEMENT

As shown with the ethnographic examples thus far, the production of racial stereotypes formed recursive sets of identity models based on school-normative discourses about good and bad students. But rather than being constituted via explicit racial labels or talk, their identity models functioned via indexicality, where "having an attitude" was locally constructed as a noncompliant stance that drew its wider meaning from the racializing stereotype of "resistant Black students." This ideologized representation of compliant ("good") and noncompliant ("bad") students was a locally empowering form of identity work that allowed them to deflect racial stigma but ultimately, it had the effect of recursively constructing Blackness as unassimilable Otherness in relation to both short- and long-term goals of academic learning and achievement.

Students also reproduced racialized ideologies of intelligence and achievement. Even in the absence of explicit reference, achievement and intelligence are made apprehensible in relation to ideas about racial difference. For example, Kromidas (2016) documents how collaborative learning activities among multiethnic fourth-grade children become sites for renegotiating ideas about who is smart and who is not smart in relation to a prevailing racial hierarchy that constructs intelligence as an innate property of whiteness. As she argues, "Schools not only produce smartness as a measurable and incrementally variable property of individuals, but also naturalize these distinctions as innate properties, and justify differential educational treatment on this basis" (2016, p. 81, citing Stark 2014). The meritocratic myth, then, presents the contradictory claim that whites are innately smart via individual merit while ethnoracial minorities are almost always interpellated as members of a racialized group and policed for any signs of intellectual deficit or deviance.

From this analytical standpoint, and given other ways in which racial Otherness is constructed as intellectual and moral lack, one can infer that racialized minorities come to learn that inhabiting smartness as identity category elevates them not just as individuals, but as exceptional members of the racialized group to which they have been assigned. Similar to how students discursively constructed good and bad identity models, this kind of *enlightened exceptionalism* (Alim & Smitherman 2012, citing Wise 2009) functioned as a status marker among students, who frequently participated in smartness contests. I argue that doing so was a local tactic that allowed them to avoid what Steele (2003) calls *stereotype threat*: fear of confirming the negative racial stereotype that African Americans are less intelligent than whites (see also Fordham 1996).

Consider the following exchange between Alisha and Mary, two nine-year-old best friends who often completed homework together. The turns at talk are sequential, but I have thematically parsed sections of the transcribed speech to show the main interactional focus of each segment and the points where Alisha intervenes with evaluative commentary about being "smart" (Section 1.2, lines 17–19) and Mary being "slow" (Section 5.4, lines 35–36):

5. Alisha and Mary doing homework
    <u>5.1</u>   <u>Answering homework questions</u>
       1   Alisha   This-hold up. This is the first one!
       2   Mary   Where?
       3   Alisha   ((reading worksheet)) "In nineteen forty-six."

4	Mary	What is number one, I do not get it.
5		Oh!
6	Alisha	((impatient)) ONE.
7	Mary	Oh.
8	Alisha	Write the one there.
9	Mary	Huh?
10	Alisha	I ain't put no three right there!
11	Mary	((laughs))
12		I did that.
13	Alisha	I put the two, and I put the three.
14	Mary	Oh!
15	Alisha	The two is right here where that ((inaudible)) at.
16	Mary	((annoyed)) Okay! Okay!

5.2   "I'm smart"

17	Alisha	I'm smart.
18	Mary	No you're not.
19	Alisha	Girl shut up!
		((10 s.))

5.3   Singing, dance class, and fighting

20	Alisha	((singing)) He wa:s, on her-
21	Mary	((inaudible)) girl she said you-
22	Alisha	((singing)) You-you gotta go, to dance class today!
23		((performed laughter)) Ha ha ha:h!
24	Mary	No I don't.
25	Alisha	You ain't going?
26	Mary	I don't-I mean, I don't wanna end up fighting. Cos
27		I'm fighting.
28	Alisha	That little girl?
29		((disbelief)) Yeah, right!
30	Mary	((inaudible)) I was, ((inaudible)) see how she
31		acting, when she-when she come today, when she
32		come up in my face.
33		((sounds of eraser contacting worksheet)) She kept
34		messing with me, so I said, "Who do you think you
35		is?"
		((5 seconds silence))

5.4   Alisha calls Mary "slow"

| 35 | Alisha | ((sucks teeth)) You so slow! |
| 36 | Mary | Girl, I'm only erasing that thing I put on my paper! |

Sections 5.2 and 5.4 mark transitional moments in the conversation where Alisha puts the main topics on pause, the task itself (Section 5.1) and social talk (Section 5.3), to evaluate her intellect contrastively, against Mary's: Alisha claims to be smart while Mary is claimed to be slow. Mary attempts to save face in both

instances by denying Alisha's claim to smartness (line 18) and defending the accusation of slowness by explaining to Alisha that she is correcting an answer by erasing what she had written (line 36). Such verbal contests were not uncommon to the after school students, nor were the open comparison of grades when advisory reports (report cards) came back from school. In extract 4, Felisha had been showing her report to Alisha and Joseph, who had rushed over to take a look at it when she had pulled it out of her backpack.

All of the students seemed perpetually concerned about who was smartest, who could get their homework done the fastest, and, more often than not, how many words someone knew compared to someone else. They often introduced off-the-cuff challenges to a recipient, as in the following extract. Joseph and Deandre had walked over to J.J. while he was completing his homework, scrutinized his worksheet, and noted that he had not completed one of the answers. Joseph then claims that J.J. does not know the answer (line 1):

6. "You don't know these words"
    1 Joseph   You don't know this one.
    2 J.J.   Yes I do I was just skipping it on my paper.
                   ((5 seconds silence))
    3 Deandre   You don't know these words.
    4 J.J.   Yes I do! I do ((inaudible))!
    5   ((inaudible))
    6 J.J.   ((offering to demonstrate)) Both of these?
    7 Deandre   This one.
    8   A:nd this one.

Joseph and Deandre force J.J. into the position of explaining why his answer is blank and verbally demonstrating that he knows the words they are pointing out. J.J.'s denials in lines 2 and 4 indicate that the other two boys have introduced a face-threatening claim.

While I have noticed that students of any elementary or middle-school age at any school participated in "smartness" contests, and while I did so myself as a child, the after school students seemed to do so with much more frequency and urgency, as in extract 6. To explain further, Joseph and Deandre had taken a detour on their way to the box of Lego pieces they had been walking toward to inspect J.J.'s work. Moreover, both boys struggled with reading at grade level while J.J. did not. J.J. also was frequently rewarded for high grades and model behavior at school, in the form of paper certificates and verbal praise from the after school instructors. I wondered, then, about Joseph and Deandre's motivation in attempting to level J.J., especially since many of the students who did not meet performance standards in school displayed similar actions.

As also illustrated in extract 6, the students defined language and literacy according to school-based norms (i.e., "not knowing words"), and their uncritical acceptance of what it means to be able to read and speak properly merits further analysis.

While their baseline speech style matches what (Labov 1972) and Baugh (1983) define as vernacular styles of AAL, the students often strove to master what adults considered to be proper speech, citing reasons such as doing well in school and to get a job (see chapter 2).

To provide an example, I once witnessed and captured on the digital voice recorder Makaila telling Mr. Morris a story about how two boys had "foughted" at school. "Foughted?" Mr. Morris asked disbelievingly, eyebrows raised. "'Foughted' is not a word." Makaila paused shyly as she considered her options. "Fighted?" she offered hesitantly. At this point, Raymond had come over and repeated Mr. Morris's correction. "'Fighted' is not a word," he stated sternly. A few students, not having overheard Makaila's first choice, called over to try and help her: "Foughted!" each of them declared. After a few more seconds of publicly exchanging looks to convey the seriousness of the linguistic transgression, Raymond finally told the students, "Fought. 'Fought' is the correct word."

Here, I want to pause and explain the two men's imposition of what linguists call a *prescriptive* language ideology, which holds that there is a correct way to speak and that to do so is desirable. Prescriptivism, in other words, uncritically sponsors the idea that there is an objectively existing set of standard/proper linguistic forms. But linguists who sponsor a *descriptive* language ideology, which sees language variation as a natural effect of social and political stratification, would see Makaila as applying a logical rule to past tense formation: she attached the *-ed* suffix to the irregular past tense of fight ("fought"). Hence, we get the form *fought + -ed*. Note that two other students produced this form as well, which means that "foughted" is a possible indicator of hypercorrection, in which speakers of stigmatized languages overgeneralize a linguistic rule in order to sound correct. Hypercorrection is especially common among AAL speakers, who tend to overgeneralize hyperstigmatized AAL features, such as final t/d deletion with consonant clusters (Baugh 1983; Rickford & McNair-Knox 1994). Thus, while forms such as *foughted* or *picked-ed* are perceived as linguistically deviant speech and the speaker is assumed to lack education and exposure to "proper" English, hypercorrection actually indicates awareness of standard grammatical rules as well as heightened awareness to racio-linguistic stigma.

Similarly, when Matt, another instructor, or I would pronounce a word for a student who was struggling to read aloud, they would often try and mimic our phonological patterns as closely as possible rather than say the word according to their own AAL phonology. I noticed this especially with eight-year-old Keri, a fluent reader who, for example, once stumbled on the word "pirate." "Pirate [pai:rIt]," she repeated after I had said the word, exaggerating and elongating the diphthong /ai/. To explain the /ai/ sound would normally be reduced to an intermediate monoph-thongal sound in AAL. When reading with other students, I noticed that they often pronounced words like "mother" and "father" using a rhotic final /r/ rather than the vocalized variant common to AAL, in which the /r/ sound is reduced and otherwise modify their phonological habits to sound more proper.

All of the students, without exception, reconstructed school-normative ideas about intelligence and achievement by defining both in relation to what counts as knowledge and evidence of learning. They were more likely to complain about and refuse to do assignments when they were given out as work to do, and in connection with punishing students for having attitudes. Even though I personally found the schoolwork they brought with them to be incredibly rote and boring, most students diligently plugged away at reading comprehension worksheets with titles like, "Animals in Winter." Such assignments, which were assigned in the attempt to produce results on the high-stakes tests that would determine their reading proficiency, taught students to learn the names of creatures and landscapes few people encounter in real life. Thus, the literacy practices at school, in terms of teaching and content, rarely built on what students knew or experienced. Yet many still expressed enthusiasm for having learned something new and unfamiliar, such as the names of exotic animals.

I am not trying to make the case that students should not be taught about people and places that they might never encounter. I am after all, an anthropologist. I simply wish to note for the purposes of this chapter that the enthusiasm for learning that I witnessed among my students, as well as they ways in which they tried to advocate for themselves, often gets lost at the level of teaching, policy, and research when the school-based terms for intelligence and academic performance are uncritically accepted as neutral measures of what African American students are capable of and willing to do.

READING AND THE CONSTRUCTION OF LITERATE SELVES: AVOIDING STEREOTYPE THREAT

One area of intense competition about smartness among students occurred in the family literacy program during a group activity we called "reading aloud." In both after school programs, the preadolescents and early teens were classified as reading below grade level. Many had trouble reading intermediate to advanced picture books, and a few had trouble with basic-level picture books. This was especially the case with several of the boys who came to the family literacy program. Not only were the nine- to thirteen-year-old boys typed as struggling readers, they were also the most targeted for having attitudes, being off task, and misbehaving.

Matt and I frequently gathered the five or so boys as a small group to practice reading aloud during the hour that most students did their homework, usually because they claimed that they had not been assigned any homework in school. Many came to the program to play games or watch YouTube videos on the computers. The routine compromise Matt and I tried, often unsuccessfully, was to read aloud with them for twenty minutes before they got on a computer or played with the Legos, another preferred activity of theirs. Reading aloud was rarely a successful activity. This was not only because the boys developed avoidance strategies during the activity, but also because some of the other students in the program would draw attention to their stigmatized status as "not being able to read."

Reading aloud was practiced as a public forum in the sense that one had to perform the act of reading aloud for evaluation and critique. If only for this reason, reading aloud could introduce a significant amount of face threat, especially if a student struggled to pronounce words aloud "correctly." More often than not, the students themselves heightened the stakes of face threat: fluent readers, such as Keri or Rashid, both from the younger set of students, often tried to control or dominate the activity by correcting students who struggled or reading over their turn for them. As I show with several examples, reading aloud set the stage for students to recruit racial and gender stereotypes about who could read and who could not. Over the course of the year, the nine- to thirteen-year-old boys came to inhabit the stigmatized identity of being illiterate and resistant Others, in distinct contrast to the readers who displayed their status as "being able to read," which formed the basis for the construction of an identity position I call "literate selves."

Commonly, reading group participants spent up to the total amount of time set aside for the activity negotiating how to proceed. It was often difficult for instructors to maintain strict turn-by-turn reading sequences. Stronger readers showed competitive behaviors that undercut or marginalized less skilled participants: they attempted to choose books that were too difficult for most others and quickly offered verbal corrections or took whole turns when the others hesitated in making out the words on the page. The less skilled readers, for their part, sometimes feigned distraction—for example, bringing Lego pieces or personal games to the activity table with them—or participating in side conversations instead of performing the task of reading aloud until an instructor could coax him into joining the round robin turn-taking sequence.

Extract 7, which is extracted from a total seven-and-a-half-minute conversation that preceded the actual task of reading aloud, is a sequence of talk that was typical of reading group dynamics. Andre and Lenny, both thirteen-year-old boys, struggled to read. Thirteen-year-old J.J., ten-year-old Malcolm, and seven-year-old Rashid did not struggle to read but had joined the group. Keri attempted to join as well. As the extract shows, the students argue about who is to read first and how turn-taking should proceed as I try to retain control of this decision-making process:

  7. Reading aloud
     1   Jen   'Kay. Who's-Andre, you wanna go next?
     2   J.J.   Me!
     3   Rashid   I will go next!
     4   ((begins to read aloud))
     5   Andre   ((as Rashid is reading)) Where you at?
     6   Keri   I wanna read!
     7   J.J.   ((to Rashid)) That's rude.
     8   Malcolm   Andre was about to read!

9	Rashid	Mm ((looks down at table, throws book))
10	Jen	Yeah Rashid, you don't claim someone's turn.
11		You go when it's your turn.
12		Andre you wanna read that page?
13	Keri	I wanna read!
14	Jen	[Get a book].
15	J.J.	[He ((Andre)) don't] know how to read.
16	Andre	((sucks teeth)) [Shut up!]
17	Keri	⠀⠀⠀⠀⠀⠀⠀[He don't know] how to read.
18	Jen	You know what, Keri? Find something else to do
19		right now.
20		Okay?
21	Andre	Lenny, you read.
22	Rashid	I wanna read!
23	Jen	Okay. You're gonna have to wait.
24	Rashid	((referring to Lenny)) He don't wanna read!
		((15 seconds later, after a few turns at reading aloud))
25	Lenny	I don't know these words!
26		What's this word?
27	Jen	"Dishwasher."
28		Andre can you read that page please?
29	Rashid	I wanna read!
30	Jen	You guys need to stop! We're reading. We're not
31		talking about,
32		who gets to read and who doesn't.
33	J.J.	((inaudible)) talking about reading, boy! Cos
34		look-
35	Jen	It was the three of us.
36		If you wanna participate, you have to follow,
37		the turn taking, and you have to respect that
38		other people are reading.
39	Andre	I'm after Lenny.
40	Jen	((sighs))
41	J.J.	Go 'head, Andre.
42		Go 'head, Andre.
43	Andre	I'm not reading, I'm just looking.
44	Jen	What?
45	Lenny	It because he don't know how to read.
46	Andre	((sucks teeth)) Shut up!
47	Lenny	You don't know how to read!
48	Andre	I read way better than you.
49	Rashid	((reading the text during talk))
50	Jen	Rashid, stop. Put the book on the table.
51	Lenny	I don't feel like reading.

Note that the debate around turn-taking is structured around students' claims about who should go or not go based on reading ability. After I select Andre to go (line 1), Rashid interjects and claims a turn by beginning to read; I chastise him for being rude (lines 3–4, 7). As I continue to press for Andre leading the activity, J.J. introduces a face threatening claim: that Andre does not know how to read, a claim which Keri echoes (lines 15, 17). In response, Andre attempts to avoid and deflect: he says that he wants to read after Lenny, the other struggling reader of the group (line 21). Rashid notes that Lenny does not want to read, likely as a bid to be chosen for the first turn (line 25). After I try to restructure the activity according to my original plan, J.J. once again provokes Andre ("Go 'head, Andre"), and Andre demurs (lines 41–43). The interaction devolves further when Lenny claims that Andre cannot read and Andre rebuts that he can read "way better than" Lenny (lines 45–48).

Reading groups pitted the students against each other in competitive status contests: they aimed to display to all either that they could read or avoid the embarrassing situation of having to demonstrate quite openly that they could not, depending on how well they performed the activity. It is not surprising then that most of the struggling readers tried to avoid having to do read aloud: in line 39, Andre attempts to give the first turn over to Lenny, who in fact struggled more than Andre. In line 51, after Lenny becomes frustrated at not knowing the words in the book (line 25), he states that he does not feel like reading.

Lenny and Andre were adopting a reading strategy that Monzó and Rueda (2009) refer to as *passing*, which is characterized avoidance, deflection, and feigning disinterest. As Monzó and Rueda argue, "It may be that passing allows students to maintain a sense of dignity while silently waiting for their [literacy] skills to strengthen" (2009, p. 37). Thus, it is not the case here that Lenny and Andre did not want to read, as Rashid claims (line 24), but that reading aloud was an incredibly face-threatening activity for them to participate in.

Extract 7 suggests that students perceived interest and ability in reading to be interconnected; students who could not read were assumed to not want to. This constitutes a recursive construction of the meritocratic view of smartness, achievement, and success. That is to say, students like Lenny and Andre were perceived to be illiterate because they were choosing not to participate in reading aloud.

Yet extract 7 as well as the forthcoming example illustrate how this assumption was locally projected onto students, and that disinterest became a reality when struggling readers came to associate the activity with situational embarrassment. Joseph, for one, was actually incredibly interested in learning to read and persisted, but was often showed up by his older brother, Deandre, and his younger sister, Keri, during reading aloud activities. Both often exploited the fact that Joseph struggled, correcting him to the point of making him upset and using his affective state to construe him as an unwilling or resistant participant. Extract 8 illustrates one such instance. Matt had organized a reading group with Joseph and Malcolm and asked Deandre if he wanted to join. Joseph had been waiting for Matt to begin, reading the text on his own. By the end of the interaction shown next, Deandre upset Joseph to the point that Joseph left the reading group to read a book by himself:

8. Malcolm, Joseph, and Deandre in reading aloud

1	Malcolm	Joseph why you reading already?
2	Joseph	Who?
3	Malcolm	You!
4	Joseph	I wasn't reading boy!
5	Malcolm	Who opened your book?
6	Joseph	Me!
7	Malcolm	You WAS reading then!
8	Matt	You wanna join us Deandre? [Isn't] there another
9		one of these?
10	Joseph	((sucks teeth)) [NO!]
11	Malcolm	Up there. [Yes it is. It's the brown books.]
12	Joseph	[Dang. No! I don't want him to read
13		with us.]
14	Matt	[Chill.]
15	Deandre	[((puts on whining as if Joseph))]
16		[((continues whining))]
17	Joseph	I don't want him to read with us.
18	Matt	Why? What's the deal? Why don't you want to
19		read with Deandre?
20	Deandre	((stops whining)) He think Imma correct him.
21	Matt	Don't correct him.
21	Joseph	I don't like when he reads.
22	Malcolm	How you ain't gonna like when he read?
23	Joseph	((Deandre takes Joseph's book)) No give it back I
24		had that dang!
25	Ms. Betty	((angry)) Who was that?
26	Jen	[J h h oseph h h]
27	Deandre	[Joseph].
28		He mad cuz Im about to read.

We see in extract 8 that Joseph began the activity interested in reading, but was gradually marginalized by everyone as Deandre successfully depicts him as an unwilling and resistant participant. Reasonably, Joseph did not like being corrected by Deandre, because Deandre often used reading corrections to embarrass Joseph, as did his younger sister, Keri, as shown in extract 9:

9   Joseph, Keri, and Rashid reading together

1	Joseph	Keri stop reading fast!
2	Keri	((keeps reading))

3	Rashid	Where she at?
4	Keri	((keeps reading))
5	Joseph	Stop reading fast! Stop.
6		Rashid don't know where you at!
7	Keri	Oh right here.
8	Rashid	Where this at?
9	Keri	It's ((inaudible)) on five.
10		One, two, three, four, five. Right here.
11	Rashid	Right here?
12	Keri	Yeah.
		((reads for 30 seconds))
13	Rashid	Where she at again?
14	Keri	((reading aloud))
15	Jen	((to Rashid)) Come sit by me. We-we'll read it together.
16	Joseph	Wait wait! Is ain't your go!
17		IS AIN'T YOUR GO!
18	Jen	Keri, we're just doing paragraphs. ((explains what a paragraph is))
19		You wanna go, Joseph?
20	Joseph	Rashid.
21	Jen	Rashid.
22	Joseph	Go 'head, Rashid.
23		((Keri reads for him every time he pauses))
24	Jen	Give him a chance, Keri.
25		You need to slow down.
		((two minutes later, Joseph's turn))
26	Keri	((reads Joseph's turn)) They. Broke.
27	Joseph	They-wait, girl!
28	Keri	You don't know how to read!
29	Joseph	((ignores Keri, reads text))

Unlike Lenny and Deandre in extract 7 and unlike in extract 8, where he becomes upset and leaves the group, Joseph is trying to advocate for himself as well as for Rashid, who cannot follow along due to Keri's rapid reading pace. I try to help Joseph temper Keri's showing off, which not only includes reading rapidly, but also taking others' turns and preemptively correcting Joseph. Joseph's reading cadence was relatively slower, and Keri often used it as an opportunity to read the word for him (lines 25–27). And when Joseph tells her to wait, she levels the claim, "You don't know how to read!" (line 28). Still, Joseph persists by ignoring her and continuing to read.

Unlike the other students who were stigmatized as illiterate Others, Joseph did not adopt passing strategies to mask the fact that he did not know how to read. As shown in extract 10, he not only claimed an alternative identity as a potential reader in the making, but also disrupted the reader/nonreader binary identity model by introducing a collaborative reading aloud logic: "Words that you don't know, we prob'ly know . . . . The words that we don't know you prob'ly know" (lines 13, 16):

10. Giving others a chance to read

1	Joseph	You don't even give nobody the chance to read!
2	Jen	Yeah Keri, you need to be quiet when other
3		people are reading.
		((6 minutes of reading aloud))
4	Keri	((has trouble pronouncing "cutlass"))
5	Joseph	See that's why you don't never 'posed to correct
6		nobody.
7	Keri	((sucks teeth)) I still know how to
8		read!
9	Jen	Everybody here knows how to read. You're just
10		impatient and you're rude. You don't let people
11		take their turns.
12	Keri	I was telling him what to-
13	Joseph	Words that, you don't know, we [prob]ly know.
14	Keri	[Uh-HUH!]
15		Yes I DO know.
16	Joseph	The words that we don't know you prob'ly
17		know.

Extracts 8–10 suggest that the students who participated in reading groups typically drew on different passing strategies as well as *fronting*, in which students pretend to be more fluent than they are in reading and other literacy-based activities (Monzó & Rueda 2009) in order to avoid being stereotyped as illiterate. The situated evaluations about others and self-positioning students took up in specific reading interactions led to a general situation in which struggling readers were consistently marginalized from the activity, despite the fact that instructors, myself included, tried to use the activity to help them specifically. It was rare for students like Joseph to persist at the goal of learning how to read in light of the fact that it was incredibly face threatening for students to be typed as illiterate by peers. Ironically, students' attempts to resist or avoid the stereotype threat of being typed as illiterate assisted, in one sense, precisely the opposite outcome: students were not learning how to read according to school-based measures.

From this set of examples related to reading aloud, it is evident that students not only respond to, but recursively constitute racial stereotypes of African American students as unable to read, and as unable to read because they are unwilling to do so. But with the concepts of passing and fronting, Monzó and Rueda present an alternative interpretation: students do not lack interest. Rather, they seek to avoid stigma and retain a sense of personal dignity. I also interpret skilled readers' use of FTAs such as "You can't read!" as a passing strategy that is rooted in the very real possibility of being racially read according to normative stereotypes themselves. In other words, they are also likely seeking to avoid stereotype threat by projecting those stereotypes outwards onto others in order to constitute themselves as socially desirable figure-types (Reyes 2017).

DISCUSSION

At the end of their study on Latino immigrant children, Monzó and Rueda present the idea of students taking on English-fluent identities as a way of developing "possible selves." As they explain:

> It may be that by figuring the world of English fluency and taking on the roles of English fluent by passing, children are learning about identities associated with English fluency and perhaps developing hoped-for "possible selves" (Osyerman et al. 2006). Possible selves refer to an individual's self-relevant expectations for the future. These possible selves include what a person hopes to become, expects to become, and fears that he or she might become. Hoped-for possible selves provide the individual with futures to dream or fantasize about. (2009, p. 37)

I want to use their critical reframing of passing strategies to suggest that in order to create their own hoped-for possible selves, students recursively projected received racial stereotypes about African Americans as unwilling or resistant learners onto others. They used school-normative definitions of compliance, intelligence, achievement, and language/literacy to individuate themselves within meritocratic definitions of being a model student—for example, good students "choosing" to do work or being literate because one is interested in reading. I argue that instead of examining this process as an ideological failure or misrecognition (i.e., "internalization" of commonsense ideology), we should approach it as an instrumental and locally useful tactic students used to avoid stereotype threat and claim institutionally valued identities. Students were not simply interested in learning for learning's sake; they were eager to claim the kinds of status afforded individuals who are determined to be smart and learned in school, from parents, older siblings, and peers that they would have to avoid racial stigma in order to achieve such a status.

The question remains, then, are students challenging raciolinguistic normativity in their recursive constructions of racial stereotypes? Perhaps not in the long run. In her study of French Algerian teens, Tetreault argues, "Using stereotypes in interaction can be a powerful means of exerting social control, as well as a way to have fun and even play . . . although re-voicing stereotypes can be a powerful way to get things done in interactions, their larger critical power remains ambiguous, in that they can naturalize experiences of racism and prejudice even when condemning them" (2016, p. 61). As is hopefully evident in my analysis of situated interactions, participants try to transform racial stereotypes even as they recruit them in their struggle to make sense of what they mean. And perhaps the recursive recirculation of stereotypes is less about what students believe to be true about themselves and others, and more about what is most locally useful and empowering as they construct hoped-for possible selves. As I explore further in chapter 6, effective critical pedagogies can help students participate in the goal of raciolinguistic transformation when it is used to shed light on their definitions and goals for social justice.

NOTES

1. Some readers may wonder why I choose to interpret the teacher's remark to the students as the application of a respectability discourse rather than as an act of linguistic racism. As mentioned in the ethnographic description, the teacher was also African American. From the perspective of critical race theory, people who are presumed to share racial identities in common and who recruit racialized meanings to create identities at the in-group level may sponsor prejudicial views rooted in racism, such as with the prevalence of colorism among African American elites (Graham 2003; Prince 2014), but are not in and of themselves capable of facilitating the kinds of structural domination and oppression that results from white racism (e.g., Omi & Winant 1994).

2. I do not mean to imply that there is a tension between a dialectically conceptualized "structure/agency," but rather that local practices of resistance often lead to the reproduction of oppression rather than effecting change on a large scale. For a nuanced discussion of what it means to exercise "agency," see Ahearn (2001).

6

Race, Literacy, and Power

Learning from Children about Educational Justice

Thus far, this book has described the language and identity practices of a group of children who ultimately attempted to participate in schooling on their own terms. A major part of this process involved transforming the raciolinguistic ideologies of deficit that presented them with impossible choices with respect to achieving in school. Race was an unavoidable social fact defining their existence in the world and for this reason, it figured centrally as an organizing principle of their identity models.

In the last phase of my fieldwork, I tried to practice critical pedagogy with the students to see if it made a noticeable difference in their schooling experiences, specifically in the way that they recognized themselves as legitimate producers of meaning and practice. Critical pedagogy is a theory of educational practice that places primacy on both teachers and students unlearning the structures, practices, and curriculum of normative schooling. As someone who was interested in helping students unlearn the oppressive ideas they encountered at school and in after school about language and literacy, I focused my efforts on developing activities centered on the topics of language variation and change. I drew from studies and lessons grounded in critical sociolinguistics, with the goal of getting students to see language change and variation as natural and desirable and also to recognize oppressive language ideologies for what they were. Ultimately, I wanted my students to have more tools at their disposal to interrupt language pedagogies of oppression, such as ones grounded in deficit-based language ideologies (Blackburn 2005; Godley & Minnici 2008). In proceeding with this project, I had the full endorsement of the organization's founders, parents, and local community members who heard about the activities I did from the students. The students, for their part, enjoyed some of what I had designed, but did not always finish lessons or carry them forward.

As I explain in this chapter, I believe that my efforts to do critical pedagogy partially failed. I, like other educators, was under enormous pressure to make sure

117

that students could pass their standardized tests in reading and writing. At the same time, I did not realize the ways in which critical pedagogical concepts such as "empowerment" and "critical reflection" continue to sponsor oppressive teaching practices (Ellsworth 1989). Moreover, I was not attuned to the ways in which students already brought a critical *translingual sensibility* to their learning, defined as the application of metalinguistic reflection and a critical bending of monoglossic language ideologies (Seltzer 2017). While I believed that the students were already engaging in critical thinking, I continued to work from the deficit-based position that students needed a "bridge" to academic language and literacy skills. I argue that my experience doing critical pedagogy in the after school program is evidence of how liberal and progressive teaching, while making well-intended efforts to help students overcome structural inequality can simply become a new conduit for historically colonizing processes, such as speaking for the Other (Spivak 1988; Ellsworth 1989). This chapter critically interrogates the critical pedagogy I practiced with the after school students and, consistent with the raciolinguistic perspective I hope to offer in this book, suggests that educators must recognize the ways in which students are already engaged in the work of racial transformation and social justice.

WHAT IS CRITICAL PEDAGOGY AND WHAT SHOULD IT BE?

Critical pedagogy is widely understood to have originated from the work of Paolo Freire's seminal text, *Pedagogy of the Oppressed* (1970). According to Freire, critical pedagogy aims to help practitioners move away from a teaching model in which the teacher deposits knowledge into the metaphorical empty bank of the students' mind. Rather, teachers must learn to recognize the ways in which they learn from students and conversely, students must learn to recognize how they are legitimate producers of knowledge.

Critical pedagogy has wide theoretical and practical applications. While many theorize it broadly as a way of teaching in general (Cochran-Lytle & Smith 2008; Gee 2012), some scholars use it to help young children name and navigate social injustice (Vasquez 2002), help minoritized communities act against oppression (Luke 1999; Janks 2003), or to develop culturally relevant pedagogies for students of color attending urban schools (Ladson-Billings 1994; Duncan-Andrade & Morrell 2008). Consistent with a raciolinguistic perspective, a growing number of researcher-practitioners see critical pedagogy's role as interrogating the continued workings of white supremacy in educational settings (Ladson-Billings 1994; Emdin 2016; Alim & Paris 2017). This means investigating how educators center whiteness in their teaching despite their efforts to help students value and use their cultural and linguistic practices in the classroom.

Critical pedagogues working from the perspective of *culturally sustaining pedagogies* (Alim & Paris 2017) and a raciolinguistic perspective note that pluralist approaches, which aim to create a space for students to value their "home languages" nevertheless sponsor assimilatory models of schooling. This means that educators often believe that while racially minoritized students' languages are of value, they also believe that these students lack the cultural and linguistic tools they need to participate in the "mainstream" and achieve success. Studies of bi- and multilingual classrooms disclose that even the most well-intentioned liberal and progressive educators hear and see racially minoritized students as needing to acquire "standard" or "academic" language (Flores & Rosa 2015; Alim & Paris 2017; Love 2018; Flores 2020). Furthermore, as Ellsworth (1989) notes from her own experiences teaching as a college professor, that many critical pedagogues adopt a "posture of invisibility" to define social justice in the service of a progressive agenda that they believe is best for everyone, but in fact center in white ("Western") values and models of personhood. Thus, despite the fact that many critical pedagogues believe in creating space to value students' linguistic and cultural practices, their underlying assumption is that white middle-class views, values, and interests are best equipped to help them do so.

Pluralist approaches in critical pedagogy also presume that students' linguistic and cultural practices do not include anything related to what is taught in school and in the so-called mainstream. As a result, these students are often asked to master academic language or Standard English while also performing "authentic" selves that are rooted in whites' stereotypical ideas about raciolinguistic difference (Guerra 2016; Chaparro 2019; Rosa 2019). Often, the core assumption is that the authentic linguistic identity for bilingual or multilingual students is their "home language," that linguistic forms or discourse styles typically considered standard, academic, or "mainstream" are somehow absent from what they do and say in their everyday lives, and that they need to be taught how to use these forms and styles. It should be obvious by this point that such neutralized terms for what students "need" or "lack" center whiteness.

As I argue in the introduction, monoglossic language ideologies that draw strict boundaries between "standard" and "non-standard" languages conceptualize racially minoritized people's languages as deficient in line with nationalist ideologies of belonging to the nation-state. The preceding chapters of this book have shown that the after school students' linguistic and cultural practices are inherently fluid, hybrid, and, importantly, aligned to the goals of schooling. This chapter documents my reflections on practicing critical pedagogy with the after school students and my realization that I had unwittingly sponsored the pitfalls and traps I have just described earlier. In the process, I revisited their writing and art projects and learned that their translingual sensibilities were much more sophisticated than I had realized at the time. In concluding this chapter, I discuss further why a raciolinguistic and translingual perspective is essential to helping students of color navigate and disrupt racism

Practicing Critical Pedagogy: A Lesson about Math

Finding an effective critical pedagogy to practice with the after school students was the goal from the time I first began my volunteer work and later, teaching and research, with Urban Pathways. During my fieldwork, I briefly halted the critical pedagogy I had been doing with the students to collect data. As I explain in the introduction, I had planned to reintroduce it in the last phase of research to see if it would make a noticeable difference in how the students interacted in the after school space. I introduced the lessons I planned to do to Victor, the students' parents, and other after school staff as well as the rationale for doing them. Generally, everyone was supportive of my project, but many expressed the view that critical pedagogy should be reserved for times when students were not doing their homework or more "traditional" modes of learning. After all, what was the point of teaching critical thinking if students could not read basic letters and sounds? That is to say, most staff felt that critical pedagogy was ultimately not as effective in helping students learn how to read or in preparing them for high-stakes standardized tests because they considered critical thinking to be a higher-level skill that could not be developed before more rote styles of learning.

Doing critical pedagogy with the students was therefore not considered a priority in the after school space. And when it was supported, it often got folded back into deficit perspectives, such as "giving" students critical thinking skills that they were presumed to lack. Victor, the founder and executive director of Urban Pathways, was extremely supportive of my efforts and often proposed his own ideas to me for what he thought would benefit students. But in discussing his ideas, I quickly learned that Victor believed students needed to be given the conceptual tools and lessons to think critically. For instance, he once asked me to design a math curriculum to help students learn how to budget money. The math lesson was certainly relevant in terms of core skill, but the life lesson was useless for the kind of sharp poverty the students and their families lived in: they had nothing to put aside. Moreover, as I often witnessed, students already had a sense of needing to save, to keep their more expensive items like shoes and winter coats clean for future use by someone else if not themselves, and to only take what they needed and nothing more.

The following story illustrates further that children have critical thinking skills (which they may or may not learn from adults but then use them for their own purposes), that they use them to navigate their particular life circumstances, and that they are often misrecognized as needing to gain those skills from adults (Vasquez 2002). During one trip to the local Giant grocery store, Alisha noticed a value deal for a bigger packet of Hostess snacks and told the group that we should buy the bigger size rather than two of the smaller ones, proudly noting that we would save a small sum of our snack budget. But her older brother Joseph disagreed: he had looked at the fine print on the shelf label and figured out the cost by weight in his head. He explained to Alisha that the value price was a trick and that we should buy two of the smaller packets as originally planned. While they argued, I did the math in my head and realized that Joseph had been right. I was astounded: Joseph had been in a remedial math class at school since I had known him, and we often spent at least the whole hour of homework time doing multiple line addition and subtraction problems. But he had exactly the kind of critical math skills he needed to calculate costs on a severely limited amount of money.

A *culturally relevant* or *culturally sustaining* pedagogy recognizes that teachers need to recognize the assets racially minoritized students bring to the classroom and use them to develop lessons that address and help them act with more agency given their lived experiences (Ladson-Billings 1994; Alim & Paris 2017). Had I followed

Victor's suggestion on the math lesson, I would have been teaching a mistargeted lesson that might have made the students feel irresponsible and at fault for being poor. Working from a critical pedagogical perspective instead would mean first taking note of students' math skills, where they got them from and why, and developing appropriate lessons, such as cost calculations at the grocery store. Scaffolded lessons could have included helping students recognize how and why grocery stores try to convince people that they are buying deals when they are really not and if this is common across different store chains or even neighborhoods. Perhaps building even further into a learning unit, I could have helped students further investigate predatorial corporate practices in urban neighborhoods and coauthor a report or petition. For anyone who doubts that such a lesson is possible with children, note that Vasquez (2002) and her kindergarten class wrote stories about animal injustice, authored a petition, and wrote a letter to McDonald's asking them to change gender-biased Happy Meal toys in the space of a school year.

Lamentably, I did not have enough time to develop such a math unit given my other teaching activities for the year. But I do hope anyone reading this chapter finds a good lesson idea, if not pedagogical perspective, to start with. Even though in the case of math I recognized the application of a deficit perspective to the students, I myself unwittingly practiced deficit thinking in my critical language pedagogy with the after school students during the last phase of my fieldwork. Moreover, my own language ideology at the time, which was grounded in a monoglossic view of languages and discourse styles, prevented me from fully seeing the translingual and transcultural sensibilities that students brought to their writing and art projects. As an institutionalized listening subject, there are a few other shortcomings that happened in my critical language pedagogy. The section to follow describes what I did, my reflections, and analyzes students' work in the interest of showing that students are creating a (potential) critical pedagogy even in the absence of teacher guidance or cueing.

TRANSLINGUAL SENSIBILITIES AND THE AUTHENTIC SELF: DISRUPTING MONOGLOSSIC LANGUAGE IDEOLOGIES AND RACIALIZED NOTIONS OF DIFFERENCE

As I described in chapter 2, most of the students anchored their notions of identity and style in hip hop. For this reason, I decided to theme my critical learning pedagogy around hip-hop as other educators working with urban youth have done (Alim 2004; Duncan-Andrade & Morrell 2008). Using prior work on critical language pedagogy (Blackburn 2005; Godley & Minnici 2008), my goal was to teach students about language variation and change, help them identify and critique oppressive language ideologies, and help them produce a hip-hop final project that showed evidenced of their learning key concepts in sociolinguistics. I used video clips and websites from the PBS series *Do You Speak American?* as well as political speeches from different Black politicians, such as Jesse Jackson and Barack Obama, to have students engage in critical discussions about what it means to code-switch and why people do it. My plan was to scaffold those lessons into a hip-hop project that would show students' knowledge of baseline concepts such as code-switching and grammar, and to shift them away from prescriptive language ideologies.

Unfortunately, the activity did not go as planned. From the time I began the unit, students showed signs of boredom and impatience. Though we used forms of technology that they were interested in, which included computers and my audio recording device, students resisted watching the video clips and filling out the worksheets. I believe that this is because I had routinized an everyday activity the students practiced for pleasure and made it work. While hip-hop was something they listened to and practiced for fun in their everyday lives, they did not want to necessarily recruit it into their academic learning activities.

In reflecting on this project, I believe I made a mistake by deciding how I thought students should be culturally validated without their input and without having drawn from the other interests they had expressed to me in terms of their language and identity practices. As I described in chapter 2, the students had multiple kinds of linguistic styles and music genres they enjoyed working with to style their identities. Thus, their ideas about what it means to be Black drew from, but were not centered in, hip-hop exclusively.

Reflecting even further, I was working from a monoglossic perspective to think about what it meant for the students to code-switch: while slang and proper were ideologically distinct and bounded languages for me and even for the students, this did not match the reality of how they manipulated and blended codes in their everyday lives. As prior chapters have shown, translanguaging practices were just as common as styleshifting from slang to proper and vice versa.

Thus, the students were probably bored because I was trying to teach them something they already knew intimately: the power of speaking in particular ways in different settings. From my monoglossic perspective, I assumed that the preadolescent students were finding their way toward more adeptly shifting between AAL and "standard" English, and I also assumed that they needed help in feeling empowered to speak AAL in an academic setting. Thus, I imagined students' "authentic selves" to be grounded in vernacular and expressive styles of AAL and any engagement with "standard" English to be a performance of assimilation. I presumed that validating AAL as a language using the tools of sociolinguistics would give them "an identity and political position from which to act as agents of social change" (Ellsworth 1989). In reality, their translanguaging practices already evidenced their attempts to do so (Guerra 2016; Seltzer 2017; Flores 2020).

In my sincere attempt to help students "feel empowered," I overdetermined their raciolinguistic subjectivity and fell into a liberal/progressive pitfall: seeing my students as wholly different, linguistically and culturally, from anything white and mainstream. In other words, my idea of what it meant for students to be Black in a school-based setting was terribly stereotypical, and this could have been avoided by first allowing students to identify what they found interesting about language and how they used it and working from a learning agenda that they defined.

A few weeks into the unsuccessful hip-hop project, I did finally think to ask the students what interested them about language. I found that their interests went beyond their own particular lived experiences to encompass a more globally minded curiosity about other languages and societies. Denise and Marcus, both twelve-years old, wrote learning logs about Spanish and French, two languages they told me they were interested in learning to speak. After researching the languages on the activity center computers, they each produced a log that documents their particular interests with regard to each language (figures 6.1 and 6.2):

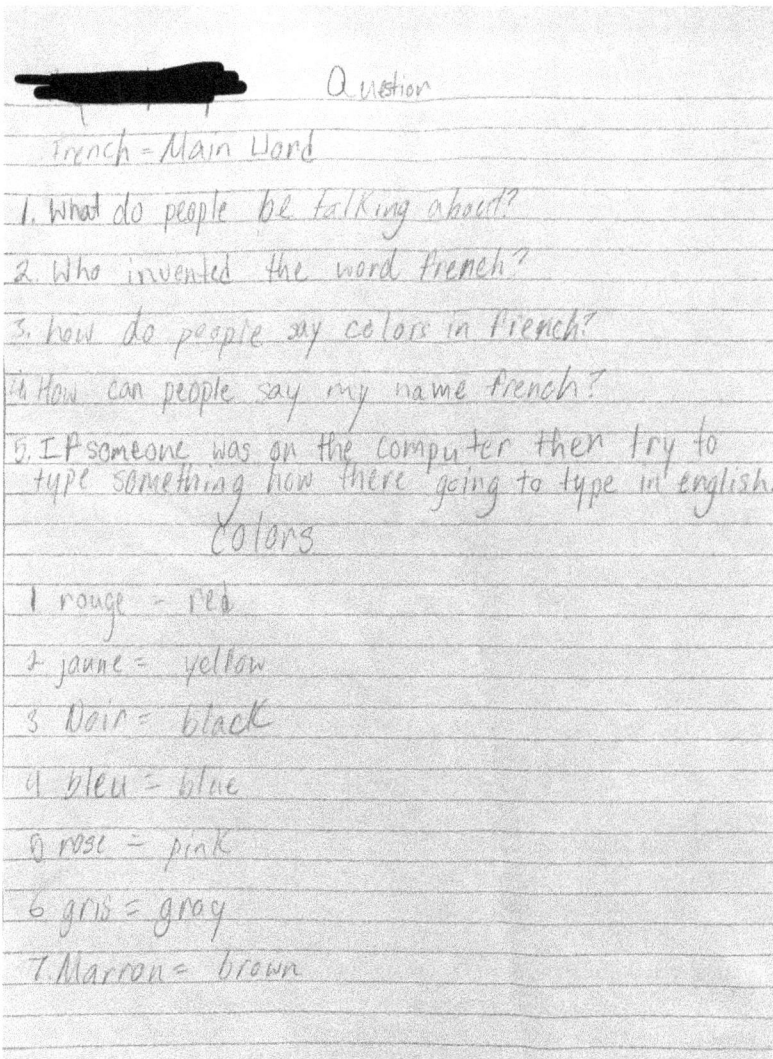

Figure 6.1   Learning Logs for French and Spanish.

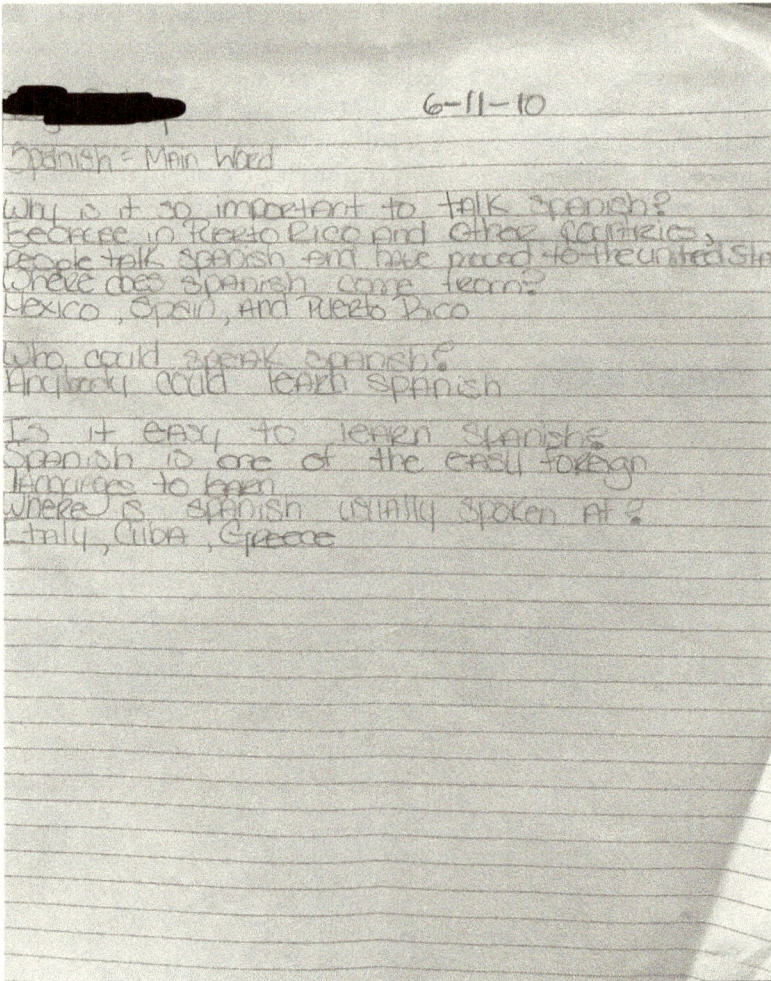

The handwritten learning log reads:

6-11-10

Spanish = Main Word

Why is it so important to talk Spanish?
Because in Puerto Rico and other countries,
people talk Spanish and have proceed to the United Sta
Where does Spanish come from?
Mexico, Spain, and Puerto Rico

Who could speak Spanish?
Anybody could learn Spanish

Is it easy to learn Spanish?
Spanish is one of the easy foreign
languages to learn
Where is Spanish usually spoken at?
Italy, Cuba, Greece

Figure 6.2   Learning Logs for French and Spanish.

While Marcus shows a general interest in the linguistic structures of French, Denise's curiosity about Spanish extends to wanting to be able to communicate with Spanish speakers who come to the United States. In her work figure 6.2, she promotes a pluralist view of language learning that de-centers the hegemonic "English-Only" and bilingual language ideologies governing public and educational spaces (Lippi-Green 2012; Rosa & Flores 2015). Thus, against the normative view that Spanish speakers need to acquire English in order to become American, Denise proposes instead that English speakers should learn Spanish to accommodate the people who "proceed" here. Her language sensibility, which promotes two-way language learning and the more general idea of multiethnic inclusion, goes against the grain of what typically happens in bilingual and two-way immersion programs: the centering of standard English acquisition and the reapplication of deficit perspectives to racialized Spanish speakers (Chaparro 2019).[1]

I do not mean to suggest that there is something wrong with drawing upon school-normative literacy practices. But my example of failure has taught me that a successful critical pedagogy recognizes the translingual and transcultural sensibilities of students and centers them in teaching, even when these sensibilities conflict with the educator's notions of difference and empowerment.

It bears mentioning that my position as an institutionalized listening subject was constrained not just by ideology, but also by the circumstances and contexts in which I was asked to produce "measurable results" for students' language and literacy learning. I had to show evidence that students were prepared for the standardized, high-stakes they took at school in order for the after school program to continue to receive federal and local sources of funding. I was afraid that if I did not use traditional learning formats, that no one would take seriously my efforts or those of the students. I was therefore more concerned with assimilating their cultural interests into these methods rather than drawing from what they already were doing and letting them self-direct more independently within learning activities. It is no accident that my failure happened because I fell into the trap of being more concerned with how the hip-hop project would be institutionally evaluated than how it would benefit the students. As Campano (2007) and Ladson-Billings (2017) have shown, prioritizing student learning tends to produce results regardless of the particular standards put in place that measure what counts as learning in the first place. In the following section, my analysis of students' writing and art projects from a language architecture perspective (Flores 2020).

WHAT SCIENTISTS AND POLITICIANS DO: STUDENTS CONSTRUCTING DISCURSIVE POWER

In addition to critical pedagogy, students participated in science, art, and other informal learning activities. After school learning activities that were not centered on homework help or other projects students brought from school included subjects such as science and politics. Urban Pathways' staff was highly attuned to the fact that instruction at school was increasingly restricted to the subjects of reading and math in order to "teach to the test" and so we, with the help and encouragement of Caleb, Victor's son who taught third-grade science at a DCPS school, developed science activities for the students. In the spring of 2011, Urban Pathways also hired a Howard University graduate student, Keegan, to start a voluntary science program at the community center. The idea was that through hands-on science lessons, students would develop skills in observation, logic, and empirical methods while also building literacy skills in the form of written and oral reporting on their topics or experiments. We believed it would not only increase their exposure to multiple forms of knowledge, but also allow them to engage in experimentation and experiential learning.

One student-generated theme that emerged in activities themed around learning about science and politics was a concern for using both to study injustice and to use positions of expertise and power to act against inequality. As I mentioned in chapter 2, one of the science activities that I led was called, "What Does a Scientist Look Like?" As I show in that chapter, the activity revealed students' transracial

models of power and authority. Science activities also showed evidence of students'
keen awareness of science's applications toward educating the public about social
justice issues, as the following examples show. For example, a major world disaster
that a group of fourth-grade students expressed concern about was the 2010 Haiti
earthquake. They not only drew a scientist who was ameliorating the destruction
caused by the tsunami that followed the earthquake, but they also decided to
author a written report on the topic, shown in figure 6.3. Following figure 6.3, I
have reproduced the report in typeface, following all original text and formatting as
closely as possible so that readers can follow my analysis (line numbers are mine):

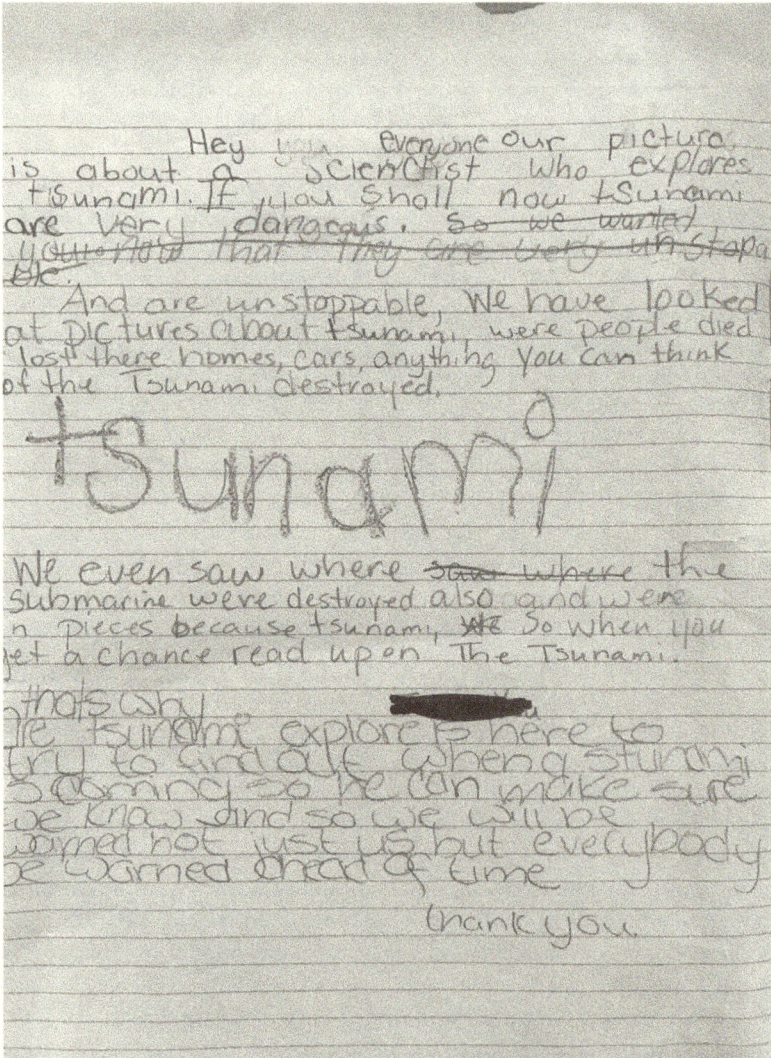

Figure 6.3   Tsunami.

1. Hey ~~you~~ everyone our picture is about a scienctist who explores tsunami. If you shall now
2. tsunami are very dangerous. ~~So we wanted you now that they are very unstopable~~.
3. And are unstoppable, we have looked at pictures about tsunami, were people died lost
4. there homes, cars, anything you can think of the Tsunami destroyed.
5. tsunami
6. We even saw where ~~saw where~~ the submarine were destroyed also and were in pieces
7. because tsunami, ~~We~~ So when you get a chance read upon The Tsunami.
8. That's why ██████████ ←(Thank You)
9. Are tsunami explore is here to try to find out when a tsunami is coming so he can make
10. sure we know and so we will be warned not just us but everybody be warned ahead of
11. time.
12. thank you.

¹This is the text that lay underneath the bolded-out strip.

To many readers, this text as reproduced signals the need for students to learn and use "academic language." However, a *language architecture perspective,* which recognizes how students manipulate language to accomplish a specific purpose (Flores 2020), shows that students are already oriented to the need to convince their audience of the importance of studying tsunamis by using an effective discourse style. But rather than use a monologic strategy, such as sticking to an informational style, the students actually drew on multiple styles of expression in order to argue their point. First, the students were aware that they needed to legitimate their knowledge, expertise, and arguments by detailing their observations. After a friendly greeting, the students begin with a thesis statement, arguing that tsunamis are very dangerous (line 2). To support this claim, the report explains that the scientists studied pictures of the tsunami's aftermath and noted the loss of human lives and property that the disaster engendered (line 3–4). Following is more evidence of what the scientist observed, an appeal for others to research tsunamis, and a concluding argument about its importance: to try and warn others ahead of time, presumably so that people can prepare in advance to mitigate the disaster's effects. Thus, the informational arc of the report follows a school-typical style of scientific reporting: thesis statement, evidence, conclusion, and future directions.

The authors of the report also appear to have attempted a friendly and accessible informational tone, perhaps to draw readers in and build sympathy for the people who had been affected by the disaster. The first line of the text, "Hey ~~you~~ everyone," is corrected for formality and politeness, perhaps to mitigate the pointed aggressiveness implied in the initial construction, "Hey you." Since the report had multiple authors, it is likely that this correction and the ones that follow are a result of students acting as co-authors. A general attempt at politeness, and also humility, is further suggested in the reports closing, in which the authors thank readers. The students, then, draw on evidential statements, evidence, and logic to construct a credible argument, but also recognize the necessity of relating to a general public by balancing this form of authoritative discourse with friendly address terms and politeness. Finally, some of the corrections in the text convey an awareness of school-based prescriptive norms that govern spelling and grammar. The students, then, drew on multiple discourse styles to create a legitimate science report with a logical structure and accessible tone, whose credibility they know rely on academic writing conventions. As evidenced in their creative use of language, the students are aware that one needs to be both knowledgeable and approachable in convincing people to pay attention to important information and to act for the greater good.

In this example, the authors of "Tsunami" are quite literally acting as language architects. As Flores explains:

> Like a building architect, language architects are not free to simply do whateverthey want. If this were the case, buildings would be unsafe and communicative efforts would fail. yet, beyond some broad general parameters both must adhere to in order to successfully complete their tasks, there is a great deal of decision-making that both make that reflect their own unique vision and voice. (2020, p. 25)

A language architecture perspective, then, allows us to see students as already engaged in the kinds of language work teachers and school institutions are asking them to do. Flores notes further, "From this perspective . . . [Common Core and other] state standards are not demanding mastery over academic language, but rather are calling for students to be language architects who are able to manipulate language for specific purposes" (2020, p. 25). The lesson for educators here is to look beyond what is normally considered writing errors or failures and to realize that students are in fact displaying their knowledge of how to use language to achieve a particular purpose.

One of the common themes in students' language architecture practices was the blending and mixing of informal and formal styles of writing. This is evident in Delonte's "Mayor Election" essay and in a creative project Matt designed and called, "If I Were President of the United States," in which students were asked to draw and write about what they would do in that role. To explain, at the time of my fieldwork, there were two major events that had shaped students' interest and involvement in politics and what it could do: the 2008 election of President Barack Obama and the upcoming 2010 mayoral election, the latter of which followed the locally debated merits of what turned out to be Adrian Fenty's first and only term as city mayor. As I described in chapter 1, Mayor Fenty had been widely perceived among the city's African American communities to be pro-gentrification in ways that benefited whites and which did not serve their interests (see also Prince 2014). During the time of the 2010 election, Vincent Gray, a Ward 7 resident, was perceived to be the mayoral candidate who would promote the interests, perspectives, and concerns of African Americans, especially those who lived in Southeast and other Black-majority neighborhoods.[2] Ten year-old Delonte Reed wrote a personal essay about why he would vote for Vincent Gray, noting that he had placed a bet with his mother about who would win the "Mayor Election":

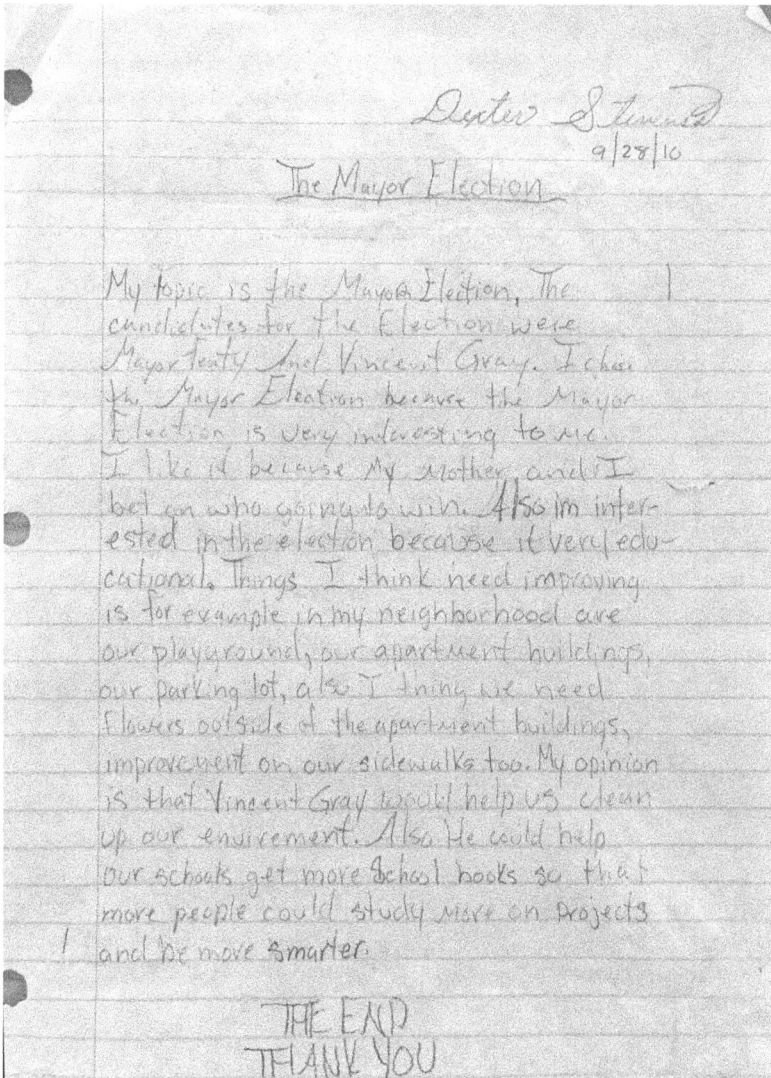

Figure 6.4   The Mayor Election.

Delonte Reed
9/28/10

The Mayor Election

My topic is the Mayor Election. The candidates for the Election were Mayor
Fenty and Vincent Gray. I chose the Mayor Election because the Mayor Election
is very interesting to me. I like it because my mother and I bet on who going
to win. Also I'm interested in the election because it very educational. Things I
think I need improving is for example in my neighborhood are our playground,
our apartment buildings, improvement on our sidewalks too. My opinion is that
Vincent Gray would help us clean up our envirement. Also He could help our
schools get more School books so that more people could study more on projects
and be more smarter.

THE END
THANK YOU

Delonte's essay reflects wider discourses about why communities in Southeast preferred Gray as a candidate: many believed he would focus on improving the conditions of local neighborhoods and schools for the people who already lived and went
to school in them. Delonte's essay indicates a keen awareness of how poverty affects
quality of living and educational opportunities, and he conceptualizes the mayorship
as a position of power that should be used to help fix structural neglect caused by
impoverishment. The essay, then, construes the mayor as a person who is and who
should be empowered to act against structural forms of inequality, with a focus on
education. The writing style itself is relatively formal, and reflects that of a traditional
essay: it names the topic, why the topic is important, and gives the key information
needed to support his position. Like the writers of "Tsunami," Delonte also includes
a closing, which thanks readers: "THE END/THANK YOU."

The after school students, like most children, were aware that language is a powerful form of discursive expression in society and constructed their essays accordingly
(cf. Vasquez 2002). Given the way that they were socialized by parents, teachers, and
other adults who participated in forms of raciolinguistic socialization that included
policing, the students had learned that politeness was an integral component of
"proper" speech and thus to being heard, especially by people in positions of power.
This may explain why the essay writers in figures 6.3 and 6.4 elected to greet or thank
their readers for their attention to their pieces. The greetings also indicate a position
of deference or perhaps humility with respect to their arguments, which challenges
the normative social conceptualization of arguments as "like war" (Lakoff & Johnson
1988). Thus, while recognizing the importance of a traditional writing structure and
attention to orthographic and grammatical "correctness," the students also modify
Western rhetorical style by explicitly drawing attention to the dialogical nature of

meaning and perspective, leaving open the friendly possibility for response. In the process, they created their own rhetorical style.

In the creative activity called, "If I Were President of the United States," several students produced a dual written and illustrated creative project that listed what they would do in that role. Figures 6.5, 6.6, and 6.7 show samples of their work, and it is followed by a reprinting of the text to help readers see what it says:

Figure 6.5   If I Were President of the United States.

Janice: If I were president of the United States I would be glad am that I am the president United States of America, ~~and~~ that I speak loud out to tell the truth to other people that do wrong and right things and Be glad that I have a job (bracketing each side: Have a nice Job).

Denise: If I were president I would give all the homeless people a house and I would bann people from having guns or any other weapons.

Keri: If I were the president I would fire all of the police Because I don't lik police Because some are crooked Because they don't like people and they lock people for no reason (I love mom).

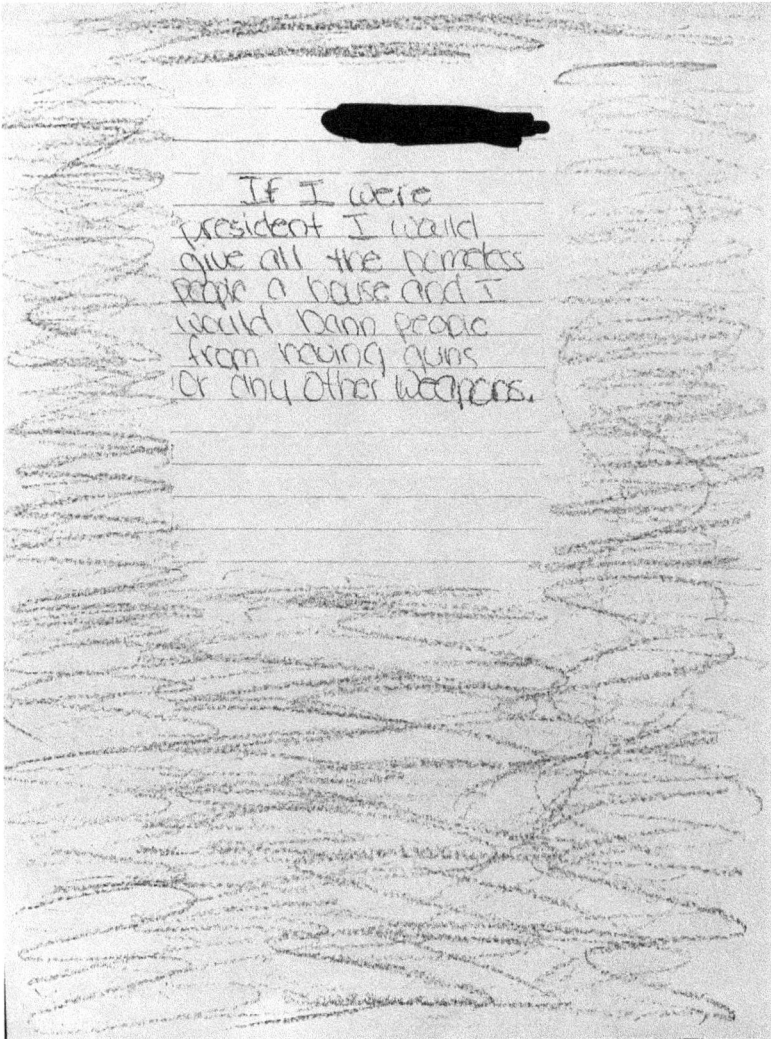

Figure 6.6   If I Were President of the United States.

Janice, Denise, and Keri's entries are reflections on their particular lived experiences and the forms of knowledge they gained. This means they each drew
from social "Discourses," which included family/home and school interactions,
their consumption of popular culture and mass media, and local neighborhood
conversations as well as social/political activism to produce their own individual
"discourses" about what the president of the United States could and should do.
As Gee explains, "Each of us is a member of many [social] Discourses and each
Discourse represents one of our ever multiple identities. These discourses need not,

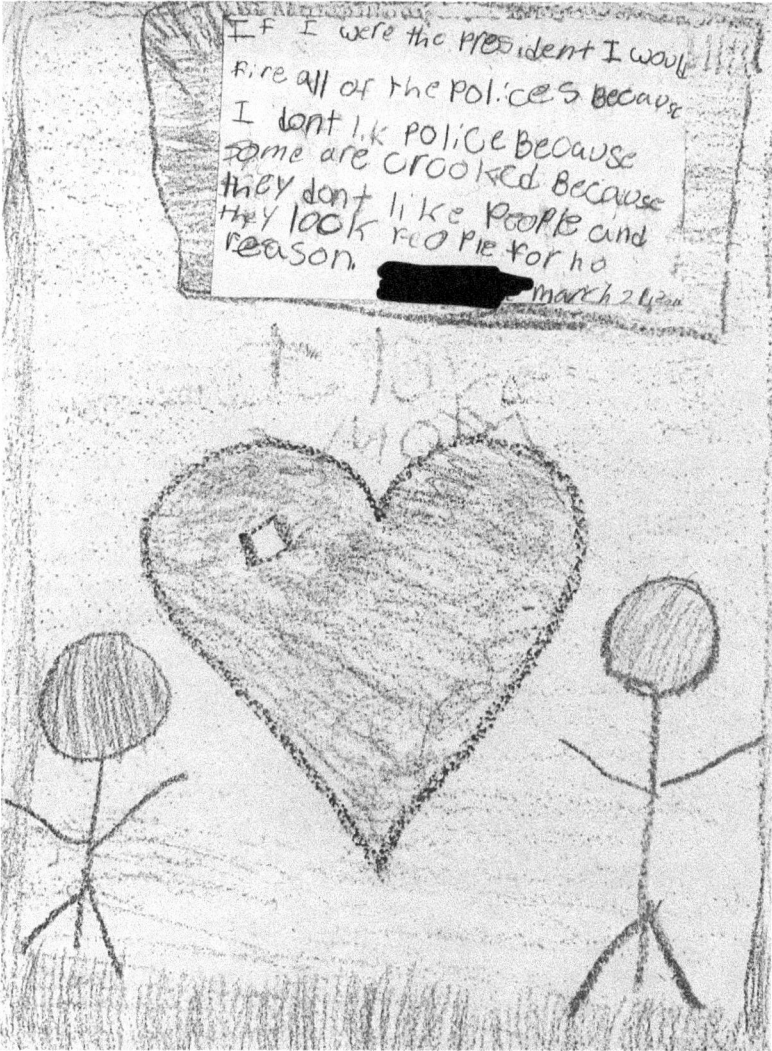

Figure 6.7 If I Were President of the United States.

and often do not, represent consistent and compatible values" (2012, p. 4). This is true within and across individuals who are socialized in a particular community. In this activity, each of the girls articulates the common view that the job of the president of the United States is to help create the conditions for social justice. For Janice, this means being able to use her voice to "speak loud out to tell the truth to other people that do wrong and right things." For Denise, it means eradicating homelessness and for eight-year-old Keri,[3] it means abolishing the police state.

While all of these particular issues affected the students and the communities to which they belonged in common, each of them had a particular personal importance for each individual student.

I want to note further that the girls' focus on the president as a social justice figure and their concern for the general welfare of society is both telling and poignant: generally, the students were interested in making connections between what they saw and experienced and using it to reinterpret what could be made better for "people" or the "world" rather than for themselves, their families, or their communities. At the time, I conceptualized critical pedagogy as an intellectual exercise that would help the students interpret and change their own particular social realities. But in the process, I was excluding the possibility of helping them connect their experiences to those of others. In terms of learning, social justice, and educational possibilities, this is an incredibly limiting frame. I only realized this in closely examining the work my students had produced years later. As it turns out, they were already doing a key component of critical pedagogy: repositioning themselves as more than just the sum of their personal experiences. In connecting their personal senses of injustice to the wider issues and structures that shaped them in their written work and art projects, the students were imagining themselves as citizens of a more broadly conceived global society. They used language architectures and social Discourses that would allow them to be heard while still being rooted in their own realities. Even without explicit teacher guidance, students were repositioning themselves outside of received identity models and discourses to act as empowered global citizens.

DISCUSSION

In reflecting on the "president" activity and others, I have learned that the after school students often cultivated their critical thinking and literacy apart from the explicit teaching or guidance of adults, and that they often had better ideas than we did about the major issues that we discussed. Imagine bilingual and language immersion programs that truly develop a pluralistic learning frame or a science report on tsunamis that reach beyond specialized experts to include the general public. I believe that students' translingual sensibilities were developed with these kinds of changes in mind, and I believe that their ideas and ways of using language could have incredible applications for structural change.

Yet unfortunately, deficit ideologies are actually applied in the education and schooling of children, which operates from an adult-centered perspective. Children are often thought of as innocent, neutral beings who need to be taught what social justice is from the perspective that they have not yet developed a sense of care or concern for others (Vasquez 2002; see Berman 2019 for cross-cultural perspective). Heath (1983) and Vasquez (2002) show that children are critical thinkers in ways that are not institutionally seen or sponsored. Heath's (1983) research is especially important for showing how in the early years, African American children develop the critical thinking skills that are recognized and valued later rather than earlier on in the schooling process. Such skills include analogical reasoning, metaphorical comparison and contrast, and the recognition of contrasting or multiple perspectives among audiences or addressees, all gained through an emphasis on storytelling. Thus, in early childhood, working-class African American children learn what is typically considered a more advanced skill but are not oriented to the rote practices that are recognized as evidence of literacy in early grades. What African American students do bring to the classroom is subsumed under deficit discourses, all with normative and often culturally irrelevant framings of what words and experiences are necessary for intellectual and social growth (see Labov & Baker 2010 for similar critique).

Students' identities are constantly changing as they engage in learning. This is a promising perspective for educators who seek to help students reposition themselves in school-based settings as producers of knowledge and social justice. This means rather than seeking to change students, educators should often step back and recognize the processes by which students are changing on their own in order to support their further growth. Often, as the previous chapters demonstrate, the ways in which students take from the school environment and engage with or reframe normative ideas or practices go unnoticed. As a result, hybrid practices are viewed from a school-normative perspective as errors in learning rather than as different ways of "taking in" what they are exposed to (Heath 1983).

It bears mentioning that deficit ideologies tend to follow students of color up through the high school years, especially for students attending schools in urban minority-majority schools (Emdin 2016; Rosa 2019). Private schools with predominantly white students, on the other hand, freely sponsor progressive or alternative models of education that are rooted in critical pedagogy, even at early ages, and they do not have to demonstrate proficiency on national standardized tests. This bifurcation of educational models suggests that racially minoritized students, especially those who are from poor urban neighborhoods, are literally being punished for not following the same literacy and language trajectories of white middle-class and wealthy students.

Looking back at the students' work has been an important exercise for me not just in learning, but in hope too, as I realize how much the after school students were producing their own ideas about race, social justice, and the power of language and literacy even in the absence of support from the structures and institutions shaping their socialization and learning. I hope seeing their work as I have since seen, it also provides learning and hope for the readers of this book as well.

To summarize this chapter, there are three lessons I took away from my experiences teaching and researching with the after school students. First, students come to the classroom as critical thinkers with their own ideas about learning and social justice. It is important for educators to learn what those are and sponsor them, and to let students help design activities and lessons. Second, promoting rigid, essentialized notions of difference, racial, cultural, or otherwise, does not serve students or honor their efforts to engage in learning. Even with the tools of expert observation and analysis is often easy to assume that there is a mismatch or clash in the classroom between the so-called "dominant" and "minority" cultures (Heath 1983; Phillips 2009). Here, I am speaking specifically to well-intentioned liberals and progressives who may or may not be aware that there is a tendency to reinforce difference by positioning oneself as a "(white) savior," or a white person who saves "brown people from other brown people" (Spivak 1988). It is essential for teachers to be able to identify and support how students make school-based language and literacy practices their own, even if the ways in which they do so appear do not appear to benefit them on the surface. Third and finally, assuming that it is an educator's job to teach students what oppression is and how to act against it reproduces deficit ideologies. A key part of a critical pedagogical perspective involves stepping back and letting students articulate their own positionality and learning interests in the classroom rather than defining those for them. Educators, in other words, should seek to co-construct learning and critical consciousness with students rather than impose it upon them.

An important part of the interpretive frame I have selected for this chapter is to reverse the dominant gaze: I am not simply looking at students' knowledge as assets, I am looking at the work it their knowledge can do in disrupting normative and hegemonic literacy practices and relations of learning (cf. Alim & Paris 2017). Many readers might still find themselves taking up a deficit perspective even by chuckling at the spelling errors and grammatical incorrectness in the students' writing. This infantilizing frame does their work a great disservice by neglecting all of the ways in which children can potentially contribute to wider conversations about race, literacy, social justice, and power. As I have tried to show with analysis, students construct their own translingual and transcultural discourses that evidence not just passive learning, but the active production and transformation of race, language, and social meaning. In this way, I hope to expand on theoretical notions of children's learning, socialization, and agency, a discussion which I expand upon in the conclusion to follow.

NOTES

1. Chaparro's study shows that not all Spanish speakers are racialized as Other and that raciolinguistic socialization is dependent on perceptions of race (i.e., phenotype) and social class.

2. Based on polling information, *The Washington Post* reported that Gray's "approval" was heavily contingent on disapproval of Fenty rather than actual support for Gray (Stewart & Cohen 2010).

3. I did not originally design the study to include children younger than nine years old. Keri asked if she could participate in my study since she was turning nine that year, and I told her no, because I knew that if I had said yes, the rest of the eight-year-olds (and then

the seven-year-olds, and then the six-year-olds) would petition me to participate in the study, and I would lose my age-specific focus for the research (and also hurt a lot of feelings by not categorically excluding the children based on age). But Keri was more likely to hang out with her older sister, Alisha, Janice, and Mary, than she was with children in her designated age group of five to eight years old, so I selectively include her talk and work in this book.

Conclusion

As a community college professor in New York, I am not terribly far away from Washington, D.C. I spend the occasional weekend there visiting friends, including Raymond and Minnie. I do not see the after school students, but I am connected with some of them on social media and hear about others from Raymond, who still keeps in touch with many or runs into them when he visits Southeast. But I always think about the after school students in teaching my college students. The children I left in 2011 would be about the age of my current students, a majority of whom would identify racially as Black, Spanish, Hispanic, or Latinx, who also attended urban schools, and who also struggle to achieve academic success against pathologizing interpretations of how they should belong in the classroom if they are presumed to belong at all. Each semester in my language, race, and ethnicity classes, I hear countless stories of how my Black students have been silenced in other classes for being loud or aggressive when speaking up in class and of how my Latinx students are treated as "the help" rather than as producers of knowledge, especially if they have or had attended college at a four-year institution with predominantly white students.

I share my research with my students, most of whom can summarize the main point of my 2016 publication on joning much more effectively than I explain in the peer-reviewed article. They use everyday language and experience to translate my jargon and analysis to their peers in class presentations and, fortunately, tell me that the article reminds them of "being in middle school again." I am glad to have confirmation that my analysis makes sense to students who see themselves as having something in common with the after school children, and perhaps it is an indication that my findings and interpretation are generalizable beyond the particular context of the after school program. And as a result of sharing my own experiences as the child of a first-generation immigrant "of color" (a label they generally agree on as formative of our shared experience), my students also see me as having something in common with them.

As my college students express their anxieties and fears about doing their writing assignments and reading responses correctly, I share with them my own insecurities in facing the results of peer review and show them some of my own works in progress, some of them replete with "mean" comments. I tell them that it took me several years to understand many of the same concepts and theories we talk about in class well enough to be able to lecture on them. And I remind them that most of my lessons are shaped in dialogue with what past students' thoughts and interpretations and that my teaching would never exist without their learning. As I do this, I find myself wishing that I had been able to have similar conversations with my after school students and wonder if it would have made a difference in the way I described in the introduction's story, in which eight-year-old Keri explained to me how "Black people talk to each other" to gently interrupt my pathologizing interpretation of a verbal conflict. But even more, I wonder how many people would listen to either my after school students or my college students, given the ways in which they are seen and heard as unintelligent, resistant, loud, angry, or otherwise unfit for social and intellectual discourse. As a professor and scholar, I realize that I have at least some influence in mediating their entry into the academic world and their desire to learn and succeed. At the same time, I make their experiences intelligible to that world and to the public because we as a society have not yet reached the point where they would be listened to as producers of knowledge in their own right.

I was reminded of the fact that the stakes of being racially read and heard as a problem are much higher than just intellectual dismissal in recently showing the film *American Son* (2019) to my classes. The film documents the angst of a couple who reunite at a police station to find their missing son, Jamal. The mother, Kendra, is African American and the father, Scott, is white. As they and the other characters debate the right way to be a young Black man in a white-dominated world characterized by racial profiling, we discover by the end that the right way does not exist: Jamal, an "articulate" and academically accomplished teenager, is a casualty of police brutality despite the fact that Kendra, to paraphrase the character's dialogue, did everything she could to minimize his hypervisibility as a social threat. Complicating the film's outcome further is the fact that the police officer who shot Jamal and his friend is African American.

In watching the film and talking about other victims of police brutality one day, some of my students noted the impossibility of being racially perceived as something other than a dangerous criminal regardless of what one does or says, relating their own experiences of being linguistically and racially policed. But despite this awareness, they also wondered about what any of those individuals could have done differently to prevent their deaths. I believe that this was less a product of "false consciousness" and more so a coping strategy: it must be terrifying to confront the possibility that one could be killed just because your skin is black. But I said what I wanted to say with a heavy heart: the film was suggesting that none of the victims could have done anything differently. It was saying that the way bodies are read should be changed, not on what they should or should not do.

The film, in other words, was taking up the kind of raciolinguistic perspective I have sought to develop in this book. I hope this book has not only demonstrated the centrality of language in terms of constructing race, but also the importance of taking up a raciolinguistic perspective that interrogates how those in power hear or do not hear racialized people as much as they are seen or not seen. I hope to impart some sense of the consequences of not hearing students such as mine outside of their raciolinguistic profiles. Some of this book is grounded in a quest to translate unfamiliar linguistic practices to a wider audience for the sake of demonstrating their integrity in the same way that cultural difference theorists of the past have. But I do not seek to explain the so-called logic of an objectively posited object we call "language." Rather, I aim to shed light on how linguistic practices, which are inherently fluid and hybrid, are grounded in the after school students' lived experiences. These experiences have one thing in common: being misheard and policed to the point where it was impossible for many of them to succeed academically despite their best efforts to the contrary. In that sense, this book is less about what the students did or did not do, but rather how they attempted to navigate around their institutional positioning as "problem students." It is an attempted acknowledgment of their efforts to transform race against near-impossible odds of being heard and understood in the way I think they might have wanted to be.

Many scholars write about the practical and policy implications of their research in the conclusion. The question still remains as to what can be done to change white people's minds about race, and it is a significant one. According to many critical race theorists, educational efforts have largely failed in the era of "racism without racists" because the effects of so-called folk theorizing are so powerful, even among scholars engaged in social justice (Bonilla-Silva 2018; see also Hill 1998 and 2008). As these scholars point out, much of the pushback is from whites who benefit from the idea that to speak and act properly is a neutral rather than a political act. Yet as the 1996/7 Oakland Ebonics controversy made evident, a lot of pushback also comes from within racially oppressed communities, from who continue to sponsor the idea of "looking white on paper" in order to pass in a society that demands racial conformity (Fordham 1996). Outside of anthropology, sociology, and other social science disciplines, radical perspectives that interrogate the foundations of difference and diversity are not common. Instead, additive approaches that approach code-switching and bilingualism as a stepping stone to "standard" language acquisition are the norm in policy and practice. Sometimes these are openly acknowledged as "lean in" strategies that get people to listen. At others, they are considered to be a truly pluralistic solution to a lingering problem. I think the trick is to figure out the intersections of ideology, critical awareness, what people believe to be possible or impossible, and whether or not they are truly willing to rearrange a system that benefits the people who are making scholarship and policy. Until radical systemic change happens, we will never change anything.

In concluding this book, I wish to point out that the after school students' racio-linguistic transformations were misrecognized and misheard as active resistance to learning. Rather than suggesting a policy solution (I do not think there is one fix-all solution), I wish to invite scholars, students, and other readers to ask themselves what they can learn from these children in order to transform their own ways of seeing and hearing people who navigate racial stigma. I ask them to also interrogate the contexts in which these individuals and groups can and cannot speak for themselves and to find a way to help them find their own credibility instead of speaking for them, as many "allies" are wont to do. I hope that eventually, this leads to a systemic transformation in which someone like me no longer has to translate on behalf of the students I teach, so that they can be seen and heard on their own terms.

References

Abrahams, Roger. (1962). Playing the dozens. *Journal of American Folklore* 75: 209–218.

Agha, Asif. (2005). Voicing, footing, enregisterment. *Journal of Linguistic Anthropology* 15(1): 38–59.

———. (2007). *Language and social relations.* Cambridge University Press.

Ahearn, Laura M. (1999). Agency. *Journal of Linguistic Anthropology* 9(1/2): 12–15.

Akom, A. A. (2008). Critical hip hop pedagogy as a form of liberatory praxis. *Equity & Excellence in Education* 42(1): 52–66.

Alexander, Michelle. (2012). *The new Jim Crow: Mass incarceration in the era of colorblindness.* The New Press.

Alim, H. Samy. (2004). *You know my steez: An ethnographic and sociolinguistic study of style-shifting in a Black American speech community.* Duke University Press for the American Dialect Society.

———. (2016a). Introducing raciolinguistics: Racing language and languaging race in hyper-racial times. In Alim, H. Samy, Arnetha Ball, & John R. Rickford (eds). *Raciolinguistics: How language shapes our ideas about race,* pp. 1–30. Oxford University Press.

———. (2016b). Who's afraid of the transracial subject? Raciolinguistics and the political project of transracialization. In Alim, H. Samy, Arnetha Ball, & John R. Rickford (eds). *Raciolinguistics: How language shapes our ideas about race,* pp. 33–50. Oxford University Press.

Alim, H. Samy & Django Paris. (2017). What is culturally sustaining pedagogy and why does it matter? In Paris, Django & H. Samy Alim (eds). *Culturally sustaining pedagogies: Teaching and learning for justice in a changing world,* pp. 1–24. Teachers College Press.

Alim, H. Samy & Geneva Smitherman. (2012). *Articulate while black: Barack Obama, language, and race in the U.S.* Oxford University Press.

Alim, H. Samy, Jooyoung Lee, & Lauren Mason Carris. (2010). "Short fried rice-eating Chinese MCs and good hair-havin' Uncle Tom niggas": Performing race and ethnicity in freestyle rap battles. *Journal of Linguistic Anthropology* 20(1): 116–133. https://doi.org/10.1111/j.1548-1395.2010.01052.x.

Anderson, Benedict. (1990). *Imagined communities: Reflections on the origin and spread of nationalism.* Verso.

Anderson, Elijah. (1990). *Streetwise: Race, class, and change in an urban community.* The University of Chicago Press.

Asch, Chris Myers & George Derek Musgrove. (2019). *Chocolate city: A history of race and democracy in the nation's capital.* The University of North Carolina Press.

Austermuhle, Martin. (2013). Cheating at D.C. public schools more widespread than originally thought, Rhee didn't investigate. *DCist*, April 12, 2013. https://www.google.com/ search?q=dcist&oq=dcist&aqs=chrome..69i57j69i60l2j0l3.878j0j7&sourceid=chrome&es pv=2&es_sm=119&ie=UTF-8. Retrieved November 20, 2019.

Avineri, Netta, Eric Johnson, Shirley Brice Heath, Teresa McCarty, Elinor Ochs, Tamar Kremer-Sadlik, Susan Blum, Ana Celia Zentella, Jonathan Rosa, Nelson Flores, H. Samy Alim, & Django Paris. (2015). Invited forum: Bridging the "language gap." *Journal of Linguistic Anthropology* 25(1): 66–86.

Bakhtin, M. M. (1981). *Discourse in the novel.* University of Texas Press.

Balibar, Etienne & Immanuel Wallerstein. (1991). *Race, nation, class: Ambiguous identities.* Verso.

Bartlett, Lesley, Marla Frederick, Thadeus Guldbrandsen, & Enrique Murillo. (2002). The marketization of education: Public schools for private ends. *Anthropology & Education Quarterly* 33(1): 5–29.

Basso, Keith. (1979). *Portraits of "The Whiteman": Linguistic play and cultural symbols among the Western Apache.* Cambridge University Press.

Baugh, John. (1983). *Black street speech: Its history, structure, and survival.* University of Texas Press.

Bauman, Richard. (1975). Verbal art as performance. *American Anthropologist* 77(5): 290–311.

Bax, Anna & Juan Sebastian Ferrada. (2018). Sounding white and boring: Race, identity, and youth freedom in an after-school program. In Bucholtz, Mary, Dolores Inés Casillas, & Jin Sook Lee (eds). *Feeling it: Language, race, and affect in Latinx youth learning,* pp. 47–71. Routledge.

Berman, Elise. (2019). *Talking like children: Language and the production of age in the Marshall Islands.* Oxford University Press.

Blackburn, Mollie V. (2005). Agency in borderland discourses: Examining language use in a community center with Black Queer youth. *Teachers College Record* 107(1): 89–113.

Blum-Kulka, Shoshana & Elite Oshtain. (1984). Requests and apologies: A cross-cultural study of speech act realization patterns (CCSARP). *Applied Linguistics* 5(3): 196–213.

Bonilla-Silva, Eduardo. (2018). *Racism without racists: Color-blind racism and the persistence of inequality in America.* Rowman & Littlefield.

Bourdieu, Pierre. (1980). *Distinction: A social critique of the judgment of taste.* Harvard University Press.

Brodkin, Karen. (1998). *How Jews became white folks and what that says about race in America.* Rutgers University Press.

Brown, Emma. (2013). Chancellor Kaya Henderson names 15 D.C. schools on closure list. *The Washington Post*, January 17. http://www.washingtonpost.com/local/education/chan cellor-kaya-henderson-names-15-dc-schools-on-closure-list/2013/01/17/e04202fa-6023 -11e2-9940-6fc488f3fecd_story.html. Retrieved January 18, 2013.

Brown, Penelope & Stephen C. Levinson. (1978). *Politeness: Some universals in language use.* Cambridge University Press.

Bucholtz, Mary. (2002). Youth and cultural practice. *Annual Review of Anthropology* 31: 525–552.

———. (2004). Styles and stereotypes: The linguistic negotiation of identity among Laotian American youth. *Pragmatics* 14(2/3): 127–147.

———. (2009). From stance to style: Gender, interaction, and indexicality in Mexican immigrant youth slang. In Jaffe, Alexandra (ed.). *Stance: Sociolinguistic perspectives*, pp. 146–170. Oxford University Press.

———. (2011). *White kids: Language, race, and styles of youth identity.* Cambridge University Press.

———. (2016). On being called out of one's name: Indexical bleaching as a technique of deracialization. In Alim, H. Samy, Arnetha Ball, & John R. Rickford (eds). *Raciolinguistics: How language shapes our ideas about race*, pp. 273–290. Oxford University Press.

Campano, Gerald. (2007). *Immigrant students and literacy: Reading, writing, and remembering.* Teachers College Press.

Chaparro, Sofía E. (2019). "But mom! I'm not a Spanish boy": Raciolinguistic socialization in a two-way immersion bilingual program. *Linguistics and Education* 50: 1–12.

Chatman, Michelle Coghill. (2016). At Eshu's crossroad: Pan-African identity in a changing city. In Hyra, Derek S. & Sabiyha Prince (eds). *Capital dilemma: Growth and inequality in Washington, D.C.*, pp. 239–254. Routledge.

Chun, Elaine. (2001). The construction of white, Black and Korean American identities through African American Vernacular English. *Journal of Linguistic Anthropology* 11(1): 52–64.

———. (2009). "Black kids who try to act white": Reading racial inauthenticity. Paper presented at the 108th American Anthropological Association Annual Meeting. Philadelphia, Pennsylvania.

Collins, Patricia Hill. (2004). *Black sexual politics: African Americans, gender, and the new racism.* Routledge.

Coupland, Justine & Nikolas Coupland. (2009). Attributing stance in discourses of body shape and weight loss. In Jaffe, Alexandra (ed.). *Stance: Sociolinguistic perspectives*. Oxford University Press.

Cutler, Cecilia. (2003). "Keepin' it real": White hip-hoppers' discourses of language, race, and authenticity. *Journal of Linguistic Anthropology* 13(2): 1–23.

Dalton-Puffer, Christiane & Tarja Nikula. (2006). Pragmatics of content-based instruction: Teacher and student directives in Finnish and Austrian classrooms. *Applied Linguistics* 27(2): 241–267.

Delfino, Jennifer B. (2014). *Negotiating achievements: Language and schooling experiences among African American students.* Unpublished Ph.D. dissertation. American University.

———. (2016). Fighting words?: Joning as conflict talk and identity performance among African American preadolescents. *Journal of Sociolinguistics* 20(5): 631–653.

———. (2020). Talking "like a race": Gender, authority, and articulate speech in African American children's *marking* speech acts. *International Journal of the Sociology of Language* 265: 57–79.

Delpit, Lisa. (1995). *Other people's children: Cultural conflict in the classroom.* The New Press.

Diner, Stephen J. (1982). The governance of education in the District of Columbia: An historical analysis of current issues. *Studies in D.C. History and Public Policy*, No. 2. University of the District of Columbia.

District of Columbia Public Schools. (2007). *DCPS reform priorities of the Fenty administration.* http://edreform.dc.gov/. Retrieved March 30, 2014.

DuBois, W. E. B. (1995[1903]). *The souls of black folk*. Signet.

Dumas, Michael J. (2016). Against the darkness: Anti-blackness in education policy and discourse. *Theory into Practice* 55(1): 11–19.

Dyson, Michael Eric. (2005). *Is Bill Cosby right? Or has the black middle class lost its mind?* Basic Books.

Eckert, Penelope. (1998). *Jocks and burnouts: Social categories and identity in the high school.* Teachers College Press.

Eder, Donna. (1990). Serious and playful disputes: Variation in conflict talk among female adolescents. In Grimshaw, Allen D. (ed.). *Conflict talk: Sociolinguistic investigations of arguments in conversation*, pp. 67–84. Cambridge University Press.

Eisenberg, Ann R. & Catherine Garvey. (1981). Children's use of verbal strategies in resolving conflicts. *Discourse Processes* 4: 149–170.

Ellsworth, Elizabeth. (1989). Why doesn't this feel empowering? Working through the repressive myths of critical pedagogy. *Harvard Educational Review* 59(3): 297–324.

Emdin, Christopher. (2016). *For white folks who teach in the hood... and the rest of y'all too: Reality pedagogy and urban education*. Beacon Press.

Ervin-Tripp, Susan. (1976). Is Sybil there? The structure of some American English directives. *Language in Society* 5(1): 25–66.

———. (1977). Wait for me, Roller Skate! In Ervin-Tripp, Susan (ed.). *Child discourse*, pp. 165–188. Academic Press, Inc.

Fanon, Franz. (2004[1963]). *The wretched of the earth*. Grove Press.

Farnsworth, Megan. (2012). Whose coming to my party? Peer talk as a bridge to oral language proficiency. *Anthropology & Education Quarterly* 43(3): 253–270.

Fasold, Ralph. (1968). *Tense marking in Black English: A linguistic and social analysis*. Urban Language Series No. 8. Center for Applied Linguistics.

Ferguson, Roderick A. (2004). *Aberrations in Black: Toward a queer of color critique*. University of Minnesota Press.

Field, Margaret. (2001). Triadic directives in Navajo language socialization. *Language in Society* 30(2): 249–263.

Flores, Nelson. (2017). From language-as-resource to Language-as-struggle: Resisting the Coke-ification of bilingual education. In Flubacher, Mi-Cha & Alfonso del Percio (eds). *Language, education, and neoliberalism: Critical studies in sociolinguistics*, pp. 62–81. Multilingual Matters.

———. (2020). From academic language to language architecture: Challenging raciolinguistic ideologies in research and practice. *Theory into Practice* 59(1): 22–31.

Flores, Nelson & Jonathan Rosa. (2015). Undoing appropriateness: Raciolinguistic ideologies and language diversity in education. *Harvard Educational Review* 85(2): 149–171.

———. (2017). Unsettling race and language: Toward a raciolinguistic perspective. *Language in Society* 46(5): 621–647.

———. (2019). Bringing race into second language acquisition. *The Modern Language Journal* 103(S1): 145–151.

Flores, Nelson, Mark Lewis, & Jennifer Phuong. (2018). Raciolinguistic chronotopes and the education of Latinx students: Resistance and anxiety in a bilingual school. *Language & Communication* 62: 15–25.

Foley, Douglas. (1990). *Learning capitalist culture: Deep in the heart of Tejas*. University of Pennsylvania Press.

———. (1991). Reconsidering anthropological explanations of ethnic school failure. *Anthropology & Education Quarterly* 22(1): 60–85.

Fordham, Signithia. (1993). "Those loud black girls": (Black) women, silence, and gender "passing" in the academy. *Anthropology and Education Quarterly* 24(1): 3–32.

———. (1996). *Blacked out: Dilemmas of race, identity, and academic success at Capital High*. Chicago University Press.

———. (1999). Dissin' "the standard": Ebonics as guerrilla warfare at Capital High. *Anthropology & Education Quarterly* 30(3): 272–303.

———. (2010). Passin' for Black: Race, identity, and bone memory in postracial America. *Harvard Educational Review* 80(1): 4–29.

Fordham, Signithia & John U. Ogbu. (1986). Black students' school success: Coping with the "burden of 'acting White'". *The Urban Review* 18(3): 176–206.

Fought, Carmen. (2006). *Language and ethnicity (key topics in sociolinguistics)*. Cambridge University Press.

Freire, Paolo. (1970). *Pedagogy of the oppressed*. Verso Books.

Gal, Susan & Judith T. Irvine. (2019). *Signs of difference: Language and ideology in social life*. Cambridge University Press.

García, Ofelia & Li Wei. (2009). *Translanguaging: Language, bilingualism, and education*. Palgrave.

Garot, Robert. (2010). *Who you claim: Performing gang identity in school and on the streets*. New York University Press.

Gatewood, Willard. (1990). *Aristocrats of color: The Black elite*. Indiana University Press.

Gee, James Paul. (2012). *Social linguistics and literacies: Ideology in discourses*. Routledge.

Godley, Amanda J. & Angela Minnici. (2008). Critical pedagogy in an urban high school English class. *Urban Education* 43(3): 319–346.

Goffman, Erving. (1981). *Forms of talk*. University of Pennsylvania Press.

Goldberg, David Theo. (2002). *The racial state*. Blackwell Publishing.

———. (2009). *The threat of race: Reflections on racial neoliberalism*. Wiley Blackwell.

Goodwin, Marjorie Harness. (1990). *He-said-she-said: Talk as social organization among Black children*. Indiana University Press.

Goodwin, Marjorie Harness & H. Samy Alim. (2010). "Whatever (neck roll, eye roll, teeth suck)": The situated coproduction of social categories and identities. *Journal of Linguistic Anthropology* 20(1): 179–194.

Gramsci, Antonio. (1971). *Selections from the prison notebooks*. International Publishers.

Green, Lisa J. (2002). *African American English: An introduction*. Cambridge University Press.

———. (2011). *Language and the African American child*. Cambridge University Press.

Griswold, Olga. (2007). Achieving authority: Discursive practices in Russian girls' pretend play. *Research on Language and Social Interaction* 40(4): 291–319.

Guerra, Juan C. (2016). Cultivating a rhetorical sensibility in the translingual writing classroom. *College English* 78(3): 228–233.

Guggenheim, Davis (dir). (2010). *Waiting for superman*. Paramount Vintage.

Gutiérrez, Kris D., Patricia Baquedano-López, & Christian Tejeda. (1999). Rethinking diversity: Hybridity and hybrid language practices in the third space. *Mind, Culture, and Activity* 6(4): 286–303.

Hackworth, Jason. (2007). *The neoliberal city: Governance, ideology, and development in American urbanism*. Cornell University Press.

Hannerz, Ulf. (2004[1966]). *Soulside: Inquiries into ghetto culture and community.* University of Chicago Press.

Harrison, Faye V. (1998). Introduction: Expanding the discourse on race. *American Anthropologist* 100(3): 609–631.

Harvey, David. (2005). *A brief history of neoliberalism.* Oxford University Press.

He, Agnes Weiyun. (2000). The grammatical and interactional organization of teacher's directives: Implications for socialization of Chinese American children. *Linguistics and Education* 11(2): 119–140.

Heath, Shirley Brice. (1983). *Ways with words: Language, life, and work in communities and classrooms.* Cambridge University Press.

Hebidge, Dick. (1979). *Subculture: The meaning of style.* Routledge.

Hemmings, Annette. (1996). Conflicting images? Being Black and a model high school student. *Anthropology & Education Quarterly* 27(1): 20–50.

Hill, Jane H. (1995). The voices of Don Gabriel: Responsibility and self in a modern Mexicano narrative. In Mannheim, Bruce & Dennis Tedlock (eds). *The dialogic emergence of culture*, pp. 97–147. University of Illinois Press.

———. (2008). *The everyday language of white racism.* Wiley Blackwell.

———. (2009). Language, race, and white public space. In Duranti, Alessandro (ed.). *Linguistic anthropology: A reader*, pp. 479–492. Blackwell Publishing.

Holland, Rosalind. (2010). Michelle Rhee, IMPACT and what this means for D.C. schools. http://www.breakthroughcollaborative.org/blog/michelle-rhee-impact-and-what-means-dc -public-schools. Retrieved November 20, 2019.

hooks, bell. (1994). *Teaching to transgress: Education as the practice of freedom.* Routledge.

hooks, bell. (2003). *We real cool: Black men and masculinity.* Routledge.

Hubbard, Lea. (1999). College aspirations among African American high school students: Gendered strategies for success. *Anthropology & Education Quarterly* 30(3): 363–393.

Hyra, Derek S. (2017). *Race, class, and politics in the Cappuccino City.* The University of Chicago Press.

Inoue, Miyako. (2006). *Vicarious language: Gender and linguistic modernity in Japan.* University of California Press.

Irvine, Judith & Susan Gal. (2000). Language ideology and linguistic differentiation. In Kroskrity, Paul V. (ed.). *Regimes of language: Ideologies, polities, and identities*, pp. 1–34. School of American Research.

Jaffe, Alexandra. (2009). Introduction: The sociolinguistics of stance. In Jaffe, Alexandra (ed.). *Stance: Sociolinguistic perspectives*, pp. 3–28. Oxford University Press.

Janks, Hilary. (2010). *Literacy and power.* Routledge.

Jones, Stephanie. (2006). Language with an attitude: White girls performing class. *Language Arts* 84(2): 114–124.

Katz, Michael B. (1993). Introduction: The urban "underclass" as a metaphor for social transformation. In Katz, Michael B. (ed.). *The "underclass" debate: Views from history*, pp. 3–23. Princeton University Press.

Kelley, Robin D. G. (1994). *Race rebels: Culture, politics, and the Black working class.* The Free Press.

Kiesling, Scott. (2001). Stances of whiteness and hegemony in fraternity men's discourse. *Journal of Linguistic Anthropology* 11(1): 101–115.

———. (2004). Dude. *American Speech* 79(3): 281–305.

Kochman, Thomas. (1972). *Rappin' and stylin' out: Communication in urban Black America.* University of Illinois Press.

———. (1983). The boundary between play and nonplay in black verbal dueling. *Language in Society* 12(3): 329–337.

Kozol, Jonathan. (1991). *Savage inequalities: Children in America's schools.* Random House, Inc.

Kromidas, Maria. (2016). *City kids: Transforming racial baggage.* Rutgers University Press.

Kryatzis, Amy. (2007). Using the social organizational affordances of role playing in American preschool girls' interactions. *Research on Language and Social Interaction* 40: 321–352.

Labov, William. (1972). *Language in the inner city: Studies in the Black English Vernacular.* University of Pennsylvania Press.

———. (1998). Coexistent systems in African-American vernacular English. In Mufwene, S. S., John R. Rickford, Guy Bailey, & John Baugh (eds). *African American vernacular English: Structure, history, and use,* pp. 110–153. Routledge.

———. (2010). Unendangered dialect, endangered people: The case of African American vernacular English. *Transforming Anthropology* 18(1): 15–28.

Labov, William & Bettina Baker. (2010). What is a reading error? *Applied Psycholinguistics* 31(4): 735–757.

Labov, William & David Fanshel. (1977). *Therapeutic discourse.* Academic Press.

Ladson-Billings, Gloria. (1994). *The dreamkeepers: Successful teachers of African American children.* Jossey-Bass.

———. (2017). The (R)Evolution will not be standardized: Teacher education, hip hop pedagogy, and culturally relevant pedagogy 2.0. In Paris, Django & H. Samy Alim (eds). *Culturally sustaining pedagogies: Teaching and learning for justice in a changing world,* pp. 141–156. Teachers College Press.

Lakoff, George & Mark Johnson. (1980). *Metaphors we live by.* University of Chicago Press.

Lazar, Sian. (2010). Schooling and critical citizenship: Pedagogies of political agency in El Alto, Bolivia. *Anthropology & Education Quarterly* 41(2): 181–205.

Leap, William L. (1993). *American Indian English.* University of Utah Press.

———. (2009). Professional baseball, urban restructuring, and (changing) gay geographies in Washington, D.C. In Lewin, Ellen & William L. Leap (eds). *Out in public: Reinventing lesbian/gay anthropology in a globalizing world,* pp. 202–222. Blackwell Publishing.

Leeman, Jennifer. (2004). Racializing language: A history of linguistic ideologies in the U.S. census. *Journal of Language and Politics* 3(3): 507–534.

Lemann, Nicholas. (1986). The origins of the underclass. *The Atlantic Monthly.* http://www.theatlantic.com/past/politics/poverty/origin1.htm and http://www.theatlantic.com/past/politics/poverty/origin2.htm. Retrieved November 20, 2019.

LeMaster, Barbara. (2010). Authority and preschool disputes: Learning to behave in the classroom. *Journal of Linguistic Anthropology* 20(1): 166–178.

Levy, Mary. (2004). *History of public school governance in the District of Columbia: A brief summary.* Washington Lawyers' Committee for Civil Rights.

Lewis, Oscar. (1966). The culture of poverty. In Gmelch, George, Robert V. Kemper, & Walter P. Zenner (eds). *Urban life: Readings in the anthropology of the city.* Waveland Press.

Liebow, Eliot. (2003[1967]). *Tally's corner.* Rowman & Littlefield.

Lipman, Pauline. (2011). *The new political economy of urban education: Neoliberalism, race, and the right to the city.* Routledge.

Lippi-Green, Rosina. (2012). *English with an accent: Language, ideology, and discrimination in the United States.* Routledge.

Love, Kristina. (2001). The construction of moral subjectivities in talk Around text in second-ary English. *Linguistics and Education* 11(3): 213–249.

Love-Nichols, Jessica. (2018). "There's no such thing as bad language, but…": Colorblind-ness and teachers' ideologies of linguistic appropriateness. In Bucholtz, Mary, Dolores Inés Casillas, & Jin Sook Lee (eds). *Feeling it: Language, race, and affect in Latinx youth learning*, pp. 91–111. Routledge.

Luke, Allen. (2018). *Critical literacy, schooling, and social justice: The selected works of Allen Luke*. Routledge.

Lytra, Vally. (2007). Teasing in contact encounters: Frames, participant positions, and responses. *Journal of Cross-Cultural and Interlanguage Communication* 26(4): 381–408.

MacLeod, Jay. (1995). *Ain't no makin' it: Aspirations and attainment in a low-income neighbor-hood*. Westview Press.

Manning, Robert D. (1998). Multicultural Washington, D.C.: The changing social and eco-nomic landscape of a post-industrial metropolis. *Ethnic and Racial Studies* 21(2): 329–355.

Marable, Manning. (2000). *How capitalism underdeveloped Black America: Problems in race, political economy, and society*. South End Press.

McFarland, Daniel A. (2001). Student resistance: How the formal and informal organization of classrooms facilitate everyday forms of student defiance. *American Journal of Sociology* 107(3): 612–678.

McWhorter, John. (2019). The origins of the "Acting White" charge. *The Atlantic Monthly*. https://www.theatlantic.com/ideas/archive/2019/07/acting-white-charge-origins/594130/. Retrieved November 30, 2019.

Mead, Margaret. (1928). *Coming of age in samoa: A psychological study of primitive youth for Western civilisation*. Harper Collins Publishers, Inc.

Mead, Sara. (2017). The capital of education reform. *U.S. News & World Report*. https://www.usnews.com/opinion/knowledge-bank/articles/2017-04-20/michelle-rhee-set-national-ex ample-of-education-reform-in-washington-dc. Retrieved November 20, 2019.

Mendoza-Denton, Norma. (2008). *Homegirls: Language and cultural practice among Latina youth gangs*. Wiley Blackwell.

Meyers, Edward M. (1996). *Political opinion and the future of the nation's capital*. Georgetown University Press.

Mickelson, Rolyn A. & Carol Ray. (1994). Fear of falling from grace: The middle class, down-ward mobility, and school desegregation. *Research in Sociology of Education and Socialization* 10: 207–238.

Mitchell-Kernan, Claudia. (2001). Signifying and marking: Two Afro-American speech acts. In Duranti, Alessandro (ed.). *Linguistic anthropology: A reader*, pp. 151–164. Blackwell Publishers, Inc.

Mitchell-Kernan, Claudia & Keith T. Kernan. (1977). Pragmatics of directive choice among children. In Ervin-Tripp, Susan (ed.). *Child discourse*, pp. 189–208. Academic Press.

Modan, Gabriella Gahlia. (2001). White, whole wheat, rye: Jews and ethnic categorization in Washington, D.C. *Journal of Linguistic Anthropology* 11(1): 116–130.

———. (2007). *Turf wars: Discourse, diversity, and the politics of place*. Blackwell Publishing.

Monzó, Lilia D. & Robert Rueda. (2009). Passing for English fluent: Latino immigrant children masking English proficiency. *Anthropology & Education Quarterly* 40(1): 20–40.

Morales, Katherine Lugo. (2020). Reimagining bilingualism in late modern Puerto Rico: The "ordinariness" of English language use among Latino adolescents. In Lee, Jerry Won & Sender Dovchin (eds). *Translinguistics: Negotiating innovation and ordinariness*, pp. 131–145. Taylor Francis.

Morgan, Marcyliena. (1994). *Language and the construction of identity in Creole situations.* UCLA Center for Afro-American Studies.

———. (2002). *Language, discourse, and power in African American culture.* Cambridge University Press.

Moynihan, Daniel Patrick. (1965). *The Negro family: The case for national action.* Office of Policy Planning and Research.

Muñoz, José Esteban. (1999). *Disidentifications: Queers of color and the performance of politics.* University of Minnesota Press.

Nakassis, Constantine. (2016). *Doing style: Youth and mass mediation in South India.* The University of Chicago Press.

Naples, Nancy. (2004). Community control: Mapping the changing context. In *Feminism and method: Ethnography, discourse analysis, and activist research*, pp. 89–108. Routledge.

Narayan, Kirin. (1993). How native is a "native" anthropologist? *American Anthropologist* 95: 671–686.

National Commission on Excellence in Education. (1983). *A nation at risk: The imperative for educational reform.* https://www2.ed.gov/pubs/NatAtRisk/index.html. Retrieved November 20, 2019.

Nielsen, Rasmus. (2010). "I ain't never been charged with nothing!": The use of falsetto speech as a linguistic strategy of indignation. *University of Pennsylvania Working Papers in Linguistics* 15(2): 111–121.

Noguera, Pedro A. (2008). *The trouble with Black boys and other reflections on race, equity, and the future of public education.* John Wiley & Sons.

Ocampo, Anthony C. (2016). *The Latinos of Asia: How Filipino Americans break the rules of race.* Stanford University Press.

Ochs, Elinor. (1992). Indexing gender. In Duranti, Alessandro & Charles Goodwin (eds). *Rethinking context: Language as an interactive phenomenon (studies in the social and cultural foundations of language 11)*, pp. 335–358. Cambridge University Press.

Ochs, Elinor & Bambi B. Schieffelin. (2009). Language acquisition and socialization: Three developmental stories and their implications. In Duranti, Alessandro (ed.). *Linguistic anthropology: A reader*, pp. 296–328. Blackwell Publishing.

Omi, Michael & Howard Winant. (1994). *Racial formation in the United States: From the 1960s to the 1990s.* Routledge.

Pagliai, Valentina. (2010). Conflict, cooperation, and facework in Contrasto verbal duels. *Journal of Linguistic Anthropology* 20(1): 87–100.

Paris, Django. (2011). *Language across difference: Ethnicity, communication, and youth identities in changing urban schools.* Cambridge University Press.

Passow, A. Harry. (1967). *Toward creating a model urban school system: A study of the Washington, D.C. public schools.* Teachers College.

Pêcheux, Michel. (1983). *Language, semantics, and ideology.* Palgrave Macmillan.

Pennycook, Alistair. (2007). *Global Englishes and transcultural flows.* Routledge.

Philips, Susan U. (2009). Participant structures and communicative competence: Warm Springs children in community and classroom. In Duranti, Alessandro (ed.). *Linguistic anthropology: A reader*, pp. 329–342. Blackwell Publishing, Ltd.

Placier, Margaret L. (1993). The semantics of state policy making: The case of "at risk." *Educational Evaluation and Policy Analysis* 15(4): 380–395.

Pollock, Mica. (2004). *Colormute: Race talk dilemmas in an American school.* Princeton University Press.

Prince, Sabiyha. (2014). *African Americans and gentrification in Washington, D.C.: Race, class and social justice in the nation's capital.* Routledge.

Rampton, Ben. (1995). *Crossing: Language and ethnicity among adolescents.* Routledge.

———. (2007). *Language in late modernity: Interaction in an urban school.* Cambridge University Press.

Reese, Ashanté M. (2019). *Black food geographies: Race, self-reliance, and food access in Washington, D.C.* University of North Carolina Press.

Reyes, Angela. (2004). Asian American stereotypes as circulating resource. *Pragmatics* 14(2): 173–192.

———. (2009). *The other Asian: Language, identity, and stereotype among Southeast Asian American youth.* Lawrence Earlbaum Associates.

———. (2016). The voicing of Asian American figures: Korean linguistic styles at an Asian American cram school. In Alim, Samy H., Arnetha Ball, & John R. Rickford (eds). *Raciolinguistics: How language shapes our ideas about race.* Oxford University Press.

———. (2017). Inventing postcolonial elites: Race, language, mix, excess. *Journal of Linguistic Anthropology* 27(2): 210–231.

Rickford, John R. & John Russell Rickford. (2000). *Spoken soul: The story of Black English.* John Wiley & Sons, Inc.

Rickford, John R. & Sharese King. (2016). Language and lingusitics on trial: Hearing Rachel Jeantel (and other vernacular speakers) in the courtroom and beyond. *Language* 92(4): 948–988.

Roberts, John W. (1982). Joning: An Afro-American verbal form in St Louis. *Journal of the Folklore Institute* 19(1): 61–70.

Roe, Donald. (2005). The Dual School System in the District of Columbia, 1862–1954: Origins, Problems, Protests. *Washington History* 16(2): 26–43.

Rosa, Jonathan. (2016). Standardization, racialization, languagelessness: Raciolinguistic ideologies across communicative contexts. *Journal of Linguistic Anthropology* 26(2): 162–183.

———. (2019). *Looking like a language, sounding like a race: Raciolinguistic ideologies and the learning of Latinidad.* Oxford University Press.

Rose, Tricia. (1994). *Black noise: Rap music and Black culture in contemporary America.* Wesleyan Press.

Roth-Gordon, Jennifer, Jessica Harris, & Stephanie Zamorra. (2020). Producing white comfort through corporate cool: Linguistic appropriation, social media, and @BrandsSaying-Bae. *International Journal of the Sociology of Language* 265: 107–128.

Sackler, Madeline (dir.). (2010). *The lottery.* Great Curve Films.

Schaffer, Rebecca & Debra G. Skinner (2009). Performing race in four culturally diverse fourth grade classrooms: Silence, race talk, and the negotiation of social boundaries. *Anthropology & Education Quarterly* 40(3): 277–296.

Schieffelin, Bambi B. (1986). Teasing and shaming in Kaluli children's interactions. In Schieffelin, Bambi B. (ed.). *Language socialization across cultures (studies in the social and cultural foundations of language 3)*, pp. 165–181. Cambridge University Press.

Scott, James C. (1985). *Weapons of the weak: Everyday forms of peasant resistance.* Yale University Press.

Searle, John R. (1975). *Expression and meaning: Studies in the theory of speech acts.* Cambridge University Press.

Selzter, Kate. (2017). *"Resisting from within": (Re)imagining a critical translingual English classroom.* Unpublished dissertation. CUNY Grad Center.

Silverstein, Michael. (2003). Indexical order and the dialectics of sociolinguistic life. *Language & Communication* 23: 193–229.

Sinclair, John McHardy & Malcolm Coulthard. (1975). *Towards an analysis of discourse: The English used by teachers and pupils.* Oxford University Press.

Smitherman, Geneva. (2000). *Talkin that talk: Language, culture, and education in African America.* Routledge.

Sperling, Rick & Phillip W. Vaughan. (2009). Measuring the relationship between attributions for 'The Gap' and educational policy attitudes: Introducing the attributions for scholastic outcomes scale-back. *The Journal of Negro Education* 78(2): 146–158.

Spivak, Gayatri Chakravorty. (1988). Can the subaltern speak? In Nelson, C. & L. Grossberg (eds). *Marxism and the interpretation of culture*, pp. 271–314. Macmillan Education.

Stack, Carol. (1974). *All our kin.* Basic Books.

Steele, Claude. (2003). Stereotype threat and African American student achievement. In Perry, Theresa, Claude Steele, & Asa G. Hilliard (eds). *Young, gifted, and Black: Promoting high achievement Among African American students*, pp. 109–130. Beacon Press.

Stewart, Nikita & John Cohen. (2010). D.C. Mayor Fenty's approval ratings plummet, poll finds. *The Washington Post.* https://www.washingtonpost.com/wp-dyn/content/article/2010/01/30/AR2010013002452.html. Retrieved December 8, 2019.

Sturm, Circe. (2002). *Blood politics: Race, culture, and identity in the Cherokee Nation of Oklahoma.* University of California Press.

Takano, Shoji. (2005). Re-examining linguistic power: Strategic uses of directives by professional Japanese women in positions of authority and leadership. *Journal of Pragmatics* 37: 633–666.

Talmy, Steven. (2004). Forever FOB: The cultural production of ESL in a high school. *Pragmatics* 14(2/3): 149–172.

Tannen, Deborah. (1995). Waiting for the mouse: Constructed dialogue in conversation. In Tedlock, Dennis & Bruce Mannheim (eds). *The dialogic emergence of culture*, pp. 198–217. University of Illinois Press.

Tarone, Elaine E. (1972). Aspects of intonation in Black English. *American Speech* 48(1/2): 29–36.

Tetreault, Chantal. (2010). Collaborative conflicts: Teens performing aggression and intimacy in a French *cité*. *Journal of Linguistic Anthropology* 20(1): 72–80.

———. (2016). *Transcultural teens: Performing youth identities in French Cités.* Wiley Blackwell.

The White House. (2009). Remarks by the president on education. http://www.whitehouse.gov/the-press-office/remarks-president-department-education. Retrieved December 28, 2010.

Thorne, Barrie. (1997). *Gender play: Boys and girls in school.* Rutgers University Press.

Turque, Bill. (2010). Rhee dismisses 241 teachers; union vows to contest firings. *The Washington Post.* http://www.washingtonpost.com/wp-dyn/content/article/2010/07/23/AR2010072303093.html. Retrieved July 26, 2010.

Urciuoli, Bonnie. (1996). *Exposing prejudice: Puerto Rican experiences of language, race, and class.* Westview Press.

———. (2001). The complex diversity of language in the U.S. In Susser, Ida & Thomas C. Patterson (eds). *Cultural diversity in the United States: A reader*, pp. 190–205. Blackwell Publishing.

———. (2016). Neoliberalizing markedness: The interpellation of "diverse" college students. *Journal of Ethnographic Theory* 6(3): 201–221.

Vasquez, Vivian Maria. (2002). *Negotiating critical literacies with young children.* Lawrence Earlbaum.

Wildhagen, Tina. (2011). Testing the 'acting White' hypothesis: A popular explanation runs out of steam. *The Journal of Negro Education* 80(4): 445–463.

Williams, Brett. (1988). *Upscaling downtown: Stalled gentrification in Washington, D.C.* Cornell University Press.

———. (2001). A river runs through us. *American Anthropologist* 103(2): 409–431.

———. (2009). Deadly inequalities: Race, illness, and poverty in Washington, D.C., since 1945. In Kusmer, Kenneth L. & Joe W. Trotter (eds). *African American urban history since World War II*, pp. 142–159. University of Chicago Press.

Willis, Paul. (1977). *Learning to labour: How working class kids get working class jobs.* Columbia University Press.

Wise, Tim. (2009). *Between Barack and a hard place: Racism and white denial in the age of Obama.* City Lights Books.

Wolfram, Walt. (2002). *The development of African American English.* Blackwell Publishing.

Wolfram, Walt & Ralph W. Fasold. (1974). *Social dialects in American English.* Prentice-Hall.

Woolard, Kathryn. (1985). Language variation and cultural hegemony: Toward an integration of sociolinguistic and social theory. *American Ethnologist* 12(4): 738–748.

Wortham, Stanton. (2007). *Learning identity: The joint emergence of social identification and academic learning.* Cambridge University Press.

Index

Note: Page numbers in italic type indicate illustrations.

AAL. *See* African American Language
academic achievement discourses: Blackness
as a deficit in, xix, 96–107; conflicting
attitudes toward, xix, xxiv, xxvi; of
Southeast residents, 9; students'
attitudes toward, xxxvii, 95–97; teachers'
employment of, xxviii. *See also* academic
success; achievement gap
academic success: adults' attitudes toward,
xxv, 98; as escape from poverty, 3;
and fear of stereotype threat, 97, 103,
107–14; as goal of educators/parents, 50,
58, 92; joning as means of negotiating,
85–92; obstacles to, in treatment of
problem students, 31, 91, 141; students'
attitudes (interest/resistance) toward,
xxv, 15, 97–114; students' recursive
creation of Otherness concerning, xxxvii,
97, 101–2, 114; withdrawal from joning
as strategy for, 83–84. *See also* academic
achievement discourses; achievement
gap; school readiness; smartness contests
achievement gap, xix, xxiv, 1, 15, 96. *See
also* academic achievement discourses;
academic success
acting/talking Black: acting/talking white
compared to, 23–24; connotations of,
24, 25–26; critical uses of, 88; identity
practice underlying, xvii–xviii, xxiii–xxiv;
marking and, 48–49
acting/talking white: academic success
associated with, 15; accusations of,
23, 26; acting/talking Black compared
to, 23–24; connotations of, 25–26;
gendering of, 65–68, 71; marking and,
48–49, 65–68, 71; styleshifting to, 34
adults. *See* African American adults; white
adults
African American adults: anxieties over
preadolescents' language and identity
practices, xxiii, xxv, xxxvi, 25, 26–29,
42, 92, 141; students' marking of, 63;
students' perceptions of, xxxvi, 64–65,
68–70
African American Language (AAL):
Black attitudes toward, xxv, 68–71;
connotations of, 30, 31; discourse theory
approach to, xxxiv–xxxv; gendering
of, 68–71; hypercorrection practiced
by speakers of, 106; joning as practice
in, 75, 79, 85–88; legitimacy of, xviii,
xx–xxi; markers of, 31, 75; marking
as practice of, 49, 63–64; negative
perceptions of, xi, xviii, 16–17, 31; oral
characteristics of, 86–88, 106; in popular
culture, xviii, 16; positive perceptions

of, 68–71; private sphere reserved for, 17; resemiotizing of, 68–71; Standard English in relation to, 32, 35, 64; and styleshifting, 35. *See also* home languages

African Americans: gentrification from perspective of, 6–7; labeled as resistant to achievement, 15; political engagement of, 8–9; stigmatization of, xxi, 7, 14

African American students. *See* preadolescents

after-school program: achievement standards imposed on, 125; educational structure and practices of, xxix, xxxii, 2, 90–91, 107; goals of, xxviii, 2, 18, 19, 58; neighborhood context for, xxvii–xxviii, 3–6; philosophy of, 1–2; as research site, xxvii–xxxiv, 2; staff of, 18–20; white people involved in, 18. *See also* education

agency: culturally sustaining pedagogies and, 120; limitations placed by social norms and hierarchies on, 102; in preadolescent language and identity practices, xviii, xix–xx, xxiii, 42, 75, 136

Alim, H. Samy, 26

American Dream, 21

American Son (film), 140

AmeriCorps, 18

anti-Blackness, xi, xiii, xxi, 8, 80

appropriateness, as linguistic/behavioral standard, xviii, xxiii, xxv, xxxii, xxxvi, 2, 17, 27, 30, 43, 51, 53, 56, 64, 70, 71, 92

Asch, Chris Myers, 9

assimilation: as contradictory to needs and interests of students, xviii–xix, xxi, xxxii, 19; critical pedagogy and, 118–19; as goal of educators/parents, xviii–xix, xxi, xxv, xxxii, 2, 17, 19, 30–31, 36, 41, 118–19; incapacity/unwillingness for, xx–xxii, xxvii, 15, 16, 17, 32; selective resistance to, 98; students' attitudes toward, xxvi, 36, 44

attitude. *See* behavior

Aubrey, Ahmaud, xi

Bastian, Walter, 11

behavior: appropriateness in language and/ or, xviii, xxiii, xxv, xxxii, xxxvi, 2, 17, 27, 30, 43, 51, 53, 56, 64, 70, 71, 92; assumptions of Black deficit influencing interpretations of, 98; "loud," xviii, 42–44, 68, 75, 84, 87–88, 91, 139; policing of, xxv, xxxii, 2, 27–30, 97, 100; "proper" speech and/or, xxv, xxxvi, 10, 19–20, 23–26, 34–36, 43, 64–65, 106, 130

Black Lives Matter movement, xi

Blackness: as deficit in academic settings, xix, 96–107; students' construction of, 40–42, 44–45. *See also* anti-Blackness

Black-white binary, 41

Bland, Sandra, xi

Board of Education, 10–12

Bolling v. Sharpe (1951), 11

The Breakfast Club (film), 38

Brown, Chuck, 38

Brown, Michael, xi

Brown v. Board of Education (1954), 11

Bucholtz, Mary, xxii, xxxv

Bush, George W., 13, 89

Campano, Gerald, 125

Capital Area Food Bank, 3

Chaparro, Sofía E., 24, 25

children, co-construction of race and language by, xix–xx. *See also* preadolescents

City Council, 11

Clinton, Bill, 13

clothing: school uniforms, 38–39, *39*; styles in, 38–40

code-mixing/switching, xx, xxi, xxv, xxvii, 122, 141. *See also* language crossing; styleshifting

colorblindness: academic achievement from perspective of, 15; language as field for asserting, 16–17; neoliberal multiculturalism and, 16–17; pervasiveness of ideology of, xxvi; societal claims of, xii, xxv. *See also* postracialism; racism without racists

competitive irreverence, 87–88

conflict, preadolescent socialization through, 50, 79–81

Consolidated Parent Group, 11

consumption, as source/indicator of style, 37–42

coolness, 37–38

Cosby, Bill, 15

Coupland, Justine, 55

Coupland, Nikolas, 55

criminalization of African Americans: adult anxieties over, xii, xxv, 26–28; behaviors/language associated with, xii, 27–28, 79, 84–85, 92; sociocultural practices of, xvii–xviii, xxv, xxvi, 29, 80, 140; stereotypes associated with, xxxvi, 92; students' responses to, xxxvi, 140

critical consciousness, xxxii, 9, 139

critical pedagogy, xx, xxxii; lesson based on, 121–25; outcome of practicing, 117–18, 122, 125, 135–36; students' tacit practice of, xxxvii, 118, 120–25, 134–35; theory and practice of, 117–19; traditional pedagogy compared to, 120; unintended consequences of, 118–19, 121

critical race theory, 44, 115n1, 141

culturally sustaining pedagogies, 118, 120

culture of poverty, xii, 12–13. *See also* poverty

cursing, 36, 42–43, 60

DCPS. *See* District of Columbia Public Schools

deficit ideologies: AAL from perspective of, xx–xxi, xxxv; in after-school program, 2, 18, 20, 121; Blackness as subject of, xix, 96–107; critical pedagogy and, 118–19; education seen from perspective of, 3, 7, 20, 118–19, 134–35; multiculturalism as instance of, 3; questioning the concept of, xii, xxvii; raciolinguistic perspective and, 17; sociocultural entrenchment of, 2; well-intentioned adults' use of, xxvi, 18, 121, 134, 136

descriptive language ideology, 106

Diner, Stephen J., 11

directives, xxxvi, 48–63; animation of adults through, 61–63; authoring of, and recruitment of adults, 52–57; defined, 48, 50; families implicated in, 57–58; ironic uses of, 58–61; marking as, 48–49, 63–70; moral claims made through, 51, 53, 56, 58, 62–63; purposes in students' use of, 48, 50–52, 57, 61, 70; reanimating adult-authored, 57–58; revoicing of adult authority in, 58–61; social face tested by use of, 50; teachers' use of, 50–51

discipline/punishment: adults' use of, for "inappropriate" behaviors, 27; assignment of academic work as, 99; Black adults' attempts at, 64–65, 68–70, 99; fighting as occasion for, 67, 77; students' modeling/critique of, 48, 51, 64–71; students' responses to, 70, 99–100; white adults' attempts at, 64–68; withholding of academic time as, 31

District of Columbia Public Schools (DCPS): neoliberal reforms in, xix, xxiv, 13–16; population of, 16; Reform Priorities of the Fenty Administration, 15

double-voicing, 57, 59, 71

Do You Speak American? (television series), 121

dual component model, *34*, 35

DuBois, W. E. B., 10

Dunbar High School, 10

education: accountability models of, xix, xxix, xxx, 1, xxxviiin9, 14–15; assimilatory racial logic underlying policies and practices in, xviii; causes of failures of, 12–13; history of African American, in D.C., 10–13; neoliberal reforms, xviii, xix, xxiv, 2, 13–16. *See also* academic achievement discourses; achievement gap; after-school programs

Ellsworth, Elizabeth, 119

Empower DC, 14

English language. *See* Standard English

enlightened exceptionalism, 103

Facebook, 27, 28–29

face threat: academics as occasion for, 85, 88, 97, 104–5, 108, 110; adults' response to, 60, 66; joning as occasion for, 74–75, 79–82, 84–86; preadolescent socialization and, 50, 79–81; race as occasion for, 19; street culture as occasion for, 30, 36, 84

false consciousness, xxxiii, 44, 140

Fenty, Adrian, 1, 7, 9, 13–15, 128

fighting, 67, 77

Flores, Nelson, xiii, xx, xxxvii, 3, 17, 64, 80, 128

Floyd, George, xi

Fordham, Signithia, 8, 9, 97

fractal recursivity, 97, 102. *See also* recursive construction

Freire, Paolo, *Pedagogy of the Oppressed*, 118

fronting, 113

Gal, Susan, 102

gambling. *See* dice (gambling)

gangs, xi, xxviii, 26, 28–29, 76, 77, 92

gangsta rap, 38, 69–70

Garner, Eric, xi

gatekeepers, xxv

Gee, James Paul, 132–33

gender: AAL and, 68–71; hip-hop and, 69–70; and joning, 43, 91–92; slang usage affected by, 43; and street talk, 42–44; white language seen from perspective of, 65–68, 71

gentrification, 6–7, 13–14, 16, 31, 128

"ghetto": behaviors associated with, 84, 87–88, 91; joning associated with, xxxvii, 84, 87–88; linguistic practices associated with, 24, 31; Southeast regarded as, xi, xxviii, 31; street toughness associated with, xxxvii, 24, 42. *See also* street toughness

Goffman, Erving, 56

go-go, 37–38

Goodwin, Marjorie Harness, 49–51, 56

Gray, Vincent, 9, 14, 128–30

Haiti, 126

Heath, Shirley Brice, 134–35

Henderson, Kaya, 9, 14

"he-said-she-said (do this)," 49

high-stakes tests, xxx, 1, 13, 14, 20, 107, 120, 125, 128

Hill, Jane H., 34

hip-hop: assertion of social power in, 70; critical pedagogy lesson based on, 121–22; go-go in relation to, 38; masculinity associated with, 69–70; street toughness associated with, 39–40, 69–70; style/attitude associated with, 28, 29, 32, 37, 39–40, 69–70, 121

home languages: as bridge to normative language use, xxi, xxvii; critical pedagogy and, 118, 119; identities linked to, xxi, xxvii. *See also* African American Language

home rule, 11–13

homework: amount of, xxx–xxxi, 99–100; content of, xxx, 107; contests over, 85–86, 103–5; as focus of after-school program, xxx, 20, 89, 91, 120; "good/smart" students' attention to, 83, 88; parents' concern with, xxx, 62–63, 68; as punishment, 99–100; students' helping others with, 35, 47, 55–56, 103–4

Howard University, xxxviii, 10, 18, 19

hypercorrection, 106

identity construction, xxii–xxiii. *See also* language and identity practices

insults. *See* joning; ritual insults

Irvine, Judith, 102

Jackson, Jesse, 121

Jeantel, Rachel, xi

joning: as AAL practice, 75, 79, 85–88; and academic success, 83–92; adults' disapproval of, xxxvi, xxxvii, 20, 74, 77–79, *78*, 89, 92; adults' participation in, 78–79, 90; agency expressed in, 75; as conflict instigator, 76–77, 80–81; contests of, 76, 82–83, 85–89; displaying toughness as purpose of, 75–77, 79, 81–86; gender differences in, 43, 91–92; as "ghetto," xxxvii, 84, 87; initiating *vs.* defensive, 81; mastery of,

74, 79, 83; overview of, 75–77; purpose of, for preadolescents, 76–77, 81–82; risks involved in, 74, 77, 82; stereotypes of African Americans prevalent in, xxxiv, 79, 88–91; street toughness associated with, 77; students' attitudes toward, 42–43, 83–84, 92; students' use of, xxix, xxxvi–xxxvii, 20, 29, 73–93; as verbal art/play, 75–76, 79, 82–83, 85, 87–88, 91; white people's manner of, 40. *See also* slang

Kelley, Robin D. G., 69
King, Martin Luther, Jr., "I Have a Dream," 96
Kromidas, Maria, 103

Labov, William, 35, 41, 76, 82
Ladson-Billings, Gloria, 125
language: children's acquisition of, xxii–xxiii; co-construction of race and, xix–xx, xxiii–xxiv, xxxv; neoliberal multiculturalism and, 16–17; prescriptive *vs.* descriptive approaches to, 106. *See also* language and identity practices
language and identity practices: adult anxieties over, xxiii, xxv, xxxvi, 25, 26–29, 42, 92, 141; agency expressed in, xviii, xxiii, 42, 75, 136; Blackness constructed by, 40–42, 44–45; co-implication of, xxiii–xxiv; contrasting models (street toughness *vs.* school readiness) of, xxiii, 29–32, 36–37, 84; controversies over, xix; critical and transformative uses of, xxii, xxv, xxvii, xxxvi–xxxvii, 25, 32–33, 36–37, 40–42, 44, 64, 85–92, 118, 126–28, 135; global, 41; home languages and, xxi; joning associated with, 85–92; linguistic anthropological approaches to, xxxiv–xxxv; of preadolescents, xvii–xviii, xx, xxii–xxiv, 25, 37–42, 44; style in, 37–42; styleshifting as, 32–37. *See also* identity construction; language
language architecture perspective, 125–28, 134

language crossing, xxvi. *See also* code-mixing/switching; styleshifting
Latinx students: cultural difference of, 17; language use of, 15, 17; sociocultural position of, 45, 80
LeMaster, Barbara, 51
Levy, Mary, 11
liberal ideologies: deficit perspective embraced by, xxvi; multiculturalism associated with, xxxiii; negative results arising from well-intentioned, xii, xix, xx, 9, 118–19, 122, 136
linguistic anthropology, xxxiv–xxxv
linguistic policing. *See* racial and linguistic policing
listening subjects, xx, xxv, xxxii–xxxv, 17, 26, 35
literacy. *See* reading abilities and activities
literate selves, 108
loudness, attributed to African Americans, xviii, 42–44, 68, 75, 84, 87–88, 91, 139
loud talk, 68

MacLeod, Jay, 9
marking, xxxvi, 63–71; child-adult relationship tested by, 48–49; defined, 48, 64; simultaneous humor/critique in use of, 64; and stereotypes of African Americans, xxxiv; of white adults, 64–68, 71
Martin, Trayvon, xi, 28
Mendoza-Denton, Norma, xxii, xxxv
meritocratic ideology, 9, 15, 84, 95, 97, 103, 110, 114
Monzó, Lilia D., 110, 113–14
M Street High School, 10
multiculturalism: in academic circles, xxxiii; deficit ideologies underlying, xix, 3; neoliberal, 3, 16–17
Musgrove, George Derek, 9

A Nation at Risk (report), 15
NCLB Act. *See* No Child Left Behind (NCLB) Act
neoliberalism: economic and political principles of, 7, 15–16; education reforms promoted by, xviii, xix, xxiv, 2,

13–16; multiculturalism promoted by, 3, 16–17; racial project of, xxxv–xxxvi, 2
Nike, 37
No Child Left Behind (NCLB) Act, xxxviii, 13, 14–15

Oakland Ebonics controversy, 141
Obama, Barack, xxiv–xxv, 8, 9, 15, 26, 33, 89, 102, 121, 128
Obama, Michelle, 33
Omi, Michael, xxiv–xxv
oppositional cultures, 41, 70, 95, 97–98, 102

Panel on Educational Research and Development, 12
Paris, Django, xxxv
passing, as student academic strategy, 110, 112–14
Passow, A. Harry, 12–13
police brutality, 140
policing. *See* racial and linguistic policing
politeness, as linguistic/behavioral standard, 24–25, 30, 35–36, 65–67, 130
politics: local engagement in, 8–10, 128–30; students' after-school work on, 128–34, *129–33*
popular culture, 38, 41–42
postracialism: challenges to societal claims of, xviii; language as field for asserting, 16–17; neoliberal multiculturalism and, 16–17; Obama and, 8; pervasiveness of ideology of, xxvi; societal claims of, xi, xii, xxiv–xxv; students' belief in, 96. *See also* colorblindness; racism without racists
poverty: culture of, xii, 12–13; in D.C., 7, 14; in Southeast, xxvii–xxviii, xxxv, 4; students' experience of, 120
poverty gap, 1, 15
preadolescents: adult perception of naïveté of, 29; agency of, xviii, xix–xx, xxiii, 42, 75; conflict as central to social practices of, 50, 80–81; liminal status of and sociocultural pressures on, xxiii, 29; linguistic policing of, 26–29; maturation of, behaviors indicating, 36, 44, 79, 84;

siblings of, 57, 61. *See also* language and identity practices
prescriptive language ideology, 106
Prince, Sabiyha, 6–7, 9–10
problem students, xx, xxiv–xxv; adult fears concerning, 25; behaviors associated with, 31, 102; obstacles to academic success of, 31, 91, 141; raciolinguistic socialization as, 24–25, 96–98; students' critique of being considered, 85, 141; students' recursive creation of, 102
"proper" speech/behavior, xxv, xxxvi, 10, 19–20, 23–26, 34–36, 43, 64–65, 106, 130
punishment. *See* discipline/punishment

race: co-construction of language and, xix–xx, xxiii–xxiv, xxxv; defined, xxiv; ethnicity *vs.*, xxi; Otherness and unassimilability linked to, xxi, 16; reluctance to talk about, 19, 21; as sociocultural construct, xxv
Race to the Top, xxxviii
racial and linguistic policing: joning and, 80, 88–89, 91–92; neoliberal reforms linked to, xviii; pervasiveness of, in racial/ethnic minorities, xxxiv; raciolinguistic enregisterment through, 26–29, 43, 91–92; sociocultural practices of, xxvi; students' responses to, xxxvi, 80, 91; students subjected to, xviii, xxv, xxxii, 80, 92, 140; systemic/structural, 15; well-intentioned reasons for, xxv
racial indexes, xxxv, 15, 16
racial projects: commercial and residential development of D.C., xxxv–xxxvi, 2, 13, 16; concept of, xxiv–xxvi; neoliberal gentrification as, xxiv; schools as, 17
raciolinguistic chronotopes, xxvi, 75, 80, 84, 91
raciolinguistic enregisterment, 25–29, 43, 91–92
raciolinguistic perspective: critical nature of, xiii, xx–xxi, 141; critical pedagogy and, 118–19; mechanism of, 17, 32; overview of, xx–xxii

raciolinguistic resemiotization, 49, 68–71
raciolinguistic socialization, 24–25, 91, 96–98
racism: linguistic, xiii, xx, 17; shared racial identity and, 115n1; systemic/structural, xxiv
racism without racists, 141. *See also* colorblindness; postracialism
ratting. *See* snitching
reading abilities and activities, xxxvii, 90–91, 105–14
Reagan, Ronald, 15
recursive construction: of Blackness, 40–42, 44–45; of intelligence and achievement, 103–7; of Otherness in academic situations, xxxvii, 97, 101–2, 114
research context, xxvii–xxxiv, 2
resemiotization. *See* raciolinguistic resemiotization
Reyes, Angela, 65, 102
Rhee, Michelle, 9, 13–15
Rice, Tamir, xi
ritual insults, 75–76. *See also* joning
Roe, Donald, 9, 10
Rosa, Jonathan, xiii, xx, xxii, xxxv, 3, 17, 64, 80
Rueda, Robert, 110, 113–14

school readiness: as goal of educators/parents, 50; as identity model, xxiii, 29–32. *See also* academic achievement discourses; academic success
science, students' after-school work on, 32–34, *33*, 125–28, *126–27*
segregation/desegregation, in education, 10–12, 96
semiotics, xxxiv
signifying, 75
Silverstein, Michael, 64
slang: gender differences in use of, 43; racialization of, 24, 36; students' perceptions of, 35–36, 43. *See also* cussing; joning
smartness contests, 85–86, 103–5, 107–10
Smitherman, Geneva, 26
snitching (ratting, tattling), 53–56, 62
social face, 30, 36, 50. *See also* face threat

socialization: conflict as means of preadolescent, 50, 79–81; raciolinguistic, 24–25, 91, 96–98
Southeast Washington, D.C.: demographics of, xxvii–xxviii, xxxv, 4; living conditions in, xxviii, 3, 5, 6; map of, *4*; perceptions of, xi, xxvii–xxviii, 31; political engagement of, 8–9; poverty in, xxvii–xxviii; students' identification with, 40–41; style associated with, 38–41; twentieth-century history of, 6
Sponge Bob (television character), 38
Standard English: AAL in relation to, 32, 35, 64; home language as bridge to, xxi, xxvii; Latinx language use compared to, 17; marking as critique of, 64–70; as sociocultural construct, xx–xxi; students' perceptions of, 35–36
Steele, Claude, 103
stereotypes of African Americans: academic/intellect-related, xxxvii, 26, 35, 95–114; crime-related, xxxvi, 92; gender-based, 42; as lazy, 18; reinforcement of, 114; street-related, xxxvii; students' use of, xix, xxxiv, xxxvi–xxxvii, 42, 71, 79, 85, 88–91, 114–15; as uninvolved citizens, 8; used in joning, xxxiv, 79, 88–91
stereotype threat, xxxvii, 97, 103, 107–14
street toughness: authority ascribed to, 69; hip-hop associated with, 39–40, 69–70; as identity model, xxiii, 29–32, 36–37; joning associated with, 77; linguistic practices associated with, 19, 24, 29–30; negative perceptions of, xviii, xix, xxiii, xxxvi, 18, 26–29, 42; students' attitudes toward, 42; visual markers of, 28, 33–34. *See also* "ghetto"; joning
students. *See* preadolescents
style, sociolinguistic, 37–42
styleshifting, xx, 26, 32–37. *See also* code-mixing/switching; language crossing
survival: of imagined Black community, xxvi, 80, 84; joning and, 80, 84, 92
systemic/structural racism, xxiv

"talking back," 84, 92, 97, 100
talking Black. *See* acting/talking Black

tattling. *See* snitching

Taylor, Breonna, xi

teacher-researchers, xxxi–xxxiv, 2

teachers, African Americans as, xxxviiin7, 10

Teacher's College, Columbia University, 12

Teach for America, xxxviii

teaching to the test, xxx, 20, 125

Temporary Assistance for Needy Families (TANF), 3

Tetreault, Chantal, xxvii, 114

Time (magazine), 14

transculturality, xxvii

translanguaging, xxvi, 122

translingual sensibility, 118

transracial project, xxv–xxvii

US Congress, 11

Vasquez, Vivian Maria, xxxvii, 121, 134

voicing, 49, 65. *See also* double-voicing

Waiting for Superman (documentary), 14

Washington, D.C.: district wards, 5; educational history of, 9–13; gentrification of, 6–7, 13–14; mid-twentieth-century revitalization of, 6; multi-ethnic population of, 7; political, social, and economic background of, 8–10; racial project to develop, xxxv–xxxvi, 2, 13, 16. *See also* Southeast Washington, D.C.

Washington, Walter, 11

white adults: students' marking of, 63–68; students' perceptions of, xxxvi, 64–68, 71

white gaze, xii, xxiv

whiteness: as educational/intellectual standard, xxvi, 26, 71, 102–3, 118–19; societal reaffirmation of, 16; as societal standard, 24, 71, 119; as unmarked/tacit/assumed, xxxiii, 16–17. *See also* acting/talking Black

white supremacy, xx, xxiv, 118

Williams, Anthony, 7

Willis, Paul, 97

Winant, Howard, xxiv–xxv

Wortham, Stanton, 50, 91–92

Zimmerman, George, xi, 28

About the Author

Jennifer B. Delfino is a linguistic and cultural anthropologist who specializes in the study of language, racialization, and identity in the United States. She is Assistant Professor of Academic Literacy and Linguistics at Borough of Manhattan Community College, The City University of New York. While she continues to examine how schooling impacts African American students' language and identity practices, she is also working on two new research projects: the linguistic and discursive construction of whiteness among liberals and progressives on social media, and language and racialization among second-generation Filipino Americans in the New York/New Jersey area. Jennifer is also a dedicated member of a local, internationally competitive running team, Central Park Track Club, and hopes to join many of her accomplished teammates in qualifying for the Boston Marathon.

www.ingramcontent.com/pod-product-compliance
Lightning Source LLC
Chambersburg PA
CBHW022316280326
41932CB00010B/1116